Hunter Davies is the author of over thirty books, including the only authorized biography of The Beatles, *The Glory Game* and *A Walk Around the Lakes*. As a journalist, he currently writes a column about money in *The Sunday Times* and about football in *The New Statesman*. He comes from Carlisle, home base of the even more famous Eddie Stobart.

THE
EDDIE STOBART
STORY

HUNTER DAVIES

HarperCollins*Entertainment*
An Imprint of HarperCollins*Publishers*

HarperCollins*Entertainment*
An Imprint of HarperCollins*Publishers*
77–85 Fulham Palace Road,
Hammersmith, London W6 8JB

www.harpercollins.co.uk

This paperback edition 2002
6

First published in Great Britain by
HarperCollins*Entertainment* 2001

ISBN 0 00 711632 2

Set in Meridien by
Rowland Phototypesetting Ltd, Bury St Edmunds, Suffolk

Printed and bound in Great Britain by
Clays Ltd, St Ives plc

CONTENTS

The author and publisher are grateful to the following for permission to use material within the book:

Caldew School, Dalston, Carlisle; 'I Want to be an Eddie Stobart Driver' reproduced by kind permission of Andrew J. Titcombe/Tim Barker, published by Loose Music 1995; Eddie Stobart website images supplied by The Web Works; photo of Caldbeck by Brittain and Wright; panto charity event by the Northampton *Chronicle and Echo*; twenty fifth anniversary group photo by Function Photographic Services, Middlesex; Carlisle United Football Club by the *Cumberland News*, Carlisle; William Hague pictures by Martin Neeves photography 'Haulier of the Year' photo supplied courtesy of *Motor Transport*. Illustrations in second picture section by Hunter Davies: page 5 (*first three pictures*); page 6 (*top pictures*); page 7; page 8 (*bottom picture*).

ILLUSTRATIONS

INTRODUCTION

Edward Stobart is Cumbria's greatest living Cumbrian. Not a great deal of competition, you might think, as Cumbria is a rural county, with only twenty settlements with a population greater than 2500. But our native sons do include Lord Bragg.

I used to say the greatest living Cumbrian was Alfred Wainwright, though he was a newcomer, who assumed Cumbrian nationality when he fell in love with Lakeland and then moved to Kendal. Wainwright, like Eddie Stobart, became a cult, acquiring an enormous following without ever really trying. In fact Wainwright discouraged fans, refusing to speak to other walkers when he met them, not allowing his photograph to appear on his guide books, never doing signing sessions. Yet he went on to sell millions of copies of his books.

Edward Stobart, the hero of this book, not to be confused with his father, Eddie Stobart, still lives in Cumbria and the world HQ of Eddie Stobart Limited is still in Carlisle. In the last ten years, it has become a household name all over the country, at least in households who have chanced to drive along one of our motorways, which means most of us. Today, the largest part of his business is now situated elsewhere in England, yet Edward remains close to his roots.

I am a fellow Cumbrian, so I boast, if not quite a genuine one as I was born in Scotland, only moving to Carlisle when I was aged four. But I know whence the Stobarts have come, know well their little Cumbrian home village, know many of their friends – and that to me is one of the many intriguing aspects of their rise. How did they get here, from there of all places?

I had met Edward, before beginning this book, at the House of Lords, guests of the late Lord Whitelaw. It was a reception for Ambassadors for Cumbria, a purely honorary title, dreamed up by some marketing whiz. I talked to Edward for a while, but didn't get very far. He doesn't go in for idle chat, doesn't care for social occasions, doesn't really like talking much, being hesitant with strangers, very reserved and private. Despite the firm's present-day fame, I can't remember seeing him interviewed on television, hearing him on the radio and I seldom see his face in the newspapers.

So this was another thought that struck me. Having got from there, that little village I used to know so well, how did Edward Stobart then become a national force, when he himself appears so unpushy, unfluent, undynamic?

The fact that he has risen to fame and fortune through lorries, creating the biggest private firm in Britain, is also interesting. It's so unmodern, unglamorous. He's now regularly on *The Sunday Times* list of the wealthiest people in Britain but, unlike so many of the other entries, he actually owns things. There is a concrete, physical presence to his fortune. The wealth of many of our present-day self-made millionaires is very often abstract, either on paper or out there on the ether; liable to fall and disappear in a puff of smoke or a blank screen.

Haulage is old technology; so old it's practically prehistoric. Hauling stuff from A to B, real stuff as opposed to messages and information, has always been with us. And over the centuries it has sent out its own messages, giving us clues to the state of the economy, the state of the nation. By following the rise of our leading haulage firm over the last thirty years, since Eddie Stobart Limited was created in 1970, we should also be able to observe glimpses of the history of our times.

The cult of Eddie Stobart: that's perhaps the most surprising aspect of all. How on earth has a lorry firm acquired a fan club of over 25,000 paid-up members? You expect it in films or football, in TV or the theatre, with people in the public eye, who have staff to push or polish their name and image. But lorries are just objects. They don't sign autographs. Hard to get them to smile to the camera. Not many have been seen drunk or stoned in the Groucho Club. Some would say they are nasty, noisy, environmentally-unfriendly, inanimate objects – not the sort of thing you'd expect right-thinking persons to fall in love with.

I wanted to find out some of the answers to these questions, some sort of explanation or insight. I also wanted to celebrate my fellow Cumbrian. Hold tight then, here we go, full speed ahead, with possibly a few diversions along the way, for a ride on the inside with Eddie Stobart.

Hunter Davies
Loweswater, August 2001.

THE
EDDIE STOBART
STORY

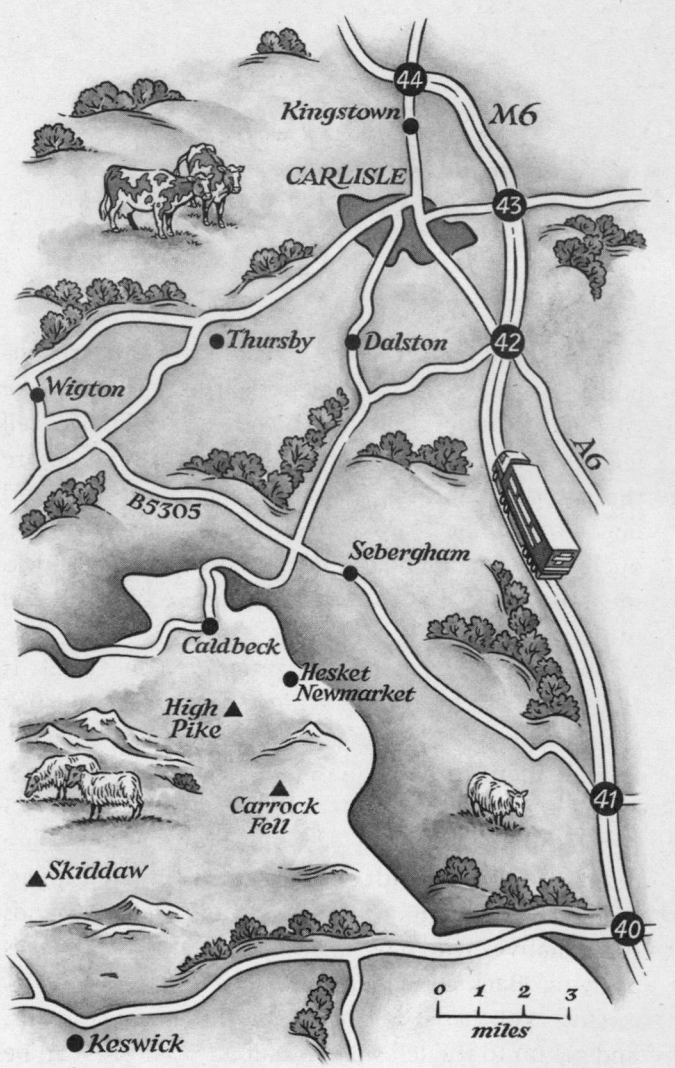

WHERE IT ALL BEGAN . . .

Caldbeck and Hesket Newmarket are two small neighbouring villages on the northern fringes of the Lake District in Cumbria, England. They are known as fell villages, being on the edges of the fells, or hills, where the laid out, captured fields and civilized hedges and obedient tarmac roads give way to unreconstructed, open countryside. A place where neatness and tidiness meet the rough and the unregimented. A bit like some of the people.

The first of the two most prominent local fells is High Pike, 2159 feet high, which looms over Caldbeck and Hesket, with Carrock Fell hovering round the side. Behind them, in the interior, there are further fells, unfolding in the distance, till you reach Skiddaw, 3053 feet high, Big Brother of the Northern Fells. A mere pimple compared with mountains in the Himalayas, but Skiddaw dominates the landscape and the minds of the natives who have always referred to themselves as living 'Back O' Skiddaw'.

Once you leave the fields, the little empty roads, and get on to the fell side, in half an hour you can be on your own, communing with nature. People think it can't be done, that the whole of Lakeland is full, the kagouls rule, but this corner is always empty. My wife and I had a cottage at Caldbeck for ten years and we used to do fifteen-mile walks, up and across the Caldbeck Fells, round Skiddaw, down to Keswick and, in eight hours, meet only two or three other walkers. Then we got a taxi back, being cheats.

You see few people because this is not the glamorous, touristy Lake District. There are no local lakes. It's hard to get to, especially if you are coming up from the South, as most of the hordes do. There used to be a lot of mining, so you still come across scarred valleys, jagged holes, dumps of debris. It's an acquired taste, being rather barren and treeless, often windy and misty, colourless for much of the year, though, in the autumn, the fell slopes turn a paler shade of yellow.

At first sight, first impression, it's not exactly a welcoming place. The people and the landscape tend to hide their delights away. Like the fells, friendships unfold. 'They'll winter you, summer you, winter you again,' so we were told when we first moved to Caldbeck. 'Then they might say hello.'

The nearest big town is Carlisle, some fifteen miles away, a historic city with a castle and cathedral, small as cities go, with only 70,000 citizens. It is, however, important as the capital of Cumbria, the second largest county in England – only in area, though; in population, Cumbria is one of the smallest, with only 400,000 people. Carlisle is in the far north-western corner of England, hidden away on the map and in the minds of many English people, who usually know the name but aren't quite sure if it might be in Scotland or even Wales.

The region, it would seem at first glance, is an unlikely, unpromising setting to produce such a family as the Stobarts. At a second glance, when you look further into their two home villages, you find more colour, more depth, more riches hidden away.

Caldbeck is the bigger village of the two, population six hundred, and has a busy, semi-industrial past. The old mill buildings have now been nicely refurbished to provide smart homes or workshops. It still is a thriving village, a genuine, working village, as all the locals will tell you. It does not depend on tourists, trippers or second-homers. It's got a very active Young Farmers Club, a tennis club, amateur dramatics. There are agricultural families who have been there for centuries, mixing well with a good sprinkling of newer, middle-class professionals who work in Carlisle.

Caldbeck's claims to national fame lie in its graveyard. At the parish church is buried the body of John Peel, a local huntsman, commemorated in a song which is Cumbria's national anthem and gets sung all round the English speaking world. (Peel never heard it himself – the words were put to the present tune after his death.) Near him lies Mary Robinson, the Maid of Buttermere, a Lakeland beauty who was wronged by a rotter in 1802. He bigamously married her and was later hanged, a drama which thrilled the

3

nation and became a London musical. More recently, it was turned into a successful novel by Melvyn Bragg. Lord Bragg, as he now is called, was brought up and educated at Wigton, a small town, about ten miles from Caldbeck. He is a great lover of the Caldbeck Fells and still has a country home locally at Ireby.

Caldbeck's church is named after St Kentigern, known as St Mungo in Scotland, who was a bishop of Glasgow. He visited the Caldbeck area in 553 and did a spot of converting after he heard that, 'many amongst the mountains were given to idolatory'. Much later, the early Quakers were very active in this corner of Cumbria, as were Methodist missionaries.

Hesket Newmarket, just over a mile away from Caldbeck, is very small, with only a few dozen houses. It is quieter, quainter than Caldbeck, a leftover hamlet from another age, one of the most attractive villages in all Cumbria and very popular with second-homers, many of whom live and work in the north-east. It's basically one street which has some pretty eighteenth-century cottages lining a long, rolling village green. In the middle is the old Market Cross, admired by Pevsner for its 'four round pillars carrying a pyramid roof with a ball finial.' Until recently, it was used as the village's garage.

There were five pubs here at one time. Now there's only one, the Old Crown, well known in real beer circles as it brews its own beer. There used to be a local school, known as Howbeck, just outside the village, which all the Stobarts attended but it is now a private home. It was opened, along with Caldbeck's village school (still going strong) in 1875 to ensure rural children received the same education as urban children. A School Inspector's report for 14 May 1890, observed that: 'a remarkable occurrence took place on Monday afternoon – viz, every child was present.'

Hesket Newmarket did have a market, established in 1751 for sheep and cattle, but it was discontinued by the middle of the nineteenth century. Hesket's annual agricultural show, held since 1877, is still a big event, featuring Cumberland and Westmorland wrestling, hound trails as well as agricultural exhibits. It draws crowds and entrants from all over the county.

William Wordsworth, plus sister Dorothy and Coleridge, stayed at Hesket on 14 August 1803. Dorothy recorded their visit in her journal: 'Slept at Mr Younghusband's publick house, Hesket Newmarket. In the evening walked to Caldbeck Fells.'

Coleridge described the inn's little parlour. 'The sanded stone floor with the spitting pot full of sand dust, two pictures of young Master and Miss, she with a rose in her hand . . . the whole room struck me as cleanliness quarrelling with tobacco ghosts.'

In September 1857, Charles Dickens and fellow novelist Wilkie Collins visited the village in order to climb Carrock Fell. They later wrote up their trip in *The Lazy Tour of Two Idle Apprentices*. They managed to get to the top of Carrock Fell in the rain, moaning all the way, but coming down, Wilkie Collins sprained an ankle.

They, too, described the parlour in which they stayed, amazed by all the 'little ornaments and nicknacks . . . it was so very pleasant to see these things in such a lonesome by-place . . . what a wonder this room must be to the little children born in the gloomy village, what grand impressions of those who became wanderers over the earth, how at distant ends of the world some old voyagers would die, cherishing the belief that the finest apartment known to men was once in the Hesket Newmarket Inn, in rare old Cumberland . . .'

I'm sure the locals didn't like the reference to their 'gloomy' village but it shows that Hesket, however hidden away, has attracted some eminent people over the centuries.

The present-day best-known resident of Hesket is Sir Chris Bonington, the mountaineer and writer: a Londoner by birth, but a Cumbrian by adoption. He bought a cottage at Nether Row, just outside Hesket, on the slopes of High Pike, in 1971 and has lived there full time since 1974. He is a co-owner of the Old Crown pub. It doesn't quite put him on the level of a Scottish and Newcastle or Guinness director: the Old Crown is now a co-operative, with sixty local co-owners.

Chris has no intention of ever leaving the area. He likes the local climbing, either doing hair-raising rock stuff over in Borrowdale or brisk fell walks straight up High Pike from his own back garden. In summer, he can manage two days in one: a working day, writing inside, then an evening day, outside at play till at least ten o'clock, as the nights are so light. 'I love the quietness up here,' he says, 'well away from the Lake District rush. I also think it's beautiful. I like the rolling quality, the open fells merging with the countryside. In fact, my favourite view in all Lakeland is a local one: from the road up above Uldale, looking back towards Skiddaw.'

As a neighbour of the Stobart clan, Chris has watched their rise and rise, but doesn't think you can make generalizations about them or their background: 'What I will say, from my observations, is that the Cumbrian is shrewd.'

Chris is currently watching the rise of another local family business from a similar background: known, so far, only in the immediate area. The founder, George Steadman, was the village blacksmith in Caldbeck in the 1900s. His son built barns. In turn, his son, Brian the present Managing Director, moved on to roofing and cladding for industrial buildings. Over the last twenty years, Brian Steadman and his wife, Doreen, have been doubling their business every year. They now employ sixty people and last year turned over nine million pounds.

Visitors to the Caldbeck area driving back into Carlisle, down Warnell Fell, will notice the Steadmans' new factory on the left-hand side. When I drive past, I always turn my head in admiration, taking care not to crash as it is a very steep hill. Their front lawns are so immaculate, their buildings all gleaming, yet it's only a boring old factory, producing boring old roofing material.

'We didn't used to be so tidy when we were based in Caldbeck,' says Brian. 'It was partly the influence of Eddie Stobart Ltd. We did a big roofing job for them in Carlisle, big for us: £400,000 it was and they paid us on the dot, which very few firms do these days.

'Anyway, while we were doing that job, I noticed how neat and tidy all his lorries were, and his premises, and how smart his staff were. We all know how successful Eddie Stobart Ltd has been. I thought we'd try to follow his lead.'

The Steadmans are following Eddie Stobart from the same local environment. Is this just by chance, perhaps, or do they think there are any connections, any generalizations to be made? 'I think what it shows,' says Doreen, 'is that people who leave school early, such as Brian and the Stobarts, who are no good academically but are good with their hands, can still create good businesses.'

'I think with us and the Stobarts,' says Brian, 'it's been an advantage being country people. Country staff are loyal, reliable people. They stick with you, through thick and thin. You need that in the difficult times, which all firms go through.'

Perhaps, then, it's not at all surprising for successful businesses to come out of a remote, rural area. Country folk are shrewd, says Bonington. Country folk are loyal, says Steadman.

Country folk can do it, as has been shown in the past. One of Cumbria's all-time successful business families came from Sebergham, the very next village after Hesket. In 1874, the village stonemason, John Laing, moved into Carlisle and set himself up as a builder. Today, Laing's are still building all over the civilized world. So much for nothing happening, nothing ever coming out of such a remote rural region.

THE STOBARTS

The Cumbrian branch of the Stobarts can trace their family back pretty clearly for around one hundred years, all of them humble farming folk in the Caldbeck Fells area. Before that, it gets a bit cloudy. Sometime early in the nineteenth century, so they think, the original Stobart is supposed to have come over to Cumberland from Northumberland, but that is just a family rumour. Originally, they could have been Scottish, or at least Border folk, as their surname is thought to have derived from 'Stob', an old Scottish word for a small wooden post or stump of a tree.

The founder of the present family was John Stobart, father of Eddie and grandfather of Edward. He was born at Howgill, Sebergham, in 1903 and worked at his father's farm on leaving school. In 1930, he secured his own smallholding of some thirty-two acres at Bankdale Head, Hesket Newmarket. By this time he had got married to Adelaide, known as Addie, and they had a baby son, Edward Pears Stobart – always known as Eddie – who was born in 1929. Eddie was followed by a second son, Ronnie, in 1936.

On John's smallholding, he kept eight cows, a bull, some horses and three hundred hens. Farming, and life in general, was hard at the end of the 1930s so, to bring in a bit more money and feed his young family, John managed to secure some work with the Cumberland County Council, hiring out himself plus his horse and cart, on occasional contract jobs.

John's wife, Addie, died in 1942. John then married again, to Ruth Crame, whose family had come up from Hastings to Hesket Newmarket during the War to escape the bombing. He went on to have six other children by Ruth: Jim, Alan, Mary, Ruth, Dorothy and Isobel. Hence the reason why there are so many Stobarts in and around the Hesket area today.

Eddie has only happy memories of his step-mother. Until she came along, there had been what he calls 'a sequence of housekeepers', so he was pleased by the stability that Ruth brought into his father's life.

After the war, in 1946, John bought his first tractor, which meant he could expand his contracting work, doing threshing and other agricultural jobs for farmers within a thirty-mile radius of Hesket.

The most important thing in John's life was his Christian beliefs. He had become a Methodist lay preacher from the age of nineteen and travelled all over north Cumberland preaching at rural chapels. Every year, he took his family to Keswick for the annual Keswick Convention, joining thousands of other Christians, mainly evangelicals, from all over England.

Some of Eddie's earliest memories are of being taken on the back of his father's BSA motorbike as he went off preaching in Methodist chapels. He recalls that one church was full when they got there, and his father, when he stood up, was having trouble making himself heard. 'Shout out, man,' said a local farmer, putting his arm round John Stobart's shoulder, 'You are working for God, you know.'

Eddie left the local village school, Howbeck, just outside Hesket, when he was fourteen. 'I was hardly there from the age of twelve. In those days, you got time off for seasonal agricultural work to help your parents. I quite enjoyed arithmetic, but my interest in history or geography or English was nil. I could never spell. I didn't really like school. I was much more interested in catching rabbits.'

He went to work with his father, helping on the farm or with his contracting jobs. When the Cumberland Council wanted a horse and cart and one man for the day, paying a daily rate of 27s.6d., they often found the man was young Eddie.

From an early age, Eddie had been making some money in his spare time by chopping logs into kindling sticks or selling the rabbits he'd trapped. He took them into Carlisle's covered market on Saturday mornings, near where farmers' wives sold their eggs and hams and cheeses.

Aged fifteen, he had saved enough money to buy an unbroken horse for thirty-three guineas. He trained it to pull the cart and a variety of agricultural machinery and sold it after a year for sixty-six guineas. With this money, he bought his own hens and hen houses. At seventeen, he passed his driving test and was able to drive his father's Morris 10.

While aged seventeen, on 16 November 1946, he attended a local Methodist chapel where a visiting preacher was in the middle of a three-week mission. Eddie was one of two people in the congregation that day who came forward and said they had been saved. From that day, he committed himself to God.

Some time later, he heard that there was a seventeen-year-old girl called Nora Boyd who had also recently been saved, and who lived only two miles away in Caldbeck. Sounded good – till Eddie discovered she had moved over the border to Lockerbie in Scotland, and was now working as a housekeeper. However, he discovered she still came home some weekends and he managed to get her address. Eddie wrote to her and said he'd heard about her conversion, adding that he too had recently been saved. He suggested perhaps they might meet next time she was home in Caldbeck.

A week later, she replied. She thanked him for his letter, saying she was pleased he was a Christian, and arranged to meet him the following Saturday at a Bible rally at the Hebron Hall in Carlisle.

For the next few Saturdays, Eddie drove into Carlisle in his father's shiny new Morris 10 and met Nora at church. Just before Christmas, she gave him a present: a copy of John Bunyan's *Pilgrim's Progress*.

What Eddie didn't know about Nora Boyd when they first met was that she was an orphan and had never known her father. Her mother had died when she was aged four and she had been placed in two children's homes before being fostered by a family called Lennon in Caldbeck.

'At school in Caldbeck, I wasn't very happy,' says Nora today. 'I would get blamed all the time. If things went missing, they would look at me – you know, look at me, because nobody knew where I was from . . .'

The Lennons of Caldbeck were a Methodist family but, on leaving Caldbeck aged fourteen, Nora decided she wasn't going to believe in God any more. 'I vowed I wasn't going to church again. I blamed God for what had happened to me in my life so far.'

Three years later, aged seventeen, while Nora was staying with relations in Liverpool, she saw the light and became converted – the conversion that Eddie learned about. 'I realized then that God could only do me good, not harm.'

Eddie and Nora spent the next five years courting, until one day in 1951, Eddie heard that an uncle of his had a house to rent at Brocklebank, outside Wigton, for 12s.6d. a week, the previous tenants having just moved out. It was this that prompted Eddie to suggest marriage to Nora. Not exactly romantic, but very sensible. Their marriage took place on Boxing Day 1951, at the Methodist chapel in Caldbeck, followed by a wedding reception at the Caldbeck village hall.

Eddie by now had acquired a threshing machine,

paying for it by selling his hens and hen houses to his father. The threshing machine, a Ransome, was bought from a contractor who was giving up. It came with a Case tractor and a list of two hundred names of people who were, supposedly, regular customers. This was in the days before combine harvesters, when small farmers could not afford expensive machinery of their own. Local contractors like Eddie Stobart would thresh their corn for them and undertake other seasonal agricultural jobs which required a bit of machinery.

In 1953, Eddie and Nora bought their own house, a bungalow called Newlands Hill, just outside Hesket. The cost was £450. Eddie put down a deposit of £50 and got the rest on a mortgage from a building society.

They moved into Newlands Hill with their first two babies: Anne, born in 1952, and John, born in 1953. Their third child, Edward – never called Eddie in order to avoid confusion with his father – was born at home at Newlands Hill on 21 November 1954. There was then a slight gap before Eddie and Nora's fourth and last child came along: William, born in 1961.

Until 1957, Eddie had still been officially working with his father, and with his brother Ronnie, all three of them running the family's little agricultural business: threshing, ploughing, ditching, carting – whatever was required. John had also started to trade in hay and grain, helped mainly by Ronnie. Eddie was doing most of the agricultural contracting and had recently begun to spread fertilizers for the local farmers. He'd also begun to feel it was time to go it alone, to run his own little business.

In 1957, when Eddie was aged twenty-eight, he and his father and brother decided to divide up the family assets. After some discussion, it was agreed that Eddie's share of the family firm would be: the threshing machine, which they valued at £150, a Fordson tractor worth £250, a Nuffield tractor worth £150, fuel tanks worth £50, and cash in hand of £100. These, then, were the net assets, valued in total at £700, of Eddie Stobart's first firm, which opened for trading in 1957 as E.P. Stobart, Hesket Newmarket.

At the end of Eddie's first year in business in 1958, the firm had added to its assets a spreader and sundry agricultural instruments. The wages during the year amounted to £424, which would appear to have been casual labour, plus what Eddie had paid himself. Turnover for the year was £2329 and the profit was declared as being £630.

The following year, turnover had almost doubled to £4063, and the profit was £1600. Eddie now had a third tractor, a second spreader and a Rotovator. Wages had risen to £834 as he had now taken on his first employee, Norman Bell. Norman drove a tractor and did general labouring, but was considered part of the family, eating his meals with Eddie and Nora in their kitchen.

Eddie's main work was spreading fertilizer on fields, hence the need for two spreaders. Originally, he had simply delivered the cartloads of fertilizers from an

E. P. STOBART – HESKET NEW MARKET

PROFIT & LOSS ACCOUNT FOR THE YEAR ENDED 31ST MAY, 1958.

To Motor & Tractor Expenses	533	14	1
" Wages & National Insurance	424	7	2
" Repairs & renewals	189	14	3
" Baling Twine etc.	214	17	3
" Insurances	75	12	10
" Bank Charges & Cheques	6	11	5
" Stationery, Advertising etc.	14	2	7
" Accountancy Charges	12	12	–
" Hire-Purchase Interest	13	–	–
" Depreciation & Loss on Sale	215	–	–
" Net Profit for year	630	1	3
	2329	12	10

agricultural merchants to various farmers. Then he undertook to do the spreading for the farmers, using his own machinery. Most of his fertilizer was in the form of slag, heavy in phosphate.

By 1960, business continued to do well, with turn-over up to £7,893, though the profit had increased only marginally to £2,026. This was mainly due to a rather large capital expenditure that had occurred during 1960.

'I got this call one day from the County Garage in Carlisle,' remembers Nora, who was doing the books and answering the phone for her husband's little business. 'Someone wanted Eddie. I said he wasn't here. A voice then asked if Eddie was still interested in the guy down at the garage. I said: "What guy? I

17

BALANCE SHEET AS AT 31ST MAY, 1958.

ASSETS

Threshing Machine per last account	150	–	–			
Less Depreciation	15	–	–	135	–	–
Fordson Tractor per last account	250	–	–			
Less Depreciation	50	–	–	200	–	–
Nuffield Tractor per last account	150	–	–			
Less Depreciation	30	–	–	120	–	–
Fuel Tanks per last account	50	–	–			
Less Depreciation	5	–	–	45	–	–
Car at cost	35–	–	–			
Less Received on Sale	10	–	–			
Loss on Sale	25	–	–			
Car at cost	200	–	–			
Less Depreciation	40	–	–	160	–	–
Baler at cost	400	–	–			
Less Depreciation	40	–	–	360	–	–
Spreader at cost	45	–	–			
Less Depreciation	10	–	–	35	–	–
Sundry Implements at cost				59	8	7
Sundry Debtors				247	–	6
Cash in Hand				28	–	–
				1389	9	1

Certified correct in accordance with the books and information received.

CARLISLE.   CHARTERED ACCOUNTANTS

didn't know Eddie was going to take on someone else. What's this guy's name?'' There was silence at the other end. Then the voice explained that it was a lorry called a Guy. Eddie was apparently interested in buying it.'

Which he did; Eddie's very first lorry. Until then, he had pulled his farming machinery or had delivered loads by tractor. The lorry was a second hand Guy, a four-wheeler Guy Invincible, which he bought for £475. Ideal for carrying and tipping basic loads of slag.

Eddie decided to have the lorry painted; make it look a bit brighter. The colours he chose were Post Office red (roughly the colour of the panels on his threshing machine, which he'd always liked) and Brunswick green. On the cab door, in small but discreet lettering, he had painted the words: 'E.P. Stobart, Caldbeck 206, Cumberland'.

And so the first Eddie Stobart lorry hit the road. But, alas, not for long. The Guy turned out to be a bad buy, a load of trouble, always going wrong. Eddie sold it a few months later for £420, thus losing £55 on the deal.

Instead, he bought a new Ford Thames lorry, which cost the large sum of £1,450. He financed it through a hire-purchase agreement, putting down a deposit of £135. A big commitment, but he hoped the fertilizing business was going to be profitable in the years to come.

At the same time, Eddie and Nora decided to enlarge their bungalow. It was proving too small to hold their family of four young children plus trying to run a business from the same premises.

Then, out of the blue, Harrison Irvinson, the local agricultural merchant who had been providing work spreading slag, went out of business. Eddie was left with a full order book of slag to be delivered and spread, a lot of expensive equipment, including a new lorry, but no slag. You needed a licence to be an agricultural merchant, which was not easy to get, and Eddie didn't have one. You also needed capital to set up as a merchant and buy stock.

Eddie had a few sleepless nights but eventually managed to do a deal with a Carlisle firm of agricultural merchants, Oliver and Snowden. But, as well as spreading the fertilizer, Eddie Stobart now also had to go and collect it. Most of it came from ICI or other steel plants in Middlesbrough, Scunthorpe or Corby, a residue of the smelting process. So Eddie had to acquire more lorries and drivers.

This led one day to a visit from an ICI official who said that Eddie's premises at Hesket were right in the middle of an area where the company wanted to expand their supply of slag for agricultural purposes. ICI was lacking a suitable slag store, a dump, where slag could be kept till needed. It offered to pay Eddie to go and collect the slag, and promised regular work, but he would have to build the slag store himself, and a weighbridge, and get the appropriate planning consents – all at his own expense.

Eddie worked out that the total cost would come to some £8000. Where could he get such a sum? And if he could, would it be worth it? Eventually, with the help of Penrith accountant, N.T. O'Reilly, he managed to borrow the money and the slag store was built.

In this way, Eddie's business as an agricultural contractor continued to expand during the 1960s. He took on more lorries and drivers and acquired more customers amongst the farming community. By 1969, he had three lorries, three tractors, three spreaders and a JCB. His turnover that year was £79,700, his profit £4687 and his wage bill £6992.

He even survived what could have been an extremely serious setback when the agricultural fertilizer department of ICI was taken over by Fisons, who then decided they didn't need the use of Eddie's slag store any more. They gave him a month's notice, then pulled out of the agreement.

Once again, Eddie and Nora slept badly for a few weeks and did a lot of heavy praying. In the end, it led to them purchasing slag in their own right, rather than just collecting and distributing it for others.

During all these developments in the 1950s and 1960s, throughout the setbacks and excitements, Eddie and Nora remember doing a lot of praying. They continued to be devout Christians but were moving towards the more evangelical wing. Eddie was a lay preacher, and he and Nora became involved in the Cumbrian branch of the Gideon movement, helping to distribute Bibles to schools, hospitals and prisons. They both attended Christian meetings all over the county and were continually putting up visiting preachers at their home in Hesket.

Eddie never worked at all over the weekends, whatever the drama might be. Sunday was devoted to God; Saturdays to their young family. Business was not the most important thing in their life; it was just what they did during the week.

YOUNG EDWARD

The Stobart children were all very blonde when young, but then most native Cumbrian children are born fair-haired. You see them 'up street' in Carlisle on Saturday mornings, in from the country and shopping with their mums and dads, being dragged around, little boys and girls, so fresh-faced and fair, like little angels. It's the Scandinavian in them coming out, leftovers from the Viking Norse raiders.

The Norse influence can also be seen in the rural place names: 'beck', meaning stream, 'how', meaning small hill, 'pike', for sharp summit, 'thwaite', meaning clearing. 'Howbeck', the name of the little village school in Hesket, is a perfect example, combining two Norse words. This was the school that all the young Stobarts attended, just as Eddie himself had done.

Young Edward, the Stobarts' third child, started at Howbeck at five years old, and was taken there each day by his sister Anne, aged seven. They walked the one-and-a-half miles to get there, along with their six-year-old brother, John. Edward has no memory of his mother taking him to school; his memory of her during his childhood was that she was ill and very often in bed all day. 'I don't even remember her making my breakfast,' he says now. During her thirties, Nora did have a sequence of illness, such as gallstone problems which confined her to her bed, but she was later to recover her health.

Edward has a clear memory of what he thought about his first day at Howbeck school: 'I hated it. It was a nightmare from day one. I remember thinking: "How am I going to get through it, so that I can go home and play?"'

By playing, Edward meant watching his father's machinery in the yard, tipping and loading, or going to his grandfather's farm and playing with the animals there. His little job each day was to go to his grandfather's to pick up a can of milk for their family.

Edward's father had remained at Howbeck all his school life, such as it was, as in those days pupils could stay there until they were fourteen. By the time young Edward attended, Howbeck had become a primary school, which meant that, at eleven years old, you had to move on elsewhere. There were just two classes in the school: Class One, for those aged five to eight, and Class Two, for those aged eight to eleven. Edward reminisces: 'I remember a Miss Allcorn taking Class One – and what I remember about her was that she had a bubble car. Miss Ashbridge took Class Two and she was the headmistress.' Kathleen Ashbridge always retained pleasant memories of the Stobart boys. They were not great scholars, but she had no trouble from them.

'If I was naughty at school,' says Edward, 'I did it behind the scenes. But I wasn't a troublemaker. All I got told off for by Miss Ashbridge was for not doing well. She'd then put me in the corner with my face to the wall. I quite liked sums, that was about all. Nothing else. I spent a lot of time just sitting, drawing cars and lorries.'

According to Nora, Edward was always the most adventurous of her four children, and the one who usually got injured. 'He had accidents all the time. One of the earliest was when he was rushing into Mrs Jardine's field to feed her hens. He was in such a hurry that he ran straight into a barbed-wire fence. He cut his whole face; the blood was awful. But that was typical. He was always falling off things or stumbling over things.

'But he was also very sensitive and generous, would do anything for people. He was always quite quiet; all the boys were quiet, really. Anne was the talker in the family; she was the clever one.'

Anne was the only person to pass the eleven-plus in her year at Howbeck. 'In fact,' she says, 'I was told I was the only one to have passed it for seventeen years – the last one being my Uncle Ronnie.' She went to Wigton Nelson Tomlinson grammar school at Wigton – alma mater of Melvyn Bragg.

When it was time for Edward to sit his eleven-plus, he had no expectations. 'I never thought for one moment I would pass,' he says. 'I was useless at all school work. In the exam, I couldn't answer a single question. I just sat there, drawing tractors. I felt pretty disgusted with myself. I don't remember any one else in my year passing, so we all went to the secondary modern together.'

This was Caldew School, Dalston, opened in 1959, so still quite new when Edward arrived in 1965. It became a comprehensive in 1968, while Edward was still there. There were five hundred pupils, both boys and girls, and lots of playing fields and space, being in a semi-rural situation. Dalston itself is a rather affluent dormitory village, just five miles from Carlisle, facing towards the Caldbeck Fell. Each day, Edward went on his bike into Hesket then caught the school bus for the ten-mile journey to Dalston.

Edward remembers, 'I was put in the dunces' class from the beginning, in Mrs Carlisle's class. William got put in the same class when he arrived. We were both big dunces all the way through our school lives. They called it the Progress Class. But we all knew what it meant.

'I was never good at writing. If I concentrated really hard, I might just make six spelling mistakes on a page. But usually I got every word wrong. I could never see the point in writing. I didn't feel thick; I was just a dunce at lessons. I felt older than the others in many ways. At twelve, I felt about twenty. I knew about general things, about how things worked, which they didn't. I wasn't street-wise – I never watched television at home, ever, so when the other lads spent hours talking about TV programmes, I didn't know what they were on about. But all the same, I felt mature compared with all of them.

'I'm not sure what they thought of me. A bit strange perhaps, eccentric. I was a bit of a loner – I never wanted to be in anyone's gang and I didn't have a best friend. At playtime, I'd often go and help the school gardener. Even during lessons, I'd try to get off and go with him. I always wanted to use his lawnmower – one of the big ones, you know, that you can sit on and drive. I thought it was a brilliant machine. But he'd never let me. Instead, he'd let me help on the hedge cutting. I enjoyed it better than any lessons.

'But I had some good laughs at school, got up to mischief now and again. I once locked a teacher in the store cupboard. The deputy headmaster was Mr Mount. We called him Bouncer – I suppose because he was small and fat and bounced along.

'I got caught once for smoking by Bouncer. It was me and John behind the gym wall. It was reported to our parents. My dad wasn't very worried: "Did it make you sick?" he asked me. I said yes. "Same as me," he said. He was very laid-back, my dad. He gave us a lot of rope.'

Nora worried about Edward's bad school reports, but always told him that all he could do was his best. 'The trouble was, Edward never did his best. So I used to tell him that at least he must always be honest.'

Kenneth Mount, now retired but still living in Carlisle, remembers the Stobart boys well. He taught at

Caldew School from its 1959 opening until 1986, when he retired. He became deputy headmaster and was indeed known as Bouncer – but not for his appearance, so he says. 'I was called Bouncer because I bounced them out of school. Oh yes, I could be very tough on them.'

He confirms that Edward went into the remedial form on his arrival at the school. 'We would have had reports from his primary and knew that he wasn't very good at reading and writing. No, he wasn't ESN [educationally subnormal]. We had special schools for those sort at the time in Carlisle. If he'd been really bad, he would have gone there. He was just, how shall I put this as I have no wish to be derogatory? A slow learner. William was even slower. Academically, neither was exactly successful.

'But you have to understand that they were typical of many country lads. School was an irrelevance to them. They would be up early morning doing jobs on the farm, then working in the evening when they got home. School was just what they did during the day. And if you think about it, it was more interesting for a certain sort of boy to be at home, surrounded by machines and animals, than sitting at a desk in school. But Edward's character was excellent, and his behaviour. I knew the family; I knew he came from a good Christian home.'

On Sundays, Edward went to Sunday School and to church with his brothers and sister. Given a choice at the time, he would not have gone as he didn't enjoy it. It was just something he was forced to do, although he did believe in God.

There was some slight social demarcation at school amongst the rural children, between the various farmers' sons. Many of these were hard up, especially if their fathers were small-holders in rented farms, or if they were farm labourers or farm contractors. Some farmers were, by contrast, quite well off, or appeared well off, especially if they owned several vehicles, as the Stobarts did.

'I knew my father was a contractor, with about four or five people working for him but, no, I never felt well off,' says Edward. 'We did have a car, a Morris Oxford, but I never had a new bike. I always had a second-hand one. We did have a summer holiday, but never abroad. We usually went to a guest house in Cornwall or Devon.

'The pipes once got frozen at school and we were all told to bring our own drinks to school. I took a bottle of water. Some people brought bottles of lemonade. I remember thinking, well, they must be well off . . .'

Edward was fascinated by money from an early age and was always looking for jobs that would earn him something. From about the age of eleven, he did what his father had done as a boy, chopping up wood to sell as kindling sticks. He seems to have had it better organized than his dad, making an attempt at mass production. Edward got his dad to order a load of old railway sleepers, which he paid for, then had them

sawn up into lengths. He chopped them into sticks
and bagged them in old animal-feed bags he got from
his Uncle Ronnie's cattle-feed mill. Each day, he would
take two bags of sticks on the school bus to Dalston,
thereby getting free transport, where he sold them to
teachers at three shillings a bag.

Very soon, Edward's earnings mounted up. He
always kept his money in cash, in his pocket, and
when the coins grew too bulky, he changed them into
notes. By the age of fourteen, he was carrying around
with him £200 in notes: an enormous amount for a
boy of fourteen in 1968. Today, of course, we would
immediately suspect a schoolboy with such a sum of
selling drugs. Not Edward, though, from his God-
fearing family, in rural Cumbria.

Edward isn't sure why he didn't put the money in
a bank or the post office, to make it earn a little bit of
interest: 'I don't know – I just liked the feel of it. I
always kept it in this trouser pocket, at the front, all
the time – even when I was at school.' Nor is Edward
sure why he didn't leave the money at home, if only
under the bed. 'Perhaps I worried about burglars,'
he muses. 'It just seemed safe, always having it on
me.'

Edward didn't, however, leave the money in his
pocket when he changed at school for PE or games.
'Oh, I took it out of my pocket then. I'd hide it in a
secret place: in my satchel . . .' That must have fooled
everyone. Yet Edward insists that he didn't even half-
want people to know, to be aware that he was a boy

of means. 'I never told people. I didn't go around boasting at school. My parents didn't know either. I can't really explain it, except to say I just liked the feeling of having my money on me.

'But it wasn't the money itself that was so important. It was the sign that I'd achieved something. I was always like that, setting myself little aims, to sell so many bags in a week, make so many pounds in a month. I liked beating my own targets which I'd set for myself. No one else knew.

'My older brother, John, also did jobs around the place; he wasn't lazy, but he was never at all interested in money. Not like me: I'd agree to wash my dad's car for a certain price and try to do it in a certain time.

'It felt good, to watch it mount up. I didn't spend it, well, not much of it. Perhaps some clothes as I got a bit older. As it got bigger, I told myself I was saving to buy my own car but, really, I was mainly saving the money because I liked seeing it mount up.

'I suppose you could say I was insecure, which I probably was. Having money made me feel a bit more secure. But, then again, nobody ever knew what I'd saved, so how did I gain by that?'

There is one other explanation why Edward got such secret satisfaction out of salting his little earnings away; why having a stash in his pocket, on his person, made him feel good, perhaps even better than most others. It happened when he was aged seven. At that time, work was being done on the house and the family was living in a caravan on the site. 'One day,' says Nora, 'Edward decided to climb up on the roof. I've no idea why. That was the sort of thing he was always doing – to see how the slates fitted, I should think. Anyway, he fell off and was badly hurt. And that was when it all began. The shock of it brought on his stammer.'

Edward clearly remembers the day of his fall. 'It wasn't the house roof. It was the roof of an outside toilet. The builders had left stuff lying around, so I just decided, for no reason, to climb up on some oil drums they'd left; take a look at the roof. It was a slate roof with a big hole in it where they were repairing it. And I just fell right through. I wasn't seriously hurt, not that I can remember. But, in about a day, I realized I'd developed a stutter. Fear, you might say. That's what caused it suddenly to happen like that.'

Nora took Edward to a speech therapist in Wigton for several years but it didn't seem to help that much. It didn't help William either. 'Oh yes,' says Nora, 'the same sort of thing happened a bit later to William. So I was then taking both of them. It was bad throughout all their childhood and youth.'

Around 1.2 per cent of children (about 109,000) in England and Wales between the ages of five and sixteen develop a stammer each year. No one has ever conclusively explained the causes or the triggers or why, over the decades, the figures have stayed roughly the same. It occurs throughout the world, across all cultures, all social groups. And everywhere it shows the same remarkable characteristic: four times as many boys are afflicted as girls. Hard luck on the Stobarts, having it happen to two of their number.

Edward's own theory is that it's all to do with trying to speak too quickly: 'That's when I always have trouble, when I want to say too much, all at the same time. I start one sentence before I've finished another, so it comes out as a stutter. I'm thinking too far ahead, that's it. Same with eating: I eat far too fast. Always have done. I used to bolt all my meals – in fact, really, I didn't like eating. What used to happen was that I couldn't really taste what was in my mouth, so I was rushing to the next bite, to see if that tasted better. I used to say I wished they would invent pills that would save the bother of sitting down and eating.'

Edward doesn't recall his stutter being a particular handicap at school. 'It was just embarrassing, that was it really. I don't think it got me down, not that I can remember. There were certain words and sentences I couldn't say. When you see them coming, you try and say something else. Which means you often don't say what you want to say.

There was one word I couldn't say: Stobart. I always hesitated on that. It's better now, because most people down South pronounce it "Stow-bart", not "Stob-burt". I find "Stow-bart" easier – it probably is the proper way. Having a stutter does make you try to speak properly. If anyone ever did try to tease me at school, then I tried to get in first. Take the mickey out of myself before they could.'

Nora says Edward's stutter has greatly improved

over the years, though she notices it can still be bad if he gets overexcited. 'Perhaps it will go in the end, now he has much more confidence. After all, Eddie conquered his.'

Eddie, too, had a stammer, although to hear him today, there is no trace of it. He so clearly loves talking, telling stories, anecdotes and moral tales. This is in contrast to Edward who, even today, clearly doesn't like talking, especially about himself. 'My stammer arrived when I was about ten years old,' says Eddie. 'It happened in much the same ways as Edward's – after an accident. I caught my thumb in a door and the shock made me stammer from then on. But it left me at the age of seventeen. And I'll tell you exactly how. It was the first day I was ever asked to stand up in chapel and talk. I didn't want to. I was scared to, because of my stammer. But God took me by the hand. God helped me to cure it.'

During the years he had his stammer, Eddie can't remember being worried by it. 'A stammer can be useful, you know. When I was queuing up for sausage and chips, I would say s-s-s-sausages and ch-ch-ch-chips p-p-p-p-please, and I would always get given two more sausages than the others!

'I'll tell you a little story about a man with a stammer. He was a Bible seller, going round the doors, selling Bibles. And he was a great success, this Bible seller, the best Bible seller in the region. Naturally enough, all the other Bible sellers wanted to know the secret of his success, how he could possibly manage with his stammer. "It's really very easy," he said. "When they open the door, I say to them 'Would you like to b-b-b-buy a Bible, or shall I r-r-r-read it to you . . .'"'

Eddie laughs and laughs at his own story, eyes twinkling, as merry as the little gnomes in his garden. This, again, is a contrast to his son Edward. Even as a young man, Edward was always the serious one, devoted to hard work rather than God, to getting on; determined to beat his own targets, whatever they might turn out to be.

EDWARD GOES TO WORK

There was never any doubt about where Edward would be employed after he left school. He always knew exactly what he was going to do: carry on as before. He would work with his father full time, without the inconvenience of having to go to school during the day and thus waste so many precious working hours.

No other career ever entered his mind, not even something which, in an ideal world, he would like to do if things had been different. The only childhood fantasy career that ever tempted Edward was to drive cars like Stirling Moss. In a fantasy world, yes, it might have been nice to be a racing driver.

But, of course, Edward always inhabited a very real world. By his own admission, he'd hardly been a childish child or a soppy teenager, feeling grown-up from the age of twelve. From that age onwards, he'd been doing man's work for his father, driving tractors and diggers or any other bits of machinery his father was using. At the age of fourteen, he was even driving a JCB – illegally of course. 'The JCB driver had left,'

Edward recollects, 'and my father had a contract through Brown's of Thursby for some work on the new M6 between Junctions 42 and 43. It was the long summer holidays from school, so I took over the JCB and did the work.

'My job was to dig holes for the new signposts being put up along the motorway and the slip roads. You don't realize how many signs there are on the motorway: hundreds of them. When I'm driving on the M6 today, I always look out for the ones I put up. They're very deep, you know. They can be ten feet in the air, but they probably go ten feet into the ground as well.

'I worked with an Irish gang. I dug the holes with my JCB, the Irish lads put the signs in. They didn't know how young I was, or anything about me. I never told anyone at school, never boasted I was driving a JCB. I loved it – loved every minute.'

Edward estimates he did that job for six months, despite the fact that his school summer holidays were only six weeks long. 'In the whole of my last year, I probably only spent three months of it at school.'

Some grammar schools at that time, in the big metropolis of Carlisle and even in smaller towns like Wigton, taught the classics and had modern-language groups and science sets. Instead of this, Caldew School, a newly emerging comprehensive serving a rural community, tried to specialize and suit its pupils to their future careers by creating an agricultural course for those about to leave. Edward took this course in his fourth and final year at school. He enjoyed it, as it mainly meant visits to farms and places of agricultural interest.

Edward finally left school in the summer of 1970, aged fifteen. His leaving report, signed by his form tutor, Mr Monaghan, and his headmaster, Mr Douglas, indicates that Edward's frequent absence made a true assessment of him difficult. The leaving report does, however, manage to praise his 'natural flair for repairing machinery' and how on 'numerous occasions [he has] shown good organizing ability in practical tasks connected with his agricultural studies'. The mention of some sort of organizing ability is interesting, though it appears to refer to organizing himself rather than others in practical tasks. The report makes it pretty clear that he had made 'limited academic progress', but that he should prove to be 'an excellent employee'.

On leaving school for good, Edward just carried on working for his father. His next contract was with a firm called Sidac at Wigton that was building a new factory. Edward's job was to dig the foundations. His wage, paid by his father, was £5 a week. When that contract came to an end, Edward returned to helping his father at home in the yard, working on the fertilizing side of the business.

For the next two years, till the age of seventeen, this was Edward's main occupation: spreading lime on farmers' fields. This business was expanding all the time, as Edward's father had now built the slag store and was both collecting and delivering as well as spreading lime.

CUMBERLAND EDUCATION COMMITTEE

CALDEW SCHOOL   ::   DALSTON   ::   CARLISLE
Telephone No. DALSTON 418   Headmaster J. H. DOUGLAS, B.A.

EDWARD STOBART

4TH YEAR AGRICULTURAL COURSE

Sept. 1969 - April 1970

Frequent absence has made a true assessment of
Edward's capabilities more than usually difficult but on
the occasions he has attended school he has shown obvious
practical talents. Although his performance this year in
metalwork and woodwork had not been too encouraging he has
demonstrated a natural flair for repairing machinery and
on numerous occasions shown good organising ability in
practical tasks connected with his agricultural studies.

He has shown a keen interest in agriculture and taken
an active part in the numerous visits to places of agricultural
interest which have been part of the course. In spite of a
limited academic progress this year Edward has more than com-
pensated with his well developed all round practical ability
and will prove to be an excellent employee.

We wish him well in the future.

.... Form Tutor

.... Headmaster

Edward worked all hours and weekends if necessary, as ever setting himself little targets, aiming to get so many fields spread in an hour, so many farms in a week, aiming to do more than all the other Stobart workers. His father was pleased that Edward worked so hard, but thought the weekend work was a bit unnecessary.

By this time, Eddie had half-a-dozen drivers and half-a-dozen assorted vehicles. There was still little demarcation between the employees and the Stobart family; everyone mucked in, did what jobs had to be done.

By the time he was seventeen, Edward was beginning to think that perhaps his father's attitude to business was, well, perhaps a bit laid back. No words were exchanged. No arguments took place. Edward did everything asked of him, and a great deal more besides. It was just that, in his head, young Edward could see ways, so he thought, of doing things differently, doing things more efficiently.

'Norman Bell, my dad's original driver, would go home on Friday evening often not knowing what his job was going to be on Monday. I always thought this was terrible. Or my dad would let a lorry drive empty all the way to Scunthorpe to pick up slag without bothering to try and get some sort of load to take there. I thought this was all wrong. Sometimes my dad would wake up on a Monday morning with no plans made for the week: terrible.'

Edward began to suggest his own ideas to his father. 'Well, we never fell out, let's say that. But as I got older, I might point out he had no Plan B. Plan A would be to spread lime on Monday morning. Now we all knew that always couldn't be done; you need a dry day for lime-spreading, no wind and that. So, if the weather turned out not right, you couldn't do it. Fair enough – but my father never seemed to have Plan B lined up. That meant the driver and vehicle were often standing around, doing nothing.

'Spreading fertilizer is seasonal work anyway. It's vital to have other contracts, such as quarry work, to keep the men and vehicles occupied. My father never seemed to me to think far enough ahead. That did upset me.

'He thought I was a good worker. He'd often say he wished all his workers were like me. But he also thought I was crackers. Especially when I spent my Saturdays and Sundays getting filthy black, washing all the vehicles after the drivers had all gone home.'

Mr Stobart, Senior, admits that he and young Edward did not always see eye-to-eye on how the work was planned, but then he wasn't too bothered. That was just Edward's opinion, how he saw it. Eddie had a different attitude to work and the business, which was anyway doing very well – especially in a time of inflation.

As Eddie was well aware, and perhaps young Edward did not quite appreciate, if the weather was bad and the lime could not be spread, this was not necessarily bad news or bad business. While the lime lay there in Eddie's slag store, the chances were that, by the time it was spread, the prices might have gone up. Because Eddie now owned the slag, which he paid for and collected then sold on in due course to farmers, it often paid him to be laid-back, not rushing things.

But, of course, the basic difference between father and son was not in business acumen or business economics but in their different philosophy to work as a whole. Eddie wouldn't break his own rule about weekends, keeping Saturdays for his wife and family, to have a run into the Lake District, a trip to the coast at Silloth or into Carlisle to go shopping. Sundays were always sacred. Mondays, well, they could look after themselves.

As the years had gone by, and Eddie's business had expanded, he had also grown to like parts of it better than other parts. He was never much interested in lorries; couldn't quite see their potential or the point in maximizing their use. 'I saw my lorries as a tool for my main business, not as a way to make a return on the capital I had invested in them. My profits were in buying and selling the fertilizers. I knew where I was with them. I knew what my return would be the moment I bought them. There wasn't a lot of risk or a lot of bother – and the profits were quite good, until the margins in fertilizers started to go down.'

The part of his business that gave Eddie a lot of fun and pleasure was a farm shop, which he had bought and created in Wigton. A diversification in a way, but still part of his general agricultural business. He much preferred this to lorries. 'I didn't want the hassles of trying to find work for all the drivers, planning where they had to go, what they had to do and when. So that's why I started to let Edward look after that side of things. He was the one always interested in making the most of the lorries.'

Edward began to divide his day between sitting in the house planning loads, organizing the work, the drivers' routes and timetables, and driving the vehicles himself. One moment he would be on a tipper in the yard, unloading slag, and the next, he'd be rushing to answer the telephone.

Despite having been so useless and disinterested at school when it came to reading and writing, he was now being forced to write things down, keep records, work out itineraries. A lot of it he kept in his head; Edward had always been very good at mental arithmetic and at money matters.

But he still much preferred driving, always willing to drive anything, anywhere at any time. One evening in 1974, when he was just twenty, they got an urgent order to take a load down south, to Wisbech. Edward said he would do it, even though, at that stage, he had never driven further than Scotch Corner in a truck. He didn't, of course, have an HGV licence, nor access to any heavy vehicle, so he went off in a small seven-and-a-half-ton truck which they used for delivering fertilizers on local farms. Just to complicate things, or give himself some company, he took with him his young brother William, then aged twelve.

Halfway down the A1, Edward realized he was running out of diesel fuel, with no service station in sight. A few miles later, his truck packed up completely. 'I sat on the verge of the A1 with my head in my hands in a state of panic. I didn't know what to do next. It was now well after midnight – and I had a young boy to worry about as well as myself.

'I got out and decided to hitch a lift for help. A furniture van picked me up and took me about ten miles to a transport caff where he said there might be some lorry drivers. As he drove into the caff, the top of his furniture van hit the filling station canopy outside the caff and tore bits off it. Oh no, I thought, all the damage I'm doing by having been so stupid. The driver dropped me off and reversed out quickly.

'There were six international lorry drivers inside, all from the same firm, all driving Seddons and, by chance, they had a mechanic. They said when they'd finished their tea, they'd come and help. Luckily, they were going my way. It was about two o'clock by now. I'd left William on his own in the truck for about an hour-and-a-half.

'The mechanic bled my engine for me, which you have to do when you run out of fuel. He then filled it up with enough diesel to get me to the next garage. I offered them money, but they refused. All they said was that one day I might pass one of their lorries, parked up, and it would then be my turn to help them . . .'

By the age of eighteen, Edward's father was paying him £9 a week. He still kept his savings in his pocket, which meant that, by the time he had passed his driving test, he thought he had enough to buy himself his own car.

One day, after finishing off some lime-spreading on a farm just outside Carlisle, Edward was driving down Currock Road, Carlisle, in his tractor when he passed a garage. On the forecourt was parked a brand-new Mini Clubman. A loud notice shrieked its price, only £820.

Edward stopped his tractor and went into the garage. The proprietor was sitting at his desk in his office, smoking a cigar. 'I w-w-w-want to buy that car, yon'un car out front,' said Edward slowly, pronouncing his words as well as he could.

'You need money to buy cars, lad,' said the garage owner, swinging back and forth on his chair, without bothering to get up.

'I've got some money,' said Edward.

'Can't you read, lad?' said the garage man. 'That car costs £820. In money.'

Edward was wearing a filthy woolly hat, filthy working clothes, was covered with slag and lime and clearly didn't look as if he had a penny. His youth and stammer did not improve the general impression. He looked very much to the garage man like a potter – a Carlisle expression that does not mean one who makes pots, but someone fairly scruffy, who might be a tramp or a dosser.

In his packed little pocket that day, Edward had £1000 – all in cash. His life savings from his short life so far. He pulled some of it out to demonstrate to the garage man that he was a person of some substance. The garage man immediately got up from behind his

desk, put down his cigar and assumed his best cus-
tomer-relations smile. After some discussion, Edward,
by promising cash, all of which he said he had on him,
got the price down to £780.

So Edward had wheels; a young man with transport, able to go into dances in Carlisle of a Saturday
night, and able to offer lifts home to young ladies,
which he did, but only now and again, as he was
working so awfully hard at weekends.

He got his Mini Clubman and most of his sub-
sequent cars serviced in Hesket, in the village garage
owned by Richard Woodcock, which stood right in the
middle of the village, in what was the ancient market
cross. In 1972, Richard's sixteen-year-old sister, Anne
Woodcock, came to work for Eddie in his office, typing
letters and invoices; her first job after leaving school.

Anne Stobart, Edward's big sister, the clever one
who had gone to grammar school, had been working
with her father as his secretary until then. She moved
over to work in the farm shop in Wigton once young
Anne Woodcock had settled into her job.

'My mother had just died,' says Anne Woodcock,
'and Eddie and Nora were really kind to me, giving
me the job, looking after me. I was with them for two
years. My wage was about £15 a week and I think at
the time they had ten vehicles altogether. It was
mainly agricultural work, lime-spreading and slag, but
they did do quite a bit of haulage. I remember when
they secured some sub-contract haulage work from
Barnett and Graham: that was a big event.

'I knew the family were strong Methodists; Eddie and Nora and Anne. Every year at Keswick Convention time, they would talk about it, perhaps hoping I might go with them. I'm Catholic by birth, so it wasn't really my thing. But they were very tolerant really. Other members of their family were much stricter.'

Anne enjoyed working with the two Stobart boys around, as John and Edward were just a few years older than herself. 'Edward and John were just normal farm boys. Like most of the others in Caldbeck and Hesket, they'd go for a drink on a Saturday night in Hesket or Caldbeck, or into Carlisle to the dance at the Cosmo – the Cosmo was where all the country boys went. I went there as well.

'At work, I have to say, I wasn't aware of Edward running anything, of being in charge in any way. He did most things in the business, but Eddie the father seemed to me definitely the boss.

'I was impressed by how Edward coped with his stutter. William's was far worse, so much so that often he couldn't talk at all, but Edward never let his get him down. He was determined to carry on as normal. Edward didn't lack confidence, I'll say that, but I have to say I had no idea he would go further than he'd got to already. When I worked with the Stobarts, it was just a small family business. And it seemed as if it always would be like that.'

During the two years Anne worked with the Stobarts, Edward had a rather nasty accident. Aged eighteen, he was working as usual one Saturday morning, up at six to start lime-spreading. Having finished, he came back to the yard in the late afternoon where he met Clive Richardson, one of their drivers, who had come into the yard to pick up something.

Edward asked Clive if he had got the message about his Monday job, one which Edward had personally fixed up for him on Friday. He'd given all the details to his father, to pass on to Clive.

'Oh he cancelled it,' said Clive. 'I'm not working Monday.'

'Why not?' asked Edward.

'I'd forgotten my wagon needs four new tyres. So I'm going to do that on Monday instead.'

Edward went straight to the phone and rang Barnett and Graham, the firm through which the job had come. He cancelled the cancellation, saying a Stobart truck would be there after all to do the job, and not to worry.

Edward then searched around the yard and eventually found four half-reasonably tyred wheels, which he thought were good enough to go on the truck, an Atkinson 240.

'My dad wasn't around, of course; he never was on a Saturday. I think that day he'd gone to Wigton to see how the shop was doing. Clive, the driver, was a bit disgruntled at first, as he was in a hurry to get home, but he agreed to help me get the old wheels off.'

They were very heavy wheels and the last one was proving difficult to get off. At last they managed it but, in doing so, the wheel somehow did a bounce and crashed into Edward. He was fit enough, with all the physical labour he had been doing since the age of twelve, but he was never very tall, just five feet, six inches high and, at eighteen, he was only eight stone in weight. The impact of the large bouncing wheel knocked Edward over. He fell down in a heap, breaking his leg.

Clive rang for an ambulance, then rang to tell Mr Stobart, Senior, what had happened. Meanwhile, Edward was in agony, lying on the ground, unable to move. He was also starting to shiver, as it was a very cold afternoon.

'The ambulance men arrived first, before my dad. They got out this blow-up bag thing and put my left leg in a splint, then they laid me on the stretcher. They were about to give me a pain-killing injection, which probably would have knocked me out, when at last my dad arrived.

'With a great struggle, I managed somehow to lean over on my side, get me hand in me front pocket, and I drew out my money. It was about £600 or £700. I didn't want to go into hospital, did I, carrying all that with me? At hospital, they'd take my clothes off, put me into hospital pyjamas and that. I might never see the money again. So the last thing I remember doing, before the ambulance took me away, was handing it over. But, by then, I knew the truck was OK and the job would be done on Monday.'

Eddie remembers the incident well, and the precise

words which Edward used: 'Tek hod o' this, Dad.' Eddie wasn't totally surprised; he and Nora always knew Edward kept his money on him. Many a time, Nora had ruined some of his pound notes in the washing machine when he'd forgotten to take them out of his trouser pocket.

'When I'd been Edward's age,' says Eddie, 'my father had never given me a wage when I'd worked with him. So I always made sure that Edward and then William, when they worked with me, got a wage, just like the other workers.

'They had, of course, nothing to spend it on. There was no drugs in those days and they didn't live a wild life. So we knew Edward must have saved a bit of money. Even so, we didn't know till that day quite how much he'd been carrying around with him. That was a surprise.'

Edward was taken to the Cumberland Infirmary in Carlisle. His leg was fractured in two places and it took the next seven-and-a-half weeks for him to recover. For the first week or so, he was in agony. Then he was in total frustration, wondering about what was happening back at the ranch.

'All the drivers came in at the weekends to see me: Norman Bell, Norman Glendinning, Stan Monkhouse, Clive and Selwyn Richardson, John Graham, Gavin Clark. I used to quiz each one on what me dad was doing: "Is he keeping you working?" I'd say, "Who's planning next week?"

'I was so miserable, stuck there. It was the worst

time in my whole life. Certainly the slowest – I just lay there, thinking about the trucks, night and day. I wasn't spying on my dad, when I was asking the drivers about him. I just worried that the lorry side would collapse while I was away.'

Edward's father was very pleased when, at last, Edward could return to work. 'Oh, I wanted him back as quickly as possible as well. Edward had been doing all the planning for the trucks. And by then, he really had become daft about trucks . . . .'

EDWARD GOES TO TOWN

Until 1970, Eddie Stobart had been trading simply as 'E.P. Stobart, Hesket Newmarket'. But, as the business grew with more employees, more tax to pay, more financial responsibilities, more things to go wrong or be sued for, it was time to become a limited company. On 23 November 1970, a new company was formed: Eddie Stobart Ltd.

In the accounts for the second half of that year, under assets, eight assorted lorries are listed, including a new Scania wagon and trailer, bought at a cost of £9000. There was a reported loss of £409, but that was partly explained by the firm being reorganized and the expense of the Scania.

The new company had two shareholders. Eddie Stobart owned nine thousand of the ten thousand shares. His daughter, Anne, who reached the age of eighteen that year, was given the remaining one thousand shares. It was Eddie's plan to give each of his four children, once they reached the age of eighteen, a thousand shares.

In 1971, when John reached eighteen, he declined

the offer of the shares. He was not interested in lorries or machinery, or in business generally. He simply wanted to be a farmer, so he took his inheritance in cash and bought some sheep in order to get started.

Edward on reaching eighteen, in 1972, naturally took his shares. Working in his father's firm, looking after the lorries and machinery, was exactly what he wanted to do. Anne, by now, was approaching her twenty-first birthday and was shortly getting married, becoming Mrs Anne Fearon. She was made a director of the firm that year, along with her father.

The accounts for 1972 show a huge increase in the firm's turnover since becoming a limited company; it had reached almost a quarter of a million pounds, with profits of £17,153. It is noticeable that, on the official accounts, the business of Eddie Stobart Ltd is stated as being: 'agricultural merchants and dealers in agricultural machinery, plant etc.' The farm shop, where Anne and her husband, Ken, were working – and also Eddie for a lot of the time – was doing well, and so were their other agricultural activities. But the haulage part of the company was also proving a success, thanks to the hard work and enthusiasm of Edward for all things lorry-like. This is where the future lay, so Edward thought, this was where a lot more business was to be had.

Although Eddie himself much preferred the fertilizing and farming side of the business, he allowed Edward to build up the haulage side and was prepared to listen to ideas, opportunities or suggestions for

further developments. In May 1973, Richard Woodcock, owner of the garage in Hesket, offered Eddie the
chance to visit a proper haulage firm, to see how the
big boys did it.

Richard Woodcock's father, also called Richard, was
the owner of the village shop in Hesket. He had sent
young Richard to a public school, Ampleforth, but
Richard had left with only one real ambition: to work
with motor cars. After leaving school, Richard had
become an apprentice fitter at the firm of Sutton and
Sons of St Helen's, a family firm in Lancashire. They
were a very well known, national firm whose rise to
eminence in the haulage business had been partly
based on their connections and nearness to Pilking-
ton's of St Helens, the glass giants. As they had grown
and expanded, so had Sutton and Sons and their
lorries. In 1973, they had about two hundred lorries.

Richard hadn't expected that Edward, aged nineteen at the time, was coming with his dad on the day's
outing. 'As we drove off, I was a bit surprised when
Edward jumped in the car as well. On the way down,

53

I told Eddie that if we met Alf Sutton himself, which was unlikely, I should warn him that Alf was a bit, well, the rough-and-ready type, who used strong industrial language. I knew that Eddie was a devout Methodist and might get upset. He said don't worry, he'd met all sorts in the agricultural world.

'We had a brilliant day out, toured all the premises, met some of my old friends. Eddie and Edward were both amazed by Sutton's operation. They had their own garages and repair shops which were huge, with state-of-the-art equipment. In those days, haulage firms kept their lorries for many years, looking after them themselves.

'We had lunch in their canteen and then, eventually, we did get to see Alf himself. It was a short chat, in his office. He was very helpful, giving the Stobarts some of his time and a bit of advice.'

Edward, today, can remember the advice very clearly. 'He asked us how many lorries we had at our place. We told him we had six – that was all we had at that particular time. His advice was that we should give them all up. Haulage was too tough a business. Get rid of the lorries and the drivers, he said. We'd be better off using owner-drivers for our business. So that was pretty depressing . . .'

But they did have a most interesting day out, enjoyed by all. Richard had been aware that Mr Sutton had not been particularly encouraging, haulage-wise but, looking back, he thinks Alf's words might have had a positive effect on young Edward. 'In a way, it spurred him on to prove people wrong. I think he saw what a fantastic setup Alf Sutton had and thought he could do just as well, if not better.'

In 1975, on reaching the age of twenty-one, Edward became a director of Eddie Stobart Ltd, joining his father Eddie and sister Anne. It was another good year for the firm, judging by the annual accounts. The turn-over, from sales of goods and work done, was £407,138, but costs had been high and their net profit was just £19,647.

By 1975, Edward was looking after the haulage side of the business almost completely on his own. The accounts for the end of the year show a number of vehicles being bought and sold during that year but, on average, they were running eight lorries, plus the same number of trailers and units.

Edward was determined to improve this side of the business, but was finding many problems. He lost one good driver who didn't want to do any long-distance work and drive further than the county boundaries. Rural-based, local country drivers from Hesket and Caldbeck, the sort they had always employed, many of whom Edward had grown up with, did not like doing night work or long-distance work. They were not keen, either, on anything that might be deemed urgent, drop everything, do-it-now work.

Almost all the haulage work the firm undertook was sub-contracted. A bigger haulage firm, elsewhere in Cumbria, would have the main contract, but would pass on bits to smaller firms like Eddie Stobart Ltd if they couldn't manage it all. By definition, these were very often last-minute jobs, emergencies or night work, which Edward was keen to accept, however inconvenient. It often meant he did these rotten jobs himself, for in 1975, aged twenty-one, he had passed his Heavy Goods Vehicle licence. He could now legally drive any of the bigger trucks. But he knew he was missing a lot of work by not having suitable, willing men always available. It was also a handicap being stuck in Hesket, out in the sticks, some fifteen miles from Carlisle.

In 1976, Edward came to a big decision. He felt it was time to go it alone, in two senses. He wanted to be personally running his own show, albeit still under his father's wing as part of the firm, as it hadn't entered his head not to be part of Eddie Stobart Ltd. Edward, however, also wanted a chance to be able to work without his father looking over his shoulder every day. He felt it was time for the haulage part of Eddie Stobart Ltd to be separated, literally and physically, from the agricultural and fertilizing sides. He wanted to be in Carlisle, to employ Carlisle-based drivers, to be on the spot, for a change, when jobs came up.

He'd done some sums in his head, worked out how much time and money was being wasted each time they drove the fifteen miles empty into Carlisle, just to pick up a load. 'I was fed up being at Hesket Newmarket. We'd outgrown the site, couldn't really expand any more. The fertilizing side was not really growing and we didn't need many more vehicles or men for that side of things. But I was sure the haulage side had a better future.'

Eddie listened to the arguments, the rationale, and willingly agreed with Edward. He says he'd been thinking much the same anyway. Edward's own memory is that his father had to be persuaded. He remembers that, when he found a suitable site in Carlisle with a rent of £3000 a year, his father initially told him that he was 'crackers'.

'My dad didn't see how I was going to make enough money to pay such a big rent. It was a big step for us, but my dad did agree it was the best thing to do, for all concerned. I will say that – he didn't try to stop me.'

'Edward was always the one with ambition,' says Eddie. 'He had always been suggesting better ways to do most things. John never had any interest at all. William was too young. But Edward always had this burning ambition. He was desperate to go into haulage.'

Once the big decision was made and Eddie saw how the family firm was beginning to split, with different parts and people going in different directions, he began to arrange a way of making it all neat and tidy. Eddie Stobart Ltd, since its creation in 1970, had consisted of three main parts: fertilizers, the farm shop and haulage. Eddie and daughter Anne were much more interested in the first two. It was therefore decided to parcel it up under a new name: Eddie Stobart Trading Ltd, which they would look after.

This left Eddie Stobart Ltd to concentrate on haulage. The bold young Edward, aged twenty-two, left the family yard in deepest, rural Hesket Newmarket, and headed for the big city, new people, new problems, new excitements.

His experience of haulage had been somewhat limited until then, despite his keenness and enthusiasm to get more work. And his day trip to Sutton's, to see how a real haulage firm operated, had not exactly been inspiring. It just seemed to Edward, without really working it all out, without looking around at the wider world of haulage, that the time was right for him to go into something new. New, perhaps, for Edward Stobart, but something very, very old as far as the rest of the world was concerned.

HAULAGE – THE LONG HAUL

There were several reasons why Eddie Stobart had never really been interested in haulage. It was partly his temperament, partly that he was more interested in other things which appeared much more profitable, and partly the result of history.

At the time that Eddie first started up his own business in 1958, haulage was subject to various Acts of Parliament, endless Government rules, complicated amendments and changes, the issuing of special licences – all of which resulted in haulage becoming almost a closed shop. But it had always been like that. Politics, local or national, have usually managed to have a hand in transport, ever since transporting began.

They often say that prostitution is the oldest profession; lorry driving – or similar – must have also been one of the earliest trades. For the history of haulage is almost as old as the history of man. Ever since we stepped out of the caves, there has been a need for some sort of dragging, carrying, carting. Hunter-gatherers might have done their own hunting, but they quickly learned to get stronger people, or better sleds, to drag their spoils home.

The Romans built the first proper roads in Britain, and their military haulage system was constantly clattering up and down the country, bringing luxury goods such as shellfish to the middle of Hadrian's Wall, as well as military equipment and supplies.

In medieval England, the establishment of local markets were both the cause and result of better haulage. All through history, transport has usually been at the heart of a nation's economy – both rising and falling in tandem, each reflecting the state of the other, a gauge to what is really going on.

By the fifteenth century, most inhabitants of England were only ten miles from the nearest market, even if it was just a small one, like Hesket Newmarket. There was local transport, taking local goods to market, but also long-distance transport, humping items around the country, from market to market. Documents from as early as 1444 show that specialist carters were on the roads with their horses and carts, taking cloth from the Midlands and North to London, doing it on a regular, daily basis, although they packed up in winter when the roads, such as they were, became impassable.

In the seventeenth century, as roads improved, long-distance wagons grew heavier and quicker, capable of carrying fifty rather than twenty hundredweight of goods. This was when the authorities, local and national, first thought up the idea of getting money out of road users. In 1604, the Canterbury Quarter Sessions decided to charge carts over fifty hundredweight the sum of five shillings because, so it was said, their local roads were being damaged by the heavy traffic. Yes, traffic problems, in 1604.

When the turnpike system came in, another way of getting money out of drivers was introduced, a toll being charged on all users of the turnpikes. These were the better class of road, the motorways of their day. The tolls went towards the cost of keeping the turnpikes in good condition.

One result of the popularity and efficiency of the turnpikes was a growth of coaching inns, catering for travellers. There were some 2000 of these by the early seventeenth century. It also led to the development of special horses, short-legged draught horses, like the Suffolk Punch, strong enough to pull the heaviest loads. As with the stagecoaches, fleets of horses for the goods wagons were kept at staging posts. It was estimated that each horse needed five acres of hay and oats a year to keep it going; development in transport has always had an overspill effect, bringing about ancillary changes.

In the middle of the eighteenth century came the canals. Bad news for road hauliers, not because canals were all that much quicker but because they were very much cheaper. A ton load from Manchester to Birmingham, which cost £4 by road, cost only £1 by canal. Smart carriers such as Pickfords, already established by 1766, who were operating horse wagons between Manchester and London, quickly got themselves some canal boats while still running their horse wagons.

Alas for the canals: just when they thought they were the state-of-the-art technology, about to lord it over road haulage for centuries, along came the railways. Canal use was killed off almost overnight. This seems to be the nature of the history of transport; new forms have always come along, to either replace or reduce the old forms. (It makes one wonder how on earth motor transport has lasted so long. After a hundred years, it must be time for some new form of transport to finish off the internal combustion engine.)

In 1838, when the first railways were running, there were 22,000 miles of turnpike roads in England. Within ten years, their income from tolls had dropped by a quarter and the condition of the roads had greatly deteriorated. But, once again, established companies like Pickfords adapted. They used railway wagons for long-distance jobs and local roads for local horse-drawn traffic. These local roads became busier if they led to or from a railway station. In 1846, Pickfords had 850 horses; by 1878, this had increased to 2000.

Railways created suburbs, commuters and markets with fresh produce available daily. The population grew. Industry arrived. Railways might have become the preferred way of travelling, for both people and goods, but transport in general continued to expand.

Road transport came into its own again with the arrival of the internal combustion engine in the 1890s.

Motor cars were the new glamorous inventions, but goods vehicles were also being made, almost from the beginning, at places like Leyland in Lancashire. In 1904, there were 4000 goods vehicles on Britain's roads. By the beginning of the First World War, this figure had risen to 82,000.

Just as the seventeenth-century growth in transport had created tolls, the result this time was taxes. The Budget of 1909 imposed a graduated tax on all vehicles, starting at £2 for light cars of 6h.p., rising to £32 for heavy vehicles of between 40–60h.p. There was also a tax imposed on petrol of 3*d* a gallon. Ostensibly, the rationale was the same as the turnpike toll: to raise money to maintain and improve roads and bridges, taking the burden off the local parishes. It was soon apparent, however, that not many new roads were actually being built, despite the sums being raised by the new road taxes.

What happened, of course, was that the Government quickly realized, as any Government would, that it had hit upon a brilliant wheeze for raising huge sums, which increased all the time without its having to do very much, except collect them.

The First World War stopped all transport growth but, afterwards, there was rapid expansion again. A new haulage industry, very much as we see it today, came into being. The initial spark occurred in 1920, when the Government decided to sell off cheaply some 20,000 vehicles which had been used during the war, mainly to carry munitions. It enabled many ex-service men, with little or no capital, to set themselves up as owner-drivers, or 'tramp drivers' as they were called.

The result was fairly chaotic, causing a Wild West-like stampede of unregulated, cut-throat, highly competitive, not to say dodgy and dangerous, lorries and lorry drivers. These flooded the roads and were soon fighting each other for business. Road taxes had to be paid, of course, but no licence was needed to operate; anyone could have a go.

At the top end of haulage, business continued to be good for some well-established, well-run firms with large fleets of lorries, such as Pickfords or Sutton and Sons, but they were not best pleased by the hordes of new owner-drivers. Very soon, this new breed made up some eighty per cent of the haulage industry, giving it a bad name and, even worse, forcing down prices. The railways were also not happy at being undercut by one-man lorry firms.

A Government Commission was set up to investigate the situation, and the result was the 1933 Road and Rail Transport Act. Amongst other things, it created a regulating system for hauliers, based on different grades of licences. You needed, for example, an A-licence to carry goods over a long distance for other people – or hire and reward, as it was called. A B-licence was for shorter distances and, if you were carrying only your own goods, then all you needed was a C-licence. The existing big boys all got A-licences but new, smaller firms found it very hard to get one.

After the Second World War and the arrival of a

Labour Government, the Transport Act of 1947 brought in nationalization to road haulage. Most of the big boys, with the A-licences, were bought over and British Road Services, BRS, began. Smaller, local firms were able to stay private, with a B-licence limiting them to a distance of twenty-five miles from their base. Those with C-licences, transporting only their own goods, were also left free. There were more changes and minor messings around when the Conservatives got back into power in 1953, with partial denationalization. But a system of A-, B- and C-licences still remained in 1958 when Eddie Stobart set himself up in business.

'As I remember it,' says Eddie, 'an A-licence meant you could carry goods for anyone, anywhere, over any distance. Robsons in Carlisle, for example, always had an A-licence, but they were huge. I think the only firm in our area who had an A-licence was Tysons of Caldbeck.

'You had to go to a Ministry of Transport tribunal if you wanted to get that sort of licence. You had to prove a need for it, that there was local demand, and also that the railways couldn't do it. The railways could object, which they did, and stop you getting an A-licence.

'What I had was a B-licence. I could transport other people's goods locally, or my own over any distance. I was doing roughly half and half. When we went to ICI at Middlesbrough to pick up slag, I was transporting my own goods because I'd bought it. A C-licence meant you could only transport your own goods.'

By the time Edward fell in love with lorries and decided to move into Carlisle, the laws had changed again. In 1968, the Labour Government's Transport Bill did away with thirty-five years of restrictions. A- and B-licences were scrapped; all hauliers, of any size, were suddenly free to transport goods over any distance.

Without realizing it, Edward was fortunate to come into the haulage business at the time he did. Ten years earlier and he would have found it very much harder. On the other hand, there were immediately hordes of little lorry firms again.

In 1976, some 900,000 lorries were trundling around Britain, a great many of them owned by small-time, agricultural contractors and part-time hauliers such as the Stobarts. All were competing for business, all hoping to grow and expand.

HELLO CARLISLE

The premises Edward moved into in Carlisle in 1976 were in Greystone Road, quite near the middle of the city, not far from Brunton Park, world-famous home of Carlisle United FC. It was the time when, back in the 1974–75 season, CUFC surprised, nay amazed, everyone by getting into the First Division. On 24 August 1974, they beat Tottenham Hotspur at Brunton Park, 1–0, before a crowd of 18,426 and, after three games, they zoomed to the top of the league. A perilous position, from which they soon grew dizzy and fell fast. They lasted only one season in the top flight, before dropping back to the Second Division.

But it did mean that, on match days in 1976, there were still quite reasonable crowds coming to watch Carlisle – some of whom took advantage of temporary, match-day-only parking spaces in the rather tatty, rather limited new premises of Eddie Stobart Ltd in Greystone Road. It made Edward and his staff a few bob, which went into the joint kitty to pay for cornflakes, milk, chips and other necessities of life.

The yard staff consisted of only two people when

the premises first opened, both of whom Edward brought with him from Hesket. There was Stan Monkhouse, then aged thirty-five, who had been working with Edward's father since 1960. He was born and brought up on a farm not far from Hesket and had been a farm worker till joining Eddie, aged eighteen, as a tractor driver. At the age of twenty-one, he had graduated to lorry driver, which he did for the next ten years, going back and forth from Hesket to places like Scunthorpe and Corby, carrying loads of slag.

He'd got married, had children and a home in Hesket, and was becoming a bit fed up with being away so much. Therefore, in 1973, when Edward offered him the chance to be the lorry maintenance man at Newlands rather than a lorry driver, he jumped at it.

'I'd been off for six months at the time,' recollects Stan. 'I broke my arm, falling off a trailer. When I got back, Eddie was having problems with his maintenance man, and asked me if I was interested in the job. I said yis, aye, I'll give it a go.'

Three years later, when young Edward asked Stan to come into Carlisle to look after the maintenance of his lorries, he said 'yis, aye', again. He could still come home every evening and thought it might be interesting, being part of a new venture.

'They were very different,' says Stan, 'Edward and his father. I'd always got on with Eddie, he'd been very good to me, a perfect boss, but I just fancied a change.

'I think Eddie was a bit reluctant about the move,

but Edward had outgrown Hesket. We'd had one or two orders from Metal Box in Carlisle, in 1973 I think it was, which meant going into Carlisle to load up, bringing them back to Hesket, leaving them overnight, then delivering next day. Edward could see that being so far from Carlisle was a handicap and lost us time and money.

'Eddie liked being a bit of a wheeler-dealer, going to agricultural auctions, buying and selling produce and fertilizers, mixing with the farmers, having a crack. Edward didn't like any of that side of things. I could see Edward had a vision, though I didn't know where it would lead.'

The other member of staff at Greystone Road was Stan's apprentice, seventeen-year-old David Jackson, a very cheerful, sunny-natured lad who came from a farming family at Shap. He had been working with the Stobarts for seven months, running errands, sweeping the floor, going into Carlisle to pick up parts. He was four years younger than Edward but they became close friends, both having been poor scholars at school, both preferring to work with their hands rather than sitting at desks.

There was parking space for fifteen vehicles when they arrived at Greystone Road, though in that first year they had no more than eight. 'It was all very basic when we arrived,' says David. 'There was no pit. It meant you had to lie flat on your back on the ground to work under the vehicles. It was very hard work; we all had to knuckle down.

'Stan and Edward did most of the driving, till Edward started hiring local drivers. I was quite relieved: I didn't have a class-one licence at the time, but I was so tired after each day in the garage, I couldn't have taken a lorry out at night.

'I once went to Glasgow with Edward overnight. I think he just took me with him as company, to keep him awake. We got back at four in the morning, too late for either of us to go home. There were some old shelves in what we called the bait cabin, where we ate our sandwiches. Edward cleared the shelves and we slept on them – as if they were bunk beds. Oh, I didn't mind. I did the job for love, not for money. It was exciting.'

David smiles as he recollects the excitement of the early days. 'I can't put it into words: it just was. It felt good, being part of it. And we did have some good laughs. Edward in those days quite liked playing practical jokes.' Edward himself, when pressed, also remembers having water fights with the hose pipes, after the end of a long day's work.

Nora Stobart remembers David and Edward both larking around in those early years at Greystone Road. The drivers would be out all day on a job, leaving Stan and David in the yard, working on repairs and maintenance. Edward would be in his little office, trying to drum up work, unless he was out on an emergency job. No one could have told the difference between the three of them, as they were all in boiler suits, all pretty scruffy.

'There was a rep they didn't like who started calling, asking to see Mr Stobart,' says Nora. 'They didn't want to see him so, next time he came, Edward and David climbed on a roof and pretended to be crackers, pulling faces. When asked if Mr Stobart was in, they both said "Who?" He went away and never came back.'

Edward, in fact, frequently pretended not to be who he was, even when he wasn't well known. He says now, 'If customers saw I was driving the lorries myself, they might think what sort of firm is this, why is he behind the wheel not at his desk?'

In the evenings, after work, Edward and David went out for a meal now and again, chased girls together, now and again, and, in the summer, they usually went on their week's holiday together. One year they went to Newquay, along with two other country lads. But, mainly, it was long hours and hard work.

'If I ever did manage to get a girlfriend,' says Edward, 'work always came first. I'd cancel a date if a job came up. The way I lived, I didn't meet many girls anyway. My fingernails were always dirty and my hands oily. Most of my Saturday nights were spent at places like Beattock, eating egg and chips in a transport caff, having tipped a load at Motherwell.'

Edward did drink and smoke at the time, so he was not totally without pleasures or vices. David remembers him going through a packet of twenty cigarettes, one after the other, but then he wouldn't have another one for days. He also had long hair, like most lads in the Seventies.

'I was looked upon as the first Stobart rebel,' recollects Edward. 'I wasn't really, of course, but my father and grandfather had always been strictly religious. My father did once catch me drinking. He made out it was the end of the world, that I'd done something really bad. I'd made it worse by taking William with me. He was only eleven at the time . . .'

On the business side of matters, the new drivers the firm hired from Carlisle didn't always turn out to be as good as they would have liked. 'One of them blew an engine,' says David, 'totally ruined a new lorry, just by being inexperienced. Another time, I came in one morning to find our best lorry had been turned over by a new driver in the night. It had rolled over and the cab was all bashed in. Edward looked at it and said to Stan and me: "Tha's got to have that'un on the road by tonight." We couldn't believe he was serious. It was in such a terrible state. But Stan and me set to, using about four jacks to support it, stop it falling to pieces while we worked on it, welding it together. We got it roadworthy in eight hours, working non-stop.'

David got the odd ear-bashing from Edward if he did something wrong, but says Edward never held it against him. 'All the drivers respected him. They could see he was doing the same work as they were – and a lot more.

'When we heard him saying: "No problem" on the telephone, we knew there were going to be problems. Edward would accept any work, anywhere, even if all the drivers were out, even if it meant dumping loaded goods in our garage in order to go off and pick up another load. There was nothing illegal about this. Stuff always got delivered on time, as promised. But we wouldn't have liked, say, someone from Metal Box to arrive and find their goods piled up on our garage floor.

'Edward, from the beginning, always wanted his lorries clean. We had to do them every weekend. Even on Christmas Eve, Edward always insisted that all wagons had to be washed and parked up before Stan and me went home, even if it was eight o'clock and we'd been working hard all day. He wanted everything left spick and span. It was as if it was the lorries' Christmas Eve as well . . . .'

Edward says he could never get to sleep on a Sunday or over any bank-holiday period if he thought any of his lorries had been left dirty. 'I'd never call myself a trucker. Still don't; I'm not the sort who's in love with lorries, who would go spotting. I look upon lorries as tools, there to do a job. And as with all tools, you should look after them as best you can. Lorries are a bit like ladies, aren't they? If they look good, you're on the right track . . . .' A metaphor which probably should not be explored too closely.

In its first year, Edward's firm expanded from eight to twelve trucks, but was then hit by a steel strike. 'The whole haulage industry had a terrible time,' says David. 'Edward didn't want to lay off any of the drivers, so what he did was take the tax off six vehicles. That saved him some money. He then put our twelve drivers on one week on, one week off, till work came in again.'

After a couple of years at Greystone Road, Edward acquired an old Portakabin which gave him more space. He used this as his office, and also as his sleeping quarters, if he came back too late after an emergency driving job, up to Glasgow, or down to Birmingham. It meant that, for days at a time, often for a whole week, he would not go home to Hesket and his own bed.

He became obsessed by sending out his lorries each day as cleanly as possible, even if it meant that he was the one to stay late the night before in order to wash them. 'I didn't ask the drivers to do it,' Edward explains. 'They were paid to drive, not wash. So if I wanted them all clean, I had to do it.

'What I was trying to do was move up-market. And that, mainly, meant trying to get cleaner work. Doing tipper work, carrying slag and fertilizers, or quarry work, as we'd been doing at Hesket, was the bottom end of the market, the dirty end. I wanted to move into food and drink, the clean end. You didn't need tippers for this. You needed flat-bed trailers, where the pallets could be laid.

'I persuaded my dad we needed two flat-bed trailers, Crane Fruehauf flat-bed trailers they were, which we bought from Grahams of Bass Lake. They cost £1750 each.'

Not content with moving up to flat-bed trailers, Edward wanted them to be the very latest versions.

Most hauliers of the time had open-sided, flat-bedded lorries, as opposed to tippers, and piled the pallets or the goods on the back, covered them with a bit of canvas to keep them dry, then secured them with ropes. This often led to ungainly, dangerous loads, exposed to the elements.

Edward wanted something different. 'I wanted ours converted into state-of-the-art trailers. So I sent them to a firm called Boalloy Industries Ltd in Cheshire, where they were fitted with an aluminium frame roof. Along the sides we had what we call "curtains": strong sheets of heavy-duty plastic.'

By enclosing the back of the lorry, more volume could be carried in cleaner, safer conditions. Along the whole side of each curtain, Edward decided to have inscribed the words: 'Eddie Stobart Ltd', in a clean script lettering.

This again was unusual. The norm was to have your firm's name rather modestly printed on the door of the lorry, as Edward's father had done with his first lorries. Edward was so proud of his lorries, which of course were ever so clean and the latest money could buy, that he wanted everyone to know about them.

Despite all the hard work and long hours, the firm was not becoming appreciably bigger or more profit able. In 1977, the turnover was £455,490, only marginally more than it had been two years earlier. The staff had increased to only fifteen. Profit that year was just £377. But Edward was, of course, incurring bigger costs by buying or equipping the firm with more expensive vehicles. Edward was taking a modest salary of £50 a week, putting everything he could back into the firm.

It was still a very small firm in a very crowded industry. The local giant was Robsons, which had become one of the biggest in the north of England. It had been founded in 1925 by Stan Robson in Hethersgill, a village about twelve miles north of Carlisle. He had started with a Model T Ford which he had converted, taking the seats out to make it into a small truck. In 1936, he became a limited company, Robsons Hauliers (Carlisle) Ltd. By the outbreak of the war, he had a fleet of seven lorries and the invaluable A-licence, which he put in his windscreen showing 'GOODS – Anywhere'.

Stan Robson had always given his lorries individual names: Border Prince, Border Princess, Border Laddie, Border Patrol. 'Border' was always in there somewhere, but the names could be male, female or neutral. Stan got the idea from a bus he used to drive as a young man, which had been called Border Queen.

In 1947, Stan Robson bought over a local rival firm, Thistle Transport, and doubled his fleet size to around fifty. He painted them all in his fleet colours, two tones of red. In 1949, his was one of the big A-licenced firms that got nationalized, fifty-two of his vehicles becoming part of BRS North-West, Carlisle division. But they did leave Robson with his milk trucks. In 1953, on denationalization, he bought back most of his lorries.

In 1976, by which time young Edward had moved into Carlisle, Robsons had a fleet of 180 vehicles and some very valuable, exclusive contracts, such as one with Metal Box. It had even opened a Southern depot, very ambitious for a Carlisle-based firm, down at Biggleswade.

Edward had been inspired by Suttons, impressed by how they had their own lorry maintenance and repair side, which Stan and young David were trying to emulate. He was also very impressed by Robsons, as everyone in the trade was. It had built itself into a national force from little old Carlisle: quite an achievement.

One of the many minor changes that Edward made during the three years he was based at Greystone Road was to introduce personalized names to his little fleet of fifteen lorries. Unlike Robsons, he chose to give them all female names.

He says, now, he wasn't consciously copying Robsons in any way. He was, of course, aware of their Border names, though he didn't actually like them. 'I really did it because I had some DAF lorries and there was a big, blank space under the windscreen. I put arrows at either side, but I wanted to fill up the middle somehow.

'That's when I thought of girls' names. It was just a bit of humour, sort of down-to-earth, to make it human. I suppose it was the time in my life when I was thinking of girls. The first lorry was called Twiggy. I rather fancied her at the time . . . .'

Twiggy was followed by Tammy, after Tammy

Wynette. Later came Dolly (Parton), Suzi (Quatro) and Tina (Turner): women who were all very big, and some who were also very thin, back in the 1960s and '70s.

PINK ELEPHANTS

Metal Box was the big one, the firm that all local hauliers would have liked to get orders from. Lucky old Robsons, having secured their contract, giving them regular work and contacts all over Britain.

The company is still known as Metal Box in Carlisle today and is even bigger, even more powerful. It is probably now the world's biggest manufacturer of cans, bottles, cartons of all sorts, but its company name has changed a few times over the years. It merged firstly with a French-based firm to become Carnaud-Metalbox PLC, then with an American firm, Crown Cork, the biggest can-maker in the United States and also the world's largest producer of bottle tops. The present group today has scores of factories all over the world as well as in Carlisle.

What's probably been forgotten amid all the name changes by its thousands of workers, if of course they ever knew, is that the company originally began in Carlisle. So hurrah for Metal Box, another firm from small, local beginnings that went on, like Carrs of Carlisle and John Laing, to be a world leader.

Even more surprising, the founding father of the original Metal Box firm, Benjamin Scott, came from precisely the same little area as the original John Laing and our very own Eddie and Edward Stobart. Benjamin Scott's family came from Caldbeck, where his father was a cooper, or barrel maker. Young Benjamin was sent to London to become an apprentice printer, returning to Carlisle in 1799 to open his own printing and stationery business. When he retired in 1832, it was inherited by his nephew, Hudson Scott.

Hudson Scott was the family's real entrepreneur and businessman, alive to all the new inventions and developments, introducing steam engines into his printing works. In 1869, he opened his own factory in James Street, Carlisle, specifically for stencil printing onto tin boxes. The Victorians loved fancy, decorated boxes of all sorts, for commercial and commemorative purposes. By 1882, Hudson Scott and Sons, as the firm was called, had two hundred employees.

Hudson Scott was a model employer, being a devout Quaker. He paid his staff well, provided them with clinics, health checks, sports clubs, outings, swimming pools. Less than a mile away, in Caldewgate, Jonathan Dodgson Carr, also a Quaker, was doing much the same with his biscuit workers. The firms rose together, one making the biscuits, the other supplying the fancy tins.

In 1906, Hudson Scott had 1200 employees and was the largest metal-box manufacturer in Britain. In 1910, a branch factory opened in Newcastle followed by a Paris office in 1911. In 1921, a number of similar firms decided to merge themselves together to form the Metal Box and Printing Company. The managing director of Hudson Scott Ltd, F.N. Hepworth, became the first chairman of the Metal Box company.

The Carlisle factory remained the company headquarters, with the biggest factory. Mr Hepworth resisted all attempts to transfer his Carlisle works and offices to London. In Carlisle, the firm's design department attracted some of the most talented artists of the day, such as Thomas Bushby, Paul Hudson and Robert Forrester.

In the mid 1950s, by which time Metal Box factories were established all round the world, a second and more modern can-making plant was established in Carlisle in Botcherby – not far from Edward's yard in Greystone Road – but the James Street factory continued to be the bigger of the two factories in Carlisle.

In 1954, young Colin Rutherford, aged twenty-four, joined Metal Box at their James Street factory, after a short spell as a clerk with British Gypsum. Over the next fifteen years, Colin was promoted from Wages Clerk to Tin-store Foreman, then to Assistant Transport Officer till, finally, in 1969, he became Transport Officer on a salary of £1100 a year.

Metal Box, Carlisle, had eight lorries of its own, but most of its goods, in and out, were being transported by Robsons of Carlisle. On average, they had twenty-five lorries a day working for Metal Box. 'Nothing had ever been signed,' says Colin. 'It was a gentleman's agreement, which had gone on for years. I just inherited it.

'If Robsons couldn't do a job, then they, not us, did the sub-contracting. I wanted to change it when I became Transport Manager, being young and keen and trying to make a name for myself. But I wasn't able to do much about it.

'Then, in 1976, as we got near to Christmas, we suddenly had so much work. This often happened at that time of the year. The beer cans would be ready to go out, but there wouldn't be enough lorries to take them. Robsons had about two hundred lorries at the time, but they still couldn't cope.

'The factory manager spoke to me and asked me to sort it out. He wanted the cans shifted on the delivery date. It was my problem, as Transport Manager. I agreed but said my hands were tied, because of the arrangement we had with Robsons. I said if you take the rope from my hands, then I can do something about it.

'He agreed I should try and find another firm to help out. Robsons weren't at all pleased, when I told them what I was going to do. But they had to agree, on condition – so they said – that I didn't personally contact any of their normal sub-contractors. They didn't want me dealing with them; they'd always done that.

'So I sat there with the Yellow Pages, desperate to find someone to take a few loads. I had three foolscap pages of the names of firms I wasn't allowed to contact, so it was pretty hard to find anyone local at all.

'I saw the name Eddie Stobart Limited in the book. I knew Eddie was an agricultural contractor, who spread fertilizers, but I didn't know if he had any wagons. I made a call, left my name with someone. It was Edward who rang back.

'He said yes he had lorries, how many did we want? I said we just wanted one load done the next day, but there might be more after that. He said no problem. From the beginning of November, right through till Christmas, he baled us out. We used him for one or two loads every day for two months.

'Robsons were not at all happy when they heard. They said we shouldn't use Stobart again, once the Christmas rush was over. They had their own regular sub-contractors. But I told Edward that, as he'd helped us out, I'd try and give him some more work – if we were busy, and if Robsons couldn't cope.'

And so Eddie Stobart Ltd got a foot in the door of Metal Box. Their very first job had been a one-off in 1973, while still at Hesket, but, from 1977 onwards, they were getting fairly frequent, if irregular and small-scale, jobs. Robsons was still the contract haulier for Metal Box. There were also other firms, all much bigger than Stobart's, who got occasional work and were waiting in the wings for any crumbs.

'Stobart was just one of the many little firms we used from time to time,' says Colin. 'But I was impressed by how Edward was investing in new vehicles and new equipment. I liked his honesty and efficiency. He was always available, twenty-four hours a day, and never let us down. He said "No problem" to everything, big or small. There was once a time when we ran out of a special sort of lacquer. There were forty-two Metal Box factories in the group at the time, so I rang round and found that the Leicester factory could let us have a drum.

'When I told Edward, he went straight off in his own car. He took the seats out first, to make more room, in order to fit in the drum. He was back that same day. Nothing had been said about the money before he went. He said we could sort that out later, when he got back.

'Their lorries were always clean and immaculate, much smarter than our own. When we had the MD coming to visit us, or some directors from London, I'd shunt our lorries out of the way, all of which were eight to ten years old. I'd tell Edward to make sure there were a couple of Eddie Stobart lorries in a prominent position in the loading bays when the boss was walking round.

'That was how Edward built his business. His lorries were always smart. Nothing was too much trouble. As Transport Manager, I was always having to ring round people who would say well, I don't know, I might, we'll have to see, then they'd tell us about their problems and end up making it all so complicated. Edward always made things so easy.'

'I knew Robsons were very upset when we got that first job,' says Edward. 'They didn't like us getting the work. But it was noticeable that Robsons and the others soon had the same sort of equipment that we had. They became standard for everyone.'

But, meanwhile, Edward's firm was still scratching around for orders, from anyone, for anything. Although they were trying to go clean, they were still taking dirty jobs, including some pig iron, which meant an extra swilling down of the wagons after the day's work. 'My answer was always the same to any job request. If it was late at night, or really awkward. I didn't tell them the twenty or so reasons which might make it difficult. Then I had to sit down and sort it all out. It meant we soon had a good name with Metal Box and everyone else. They could rely on us.'

Perhaps the fact of Edward's stammer was another element that made him stick to an instant, laconic 'No problem.' and then hang up. If he'd been able to get his tongue round all the things he then had to sort out, he might have turned down the odd job . . . .

David Jackson says it was remarkable how Edward did cope on the phone, despite his verbal handicap. He would always try to say the minimum, or get others to do the phoning for him but, as customers got to know him, he was more at ease. Some of them, thinks David, rather warmed to him because of his impediment, making it almost an asset at times.

As the firm expanded and they got more orders, there was more paperwork to be done. Once a week, on a Thursday, Eddie Stobart would send his new secretary, Sylvia, over from Hesket to Carlisle to help Edward with some of his office work. She would type out the invoices for Edward and do the wages, so he could concentrate on organizing the drivers and finding more work.

'After we'd done a job for a new firm,' says Edward, 'I'd ring up and ask for any more. They usually said no. That was all the work they had. But I alerted my drivers to keep their ears open when they were delivering, to hear if there was work going, if any of the other hauliers were having problems.

'In those days, transport managers didn't move around. They were there for ever and they had their own favourite hauliers, people they'd known for ever, who gave them a bottle of whisky at Christmas; I had to break into all that. I did it by concentrating on two things: price and service. It's always that way round. In the end, price is what matters most to them, what gets you the job. But of course if the service isn't good, they won't come back to you next time.'

Edward felt he always had no option, if he wanted to expand. He had to take on every job, even if he had to do it himself. 'I once left Carlisle at 9 p.m., after a full day's work, on a Metal Box job for London. I delivered the goods, then turned straight round with another load, arriving back in Greystone Road about 10 a.m. This was probably not legal at the time, as I had been doing too many hours.

'I never actually fell asleep at the wheel, but now and again, well, it was close. I often did see pink elephants on the road. When that happened, I either opened the window to let the cold breeze in, or I stopped for a while on the hard shoulder.

'I lived that sort of life for at least ten years – from about 1976, when we moved to Carlisle, till about 1986. I worked in the office during the day and drove four or five nights a week.

'I only ever had a few hours sleep. I slept on a camp bed in the Portakabin and never ate proper meals. In the morning, when I woke up, I'd go to a shop and get a bottle of milk and some cornflakes. That was my breakfast, which I ate at my desk. At the age of twenty-five, I still weighed only eight stone.

'Looking back, I shouldn't have done such long hours. I should have kept myself fresh for each new day. But I thought it was the only way. No job was refused, even if I had to do it. I suppose it was insecurity. I still feel that, in a way, even now. I think if I don't work hard every day, we'll go bust. It was naive, I suppose. I should have used my head more. I just thought that every load could be my last load, so I had to keep at it.

'We still had no contracts at that time. We were still only sub-contractors, apart from odd Metal Box jobs. We got stuff passed on from other hauliers or from firms when their regular hauliers couldn't manage it. Nothing was ever certain.

'We worked from day to day, with nothing in the future. It might all come to an end at any moment. That's why I worked so hard. And that's why my dad continued to think I was crackers – for working so hard with such small returns. I did begin to wonder myself at times, if it was all going to be worth it.' In

1980, two things happened to change Edward's life and the firm's life: Edward got married and the firm moved into new premises.

A WEDDING AND A WAREHOUSE

All of Edward's constant work, being a slave to his lorries or his Portakabin, meant that he had little time for social life. There wasn't much chance of meeting girls or taking them out if your Saturday evenings were spent in some transport caff in the middle of nowhere. But there was one girl he did regularly see: Sylvia Turner, his dad's secretary who came in on Thursdays to help out in his office. They eventually started going out – when of course he had the time.

'We got married in 1980', says Edward, 'at the register office in Carlisle, at eleven on the Saturday morning. We had a small reception afterwards at the Crosby Lodge Hotel. Oh yes, we did have a honeymoon. We went to Morecambe on the Saturday evening, but we'd left by one o'clock on the Sunday. Ten minutes after we were back in Carlisle, I got an urgent call from Metal Box to take a vehicle to Hartlepool.'

Edward's parents were pleased that, at the age of twenty-six, Edward had found someone. However, being deeply religious, they were not too thrilled that

Sylvia had been married before and had a child. Hence the register office as opposed to a church wedding.

Edward and Sylvia moved into a brand-new, £23,000 semi-detached, three-bedroom house at Great Corby, just outside Carlisle, for which Edward had earlier put down a £3000 deposit. He had been intending to live there on his own before he had finally decided to get married.

Around the same time, there was another important development in the Stobart family which directly affected the family businesses and Edward himself. Father Eddie, having by now reached the age of fifty, was keener than ever on his evangelical work and, along with his wife Nora, was beginning to think that he'd had enough of running a business. There were more important things in his life he wanted to do.

His family was by now settled, more or less, their jobs and lives taking shape. Anne and her husband, Ken, were running the farm-shop side of things. John, who never had any interest in business, was happy farming. Edward was busy with his lorries in Greystone Road. William, the youngest, was also very keen on lorries but, unlike Edward, he had no interest at all in organizing them or doing any office work of any sort. He was much more content to be one of Edward's drivers, which is what he became, on reaching the age of twenty-one.

Eddie, however, still had a good eye for a deal, a bit of wheeler-dealing, one final business creation before giving up the helm of the family firm. He was approached in 1979 by a Carlisle contractor who knew about a large site available at Kingstown in Carlisle. This was an embryo light-industrial estate, with not many buildings or little factories created so far, but there was lots of talk about well-known local firms being interested in moving there, or establishing some sort of presence.

Kingstown is about three miles from Carlisle city centre, due north, on the way to Scotland. A fairly boring, empty suburb, with a lot of open spaces and leftover, war-time RAF bases and hangars. The main road to Scotland, the A7, runs through Kingstown from Carlisle, along Scotland Road. This used to mean it was very busy at Glasgow Fair-time, with queues stretching back for miles. With the coming of the M6 and the motorway loop round Carlisle, and the promise of a motorway all the way up towards Glasgow and Edinburgh, it was clear that Kingstown was going to be in a perfect position, transport-wise. A warehouse at Kingstown, just a mile from the new M6, would obviously be a good prospect, and the building contractor who suggested it to Eddie was willing to do the construction.

Through Edward's sub-contract work for Metal Box, which continued to roll in, both he and Eddie knew that Metal Box might be an ideal customer for any warehouse built in such a handy spot. They also knew that one of the main warehouses which Metal Box was currently using, owned by their regular hauliers, Robsons, was miles down the west coast, in an old RAF hangar at Kirkbride. This was awkward to get to and from, and in very poor condition.

Despite its size and wealth, Metal Box, like many manufacturers then and now, did not have extensive warehouse space. They made the goods, then tried to shift them as quickly as possible, either to their customers or to the next stage in the chain. They did not want their own finished products lying around, cluttering up their valuable industrial site.

But, at the other end of production, there was often a time and space gap – for example, brewers have machines capable of filling a thousand cans of lager per minute, but a can-maker might only manage to produce 400 empty cans a minute. So, to keep the brewers happy and occupied, Metal Box needed some sort of warehouse situated as conveniently as possible, to either themselves or the brewery, where empty cans would always be in stock, ready to be moved in and filled.

This was the theory that Eddie Stobart mulled over and discussed with Metal Box. However, at no stage did Metal Box ever say yes, we'll definitely use your warehouse if you ever go ahead. 'I knew about the plan,' says Colin Rutherford, 'but we gave no commitment.'

Eddie went ahead and got an estimate for building a warehouse of some 64,000 square feet and found it would cost in all £244,000. Far more than he expected, far more than he had. He could have borrowed, but that would have landed the company with huge debts.

Instead, he decided to sell his main assets. He sold Newlands Hill, his own home at Hesket Newmarket, originally a bungalow, now with many sprawling outbuildings and yards, for £100,000 to his brother Ronnie, who was running a successful cattle-feed business. The shop in Wigton was sold for £60,000.

Eddie Stobart Trading Ltd, the agricultural part of the Stobart empire, was wound up. Despite having realized all their assets, they still needed a bank loan of £140,000, which they got through a venture capitalist, in order to reach the total amount needed to build the new warehouse. 'I remember we had a struggle raising the final £70,000,' says Eddie. 'To secure it, I had to get my father to stand as guarantor. He didn't lend me any money, just helped to guarantee me. It was a difficult time, raising all the money, and very risky. We began building work with no guarantees at all that we would get customers.'

Young William, then aged twenty, worked on his own for several nights during December 1980 in order to give the concrete floor a final skim and enable the warehouse to open on time. But, even before they opened for business, with the doors not hung properly, Metal Box in Carlisle was desperate to use it, sending along empty cans for storage. 'We had a rush job for Spillers,' says Colin Rutherford, 'so it was vital to have a big enough space right on the motorway, even if the Stobart warehouse wasn't quite ready.'

Metal Box Glasgow soon followed. The site at Kingstown proved to be ideally situated, handy for empty or finished goods to be transported either north or south.

Not long after the opening, Edward moved Eddie Stobart Ltd from their rented Greystone Road premises to their own site beside the Stobart warehouse at Kingstown. It was from this moment on that Edward officially took the reins of the family haulage firm, although he had been running that side of the business for the last seven years, making most of the day-to-day decisions.

Until 1980, Eddie had still considered himself the head of the family firm, which after all bore his name. 'But, from the age of forty-five, I had always told myself that I was going to retire soon from full-time business. That's why, in 1976, I had agreed that Edward would move into Carlisle with the haulage business. When the warehouse was finished, Edward said to me, "Thanks, Dad, I can manage now."

'I was then waiting to see all my children settled, that's why I kept going a bit longer, thinking of the lads, their families and their future. I never aimed to devote my life to work. I've always thought there's more to life than work. I am by nature fairly laid-back compared with Edward. I used to think to myself, what's the point of all his worry and rush? We are here to serve God, not Mammon.

'I could have sold up completely earlier, but when the warehouse idea came up, it did seem a sensible thing. It was an investment which, once established, should not be too difficult to run, make a good profit and secure the family. Far easier than the hassle of running lorries.

'I didn't see lorries making money, not compared with storage or owning property. That's why I'd left the running of the lorries to Edward for some time. I was still a director of Eddie Stobart Ltd, but board meetings consisted of me sitting in an armchair at home while Edward was ringing me from somewhere on the M6 to tell me what he was doing . . . .

'Edward never liked to discuss things. And he was never keen on reading and writing things down. He just had a gut feeling about what he was doing, where he was going. I had total confidence in him as a worker, but I didn't know how it would all work out when he finally took over.

'I did think he was moving far too quickly. I had worried about all the new people he was taking on. Edward took a lot of risks. I did myself, in my early days, but I was never in the same league as Edward. Of course, the climate was different compared with my day in the fifties. The eighties were a time of taking risks, seizing opportunities, going for things when you saw them.

'I'll tell you a little story. There was once a man at Hesket Newmarket who was very good at making walking sticks. He always seemed to find the perfect piece of hazel wood and make it into a perfect stick. Someone asked him one day what was the best time to cut the hazel: when the sap was rising or when the wood was dead? "Cut it when you see it," the old man said.

'Do you get what he was really saying? He was saying that when you see the right bit of wood, you take it, there and then. Otherwise someone else will take it. Edward always had that mentality: take the opportunity when you see it.

'But I did worry about him. I remember talking about him with William. I said that Edward will either make us or break us. He could end up a multi-millionaire, or we could all end up bust. There will be nothing in-between.'

MOTORWAYS COMETH

For the next five years, Edward worked just as hard as he had ever done, still doing lots of driving, which he now says he should have given up much earlier. He was as desperate as ever to push the firm on, get more orders, shift more loads. It was hard graft, no question about that, not luck, that doubled the size of the firm between 1980 and 1985, with turnover reaching over one million pounds. Edward's rise, however, was also aided by the circumstances of the time.

His first stroke of luck had been to have arrived in haulage when it was comparatively easy to get in, with the end of the restrictive A- and B-licences. Now, in the eighties, he was helped by the enormous growth in the national network of motorways.

When Colin Rutherford arrived in transport managing at Metal Box in 1954, almost all their products went by rail. By 1974, when Eddie Stobart Ltd was getting its first orders from Metal Box, there had been an almost complete changeover in the transport industry. Everything was now going by road. The birth of the motorway had been a vital factor in this revolution, but it was not the only one. Various elements came together around the same time. Firstly, there was the decline in the railways themselves, symbolized by the rail cuts and closures made by Dr Beeching in the sixties and seventies. To many railway lovers, it appeared brutal at the time but it had become inevitable.

In 1948, when British Rail came into existence, it inherited 19,000 miles of railways. By 1982, this had been cut almost in half, to 10,000. Bad news for rail workers but good news for all road hauliers. (And, subsequently, excellent news for the nation's walkers and cyclists, when we eventually woke up to the fact that there were now 9000 empty and overgrown miles out there, waiting to be explored and used.)

One reason for the decline in railways was the decline in the coal and steel industries. Railway wagons had been well suited to transporting heavy, dirty stuff like coal and iron and steel, where speed was not essential and it didn't matter too much if wagons were left in remote sidings in freezing temperatures for days on end. It's hard to harm raw coal.

At the same time, more of us, from the 1950s onwards, began to own our own cars and wanted to make our own journeys, thus the number of railway passengers started to decrease. But what speeded up the decline in railway revenue, from both goods and passengers, was the arrival of the motorway.

Motorways arrived rather belatedly in Britain. They'd been talked about since 1906, but nothing had ever been done. Contrary to popular belief, the world's first motorways were not the German Autobahns of the 1930s; the Italians got in first, with a thirteen-mile stretch between Milan and Varese in 1924. After the Second World War, the USA and France followed suit, well ahead of Britain.

Britain's first, rather titchy chunk of motorway was an eight-mile stretch of bypass round Preston, opened by Harold Macmillan in December 1958. This was the first bit of the M6, on which young Edward later worked in the late 1960s.

Our first motorway proper, the M1, opened a year later, in November 1959, seventy-six miles of it from St Albans to Birmingham. The eight-mile Preston bypass had taken two-and-a-half years to build, and was beset by bad weather and other difficulties, but that first seventy-six miles of the M1, complete with 183 bridges, was built in just nineteen months by five thousand workers who completed it at a rate of one mile of motorway every eight days. Incredible, really, but then, in so many walks of life, things do seem to have slowed down since, from postal deliveries to train times.

A nation rejoiced on the opening of the M1. We all felt pleased with ourselves at this great achievement. Motorways were seen as nice things, wonders of engineering, not nasty things where madness lay and traffic chaos reigned. There were only three million vehicles on the roads in 1960, compared with thirty million today, so it was still relatively fun to drive and feel pleased by the experience. There were also no speed limits on motorways till 1965, so people could go pretty fast if they wanted to.

Too fast for the RAC and AA and their leather-gauntleted patrolmen. The birth of motorways brought about the end of their quaint habit of saluting members sporting the appropriate badge. From then on, so they were told, they only had to salute when it was safe. Which of course it wasn't any more, not on motorways with cars whizzing past them at one hundred miles per hour. They gave up the habit for ever; motorways finished off whatever style motoring had ever had.

But, of course, the speed and ease of travelling was immensely improved. Until motorways, dual carriageway roads were few, and most roads were narrow, bending, taking in every village and town, usually going right through the middle, down every high street, just as the stage coaches had once done. Cross-country journeys took for ever with endless delays. You'd often get stuck for miles behind a slow-moving lorry, and if you got stuck behind a caravan, that was it. No wonder people and goods had chosen for so long to go by rail, where at least there were timetables that could roughly be relied upon.

In 1960, when I first started driving home to Carlisle from London, to visit the family, a whole day had to be set aside for the journey, which sometimes took ten to eleven hours. Today, I can do it in almost half that time, thanks to the motorways, the M1 and M6.

The other big change that affected not just the wonderful world of transport but how we all live, was the arrival of supermarkets. Since the 1960s, when they first began to appear, they had grown bigger and bigger, necessitating bigger deliveries, more frequently, more quickly, and all of them door-to-door. Only monster lorries could manage all that, especially when all the bigger, newer supermarkets plonked themselves in out-of-town sites. Poor old railways could not cope with supermarket culture.

The rise of supermarkets went along with the rise in convenience food and convenience living. They provided cheap mass-market produce for us all, especially soft drinks and fast food. Just the market that Metal Box had been supplying, and precisely the market that Eddie Stobart had decided to enter.

There had been a reason behind Edward's decision to go up-market, to get away from dirty old slag and coal and move into cleaner stuff like tins of food and drink. This was because food and drink were required all the year round, whereas spreading lime was seasonal. What Edward could hardly have imagined, however, was that, with the coming of motorways and supermarkets, and the growth of the multi-national firms controlling so much of the food and drink trade, the market would increase so enormously in the next twenty years.

Transport economists have traditionally enjoyed dividing freight into two basic types. Firstly, there is the heavy stuff of low value. This covers coal and stone, where you try to keep the transport costs down, as the basic stuff is relatively cheap, therefore you don't mind too much about the speed of delivery. Canals were perfect for this.

Secondly, there are light goods of high value. Historically, this covered silks and fine cloths. The market always wanted them delivered as quickly as possible, so that costs could be recouped quickly. Columbus set off west, to find a new route from the East, in order to get spices and silks back as quickly as possible. In medieval England, lines of expensive pack horses were a common sight, carrying raw wool and finished goods. They were needed quickly, by whatever was the best transport of the time.

Today, you might not consider that pet food and crisps, or cans of Coke and Pepsi, are exactly precious cargo, but they are light goods and are therefore seen as high value. They must be carried cleanly and efficiently, around the clock, from manufacturer to mouth, as quickly as possible. This was the new world, created by many forces, the one that Eddie Stobart Ltd was now entering.

EDWARD FACES A DILEMMA

By 1985, Edward had roughly quadrupled the size of the firm in ten years. Turnover in 1975 had been £407,138. In 1985, it had risen to £1,291,941. The firm had expanded from eight vehicles to twenty-six vehicles, plus thirty-two trailers. The staff had shot up from twelve to forty. The premises on the Kingstown industrial estate, the warehouse and the lorry depot, were being enlarged all the time.

The annual profit in 1985 was shown as £77,355 compared with £19,647 in 1975 – again about a four-fold rise. But the wage bill had gone up almost eight times, to £294,589.

Edward was paying himself a bit more, especially when, later, he had a family to support. He and Sylvia decided to adopt a child, that was the first plan, but it led to them adopting four young children, all from the same family: three girls and a boy. They had moved to a bigger house at Houghton, just outside Carlisle, at a cost of £85,000, where Edward and Sylvia became pillars of the local Church of England.

Edward was trying, as a married man, to devote a

little less time to his business life, managing to take the odd break on a Sunday to go to church. He was still, however, obsessed by progressing the firm, making it bigger and better, and ploughing as much back into it as possible. Once he'd got to thirty vehicles, he wanted to make it fifty. Why not? That would be status and a conduit for further growth.

Naturally, Edward was still keeping his twenty-six vehicles as sparkling clean as when he'd only had eight to look after. He recollects, 'One of my earliest big expenditures when we moved to Kingstown was a fully automatic Kärcher heavy-duty washer. It cost £22,000, which seemed enormous at the time. Until then, I'd still been washing most of the lorries myself with a hose pipe. But as we got more lorries, and more drivers, there was always a queue for the hose pipes every evening. We had to get a machine if we wanted to keep every lorry immaculate. I had to borrow, of course: most of the money I spent on new vehicles and new machinery was borrowed.'

It was during 1985 that Edward started wondering for the first time whether it was all worth it. He seemed to be working so hard just to get more business, take on more lorries, yet, at the end of the day, he didn't feel any more secure than he'd done ten years earlier. Or any richer. On paper, thirty-five staff and twenty-six lorries meant more money coming in than running twelve staff and eight lorries, but they brought more pressure and more headaches. Proportionally, the firm was no better off than it had been. Turnover was up three-fold, profits up four-fold – but Edward's running costs were up about ten-fold, thanks to the huge increase in his wage bills and his borrowings.

In a moment of passing depression, or at least passing cynicism, as he always tried to be up-beat and optimistic, Edward worked out that turning everyone into an owner-driver, as Alf Sutton had recommended all those years ago, would probably benefit everyone, including himself. It would make more money in less time for less aggravation.

Although Edward managed to make a church appearance most Sundays, he was still working most evenings, most Saturdays and was never able to find time for a proper holiday. Which, naturally, did not please his wife Sylvia. 'I was getting hassled at home about never being there, but I just felt I had to be at work all the time, or it would all collapse.'

The main problem was that Edward was still doing everything himself, as he had done ten years previously, when things had been more manageable. He was getting in the orders, planning the work, dealing with the bank, buying the new vehicles, looking after the staff, running the finances. 'And I was still washing lorries myself, like. Oh there's always a bit you have to finish off by hand, even with the best vehicle wash. So I usually did that, when they'd all gone home.'

Since moving to Kingstown, he had tried to promote a few drivers to management jobs. One of these was Geoff Bainbridge, an ex-driver, who came off the road and into the office to help on the load-planning side. Edward also now had a full-time secretary but, essentially, he was a one-man management team, shouldering all the decision-making burdens himself. He had tried to persuade young William, now twenty-five, who had been driving for him for four years, to come into the office with him – for moral support if nothing else – but William had refused. He said he enjoyed driving too much.

'I felt sort of lonely and vulnerable,' says Edward. 'I had no one really to talk to, discuss things with. There was no one I could delegate things to or rely on to do important things.' Sylvia, who knew how the firm operated, tried to help out, but this arrangement was not a success. 'She did work with me in the office for about two weeks, after we got married. Then we had a row. Oh, it was just some mistake in some invoices. A girl had made the mistake, not Sylvia, but I blamed Sylvia. I said it was her fault that the girl hadn't been doing her job right. Anyway, we banged a few doors at each other. Then she walked out, never to return to the yard again.'

Edward didn't ask his father for advice. 'He wasn't interested in haulage. I had to sort it myself.' For six months, it all went round and round in Edward's mind, with him wondering what to do, how to solve all his problems, make life easier. 'I did think seriously about splitting up the firm. I then wouldn't have to worry about the staff and their problems, always wanting more money. Or the customers, always wanting lower prices. Or the bank, always wanting more security. It would stop all those problems, straightaway.

'But I never told anyone I was thinking on these lines – it was just in my head – least of all the bank. I had to go in and see them and appear all cheerful, hadn't I, tell them my plans for the next expansion, all the contracts I was about to get, or said I was about to get.

'Then I thought, if I do break up the firm, let them all go owner-driver, including myself, that would be it. For life. I'd never be able to do all this again. After all the pain I'd gone through in the last ten years, I'd simply end up throwing away everything I'd struggled for.

'The forty staff I'd built up had all been very loyal to me, many of them from the very beginning. How could I tell them I was packing it in? That I was throwing them all out of work? I tried to look at it from all angles, from their eyes as well as my eyes.

'So I made the decision not to pack up. But at the same time, I decided that I would not go on in the same way. If I was going to try and continue to grow, I needed to get in some proper management at last, people who would be able to help me.

'I worked out there were four areas I needed help in. Firstly someone on the financial side: an account-ant figure to look after all the money side, the wages, do the VAT, handle the bank, all the financial stuff I'd been doing by myself. Then I wanted a traffic plan-ner: someone to take over organizing the lorries and the loads. Thirdly, I needed someone to go out and get new customers. And, finally, someone to look after the staff, be a personnel officer, sort out their problems.'

A firm the size of Eddie Stobart Ltd in 1985 – a small, provincial business, with a turnover of only a million pounds – might well have hired a head-hunting firm or a recruitment agency. Not a national one, perhaps, but one based in Manchester. Or they might themselves have placed a small, discreet advertisement in a national newspaper. Or at least in the *Cumberland News*. After all, it would have been fairly sensible to go out and look for trained, professional people for a change, as opposed to ex-lorry drivers. Graduates from business schools did exist in 1985, people with proper professional qualifications or at least impressive CVs from well-known firms.

Perhaps, though, this might have been a bit bold and adventurous for Edward. It would have meant considering people who were not Cumbrians, who were foreigners from the Deep South such as Lancashire, the sort who would have no idea where Hesket Newmarket was or what the letters C.U.F.C. stood for.

So all Edward did was put the word around informally, asking one or two people he knew for any suggestions, not that he came across many people, having such a restricted social life. Naturally, he also asked his father if he had any ideas. In the end, he found three people – all local Cumbrians – to take over the four areas he had identified as requiring proper management figures. Edward would therefore be left to do whatever he was now going to do, taking the firm on to wherever it was about to go.

THE NEW MANAGEMENT MEN

The first member of the new management team arrived in January 1986 – and he was someone whom Edward had known well for many years. Nevertheless, his appointment was a bit of a surprise, considering he was then aged fifty-five and had just retired from work through ill health. It was Colin Rutherford, Transport Manager at Metal Box in Carlisle.

For the previous five years, Colin had been suffering from angina. It had suddenly struck him one day at Whitby in Yorkshire, where he'd gone on Metal Box business to inspect some metal coil in the hold of a ship. He thought at the time he was having a heart attack, but it wasn't as serious as he'd first feared and, with the aid of medication, he had continued working. But, in his mind, Colin saw it as a warning and had decided from then on to retire as early as possible.

'Not long afterwards, Metal Box offered me further promotion, to take on the general stores as well as transport. But I said no thanks. I was looking for a way to get out, not stay in. The chance came at the end of 1985. Some good redundancy packages were being offered, so I took mine. Yes, it was a bit delicate when, at the same time, the Eddie Stobart offer came up. I told the Metal Box management about it. They said they had no objections; I got their permission to join Edward.'

Colin's job, which was only meant to be part time, till Edward found more management people, was to be two-fold, helping Edward out in two of the areas he had worried about: looking after both new customers and the staff. Colin was ideal for both roles, being a very outgoing person with very good contacts, and also being good with people and long experienced in handling drivers.

'Edward had said, when we first discussed the job, that I could come in at 9.30 a.m. and leave at 3.30 p.m. I could even have the whole day off when I felt like it. But it didn't quite work out that way; mainly because I loved it so much.

'I was given total freedom to find new customers. Edward just let me get on with it. I knew so many of them, of course, from my Metal Box work, such as Tennents, Scottish and Newcastle – all the big brewers. I'd ring up my contacts, drive off and see them, try to get some business from them: I loved it.

'I also looked after staff problems. The drivers were still being paid in cash when I arrived in 1986. I said we can't be having that – this is old hat. Some of the drivers didn't like the change. Most didn't have bank accounts, you see. Some didn't want their wives to know how much they were earning.

'Edward himself still worked round the clock, and at weekends, even though I had arrived to take some of the load off him. I can still see him standing in the yard, washing down the trailers himself.

'When I was interviewing new staff, he'd often go out to their car in the car park, to see what their own car was like. If it was filthy, he would say, don't hire that person, they're not the sort we want.'

The second new arrival at Eddie Stobart Ltd was Barrie Thomas, who came to look after the financial side of things in July 1986, aged thirty-one. He came from Brampton and had been brought up as a devout Methodist. In his spare time, he was involved in local inter-church committees and good works in Carlisle. It was through his involvement with the YMCA that he met Eddie Stobart.

'Eddie recommended me to Edward, knowing he wanted someone with financial experience. So I went to see him at Kingstown. It was a very informal chat. He just wanted to meet me, get an impression of me as a person. I think he feared that, with my church background, I might be very serious and po-faced. Or, as Edward would put it, "not a day's work in him".'

Barrie is very outgoing and personable, fitting neither the standard image of a dry accountancy figure nor that of the strict, evangelical stereotype. Edward felt that Barrie would fit in with the firm, despite knowing nothing at all about the haulage industry. He'd previously been Company Accountant for an engineering firm in Carlisle.

Barrie's first month at Eddie Stobart Ltd was spent learning the ropes, sitting beside the traffic desk, watching Edward at work. 'It was so different from engineering. That is contract-based – you work for a long time to get a contract, then you have a long time to deliver it. In haulage, everything happens in twenty-four hours. If you make a mess of something – there are delays or things go wrong during the day – that's it. You can never reclaim the day: it's gone.'

Barrie joined as Company Accountant, but was soon promoted to Company Secretary. His main work was with the finances, which included going with Edward to the bank each time they needed to raise more money for more vehicles or equipment. 'During those early visits, so we used to discover later, the bank would ring father Eddie, just to check on us. Edward was totally in control of the business, but that wasn't the bank's perception. They didn't rate Edward, didn't have a high estimation of his ability. I suppose it was how he appeared. He wasn't good at projecting himself and he didn't really like meeting people, or putting things on paper. He didn't come over as very confident, which he wasn't, compared with later on. I'd just come from the Deaf Association, so that didn't help much either. They considered we were a couple of upstarts, coming in with big ideas. That's why they'd ring Eddie after we'd gone and say: "Is this right, is this ok?"'

When Barrie joined, there were still only around thirty-five vehicles during his first year with the firm.

'It seemed a very well-managed little business, but I could see that Edward was very tied down to the traffic desk, planning all the work. We did need someone to take over from him on traffic.

'I didn't think that was what he was best at – and, in fact, the person we eventually found turned out much better – but the main thing was to get Edward into a suit and upstairs, into his own office. He was still washing vehicles when I arrived, so it was hard for him to be taken seriously by customers, or the bank.

'I also felt that, by going upstairs, he would have different horizons, being able to look ahead, concentrate full time on where we were going. Downstairs, in the traffic room, you work solely from day to day. I suppose that was the biggest thing which struck me when I first met Edward and began working for him. He couldn't explain things very well, except when it came to figures. He was phenomenal when it came to working out costs and sums. Everything was really in his head. And, in his head, he had this clear vision of where he was going. That was what was so remarkable about him.'

The third new management man was an internal promotion, someone who had been working in the firm for several years, but as a driver. And he had been totally content as a driver, never having had any ambition to put on a suit and sit at a desk all day, even when his big brother started getting on at him. Yes, it was young William.

William Stobart, born 10 November 1961, seven

years after Edward, was the fourth and last of Eddie and Nora Stobart's children. The first three had been born close together, in 1952, 1953 and 1954, which made William feel separated from them, that they were a unit which he was not part of. In turn, they saw him as the spoiled one, the baby of the family.

But, as he grew up, William grew closer and closer to Edward. Not just through being his nearest sibling, but also by sharing an interest in trucks and anything mechanical and also, like Edward, by having a speech impediment.

When William started at Howbeck School in the village, he didn't have to walk there as the others had done. Eddie had a salesman by then, Pearson Scott, who went round the local farms selling fertilizers. His first job each morning, after he had clocked on at Newlands Hill, was to take young William to school in his van, before setting off on his rounds.

At primary school, William performed just as badly as Edward had done. He admits he had no interest or talent for reading and writing: 'My aim each day was to get home as early as possible. There was so much happening at home, compared with school. My Uncle Ronnie had his cattle-food mill next door, so if there was nothing happening in our yard, I would pop over to his place and watch the trucks or the men or what-ever. From the age of six or seven, I was allowed just to wander around the yards. You couldn't do that today – the health and safety people would soon sort you out.'

By the time William arrived at Caldew School at Dalston, Edward had left, which made him feel pretty scared, having to face a thousand new faces on his own, especially with his stammer. This, from all accounts, was far worse at that age than Edward's had ever been; there were times when William could literally not speak at all.

William remembers no childhood accident, no trauma – nor can his parents. His stammer just always seemed to be there. 'I've no idea what caused it,' says William, 'I might have picked it up from copying Edward – I don't know. All I know is that it was worse when I got frightened, when I went into a new class or I had a new teacher. They would tell you to stand up in turn and say your name. That petrified me as I knew what was coming, that I would never be able to say my own name. Which I never could. But if I was asked my name suddenly, like a teacher in the corridor suddenly saying, "What's your name, son?" I could usually get it ok.'

At Caldew, William was given a test on his second day and it confirmed that, aged eleven, he couldn't spell his own name, couldn't write down his own address and couldn't read. Looking back, William says this was mainly his own fault, never having been interested in school work, but he also thinks that the teaching at Howbeck was partly to blame.

So William was put into the same class that Edward had been in, the one informally known as the dunces' class, but officially known as the Progress Class. 'We were in room five with Mrs Carlisle,' remembers William. 'She wasn't a well woman, always going out for a fag, but I had great respect for Mrs Carlisle; she let me sit beside her. There were forty in the class. Some were thick but, the thicker they were, the harder they were. It was all ages, which meant there were big kids of fourteen and fifteen along with the eleven-year-olds.

'I was in the corridor, not long after I'd just started, and there was this kid who was taking the piss out of how I spoke. But along comes one of the fourteen-year-olds from Progress Class. He heard what the kid was doing – and he just smacked him one. I never got picked on again. So it worked to my advantage, you might say, being in the Progress Class.'

William, like Edward, didn't find that the visits to the speech therapist helped much. 'She did find out that I could use either hand – what's it called? Ambidextrous. She seemed to think it might explain why I stammered, because I couldn't decide which hand to use.

'What seemed to happen was that my mind was always jumping ahead, to the next word, the next sentence I was going to say, which made me stumble over the first one. My mind was ahead of my mouth. She tried to slow me down, make me do breathing exercises, but that didn't help either. It was just the embarrassment of it which was worrying. I always felt confident, as a person.'

For three years, William was in the Progress Class,

for all lessons except P.E. but, thanks to Mrs Carlisle's care and encouragement, when he got to the fourth year, he was put into the normal class, along with the other children of his age.

On leaving school at fifteen, William worked with his father for a couple of years, driving a tractor, on the agricultural side of the business. The family firm had split by now, Edward having moved into Carlisle with the haulage business while his father, plus brother-in-law, Ken, ran the agricultural and fertilizer side. William spread lime for a few years, which he didn't like doing much. 'My heart was always with Edward and the wagons, but I was too young to drive one.'

While William was still only ten, Edward, then aged seventeen, used to treat his little brother, and himself, by taking him into Carlisle on Saturday evenings in his Mini Clubman. They would drive down London Road, which was lined with small, cheap guesthouses, popular with long-distance lorry drivers, and ogle all the long-distance lorries parked nearby.

'What we loved best was the Scotch lorries, the fish trucks which had come from Aberdeen and were on their way to London. I can still remember the names of the firms. One was Cato – no idea how you spell it – another was Smith's of Maddiston, another was Pollock's of Musselburgh. They had massive trucks which were all in tartan livery, customized trucks with flags and banners and all sorts on them. Some were beautifully hand-painted. I loved looking at them.

'Afterwards, we'd go round to Robsons yard. We'd just walk in, there was no security worries in them days, just walk in and have a look at his lorries. Robsons had something like 150 trucks at the time. I couldn't really take it all in, there were so many. Edward used to say that, some day, he would have as many lorries as Robsons, but of course I didn't believe it.' The boys' Saturday-night excitement in the big city usually finished with a packet of chips each, then they'd go back to Hesket.

On Sundays, with Edward having reached seventeen, he refused to go with his parents to church any more, but William, the baby, still had to go. 'Edward wasn't supposed to work on a Sunday, the Lord's day, but I used to notice when we got home from church that our two trucks had been washed by Edward while we'd been in church. I don't think my father ever realized. He didn't notice whether a truck was clean or dirty.'

William thinks that Edward's passion for clean vehicles was first created, or at least encouraged by, Norman Bell, Eddie's first driver. 'Edward had it drilled into him by Norman. Norman also used to tell him not to put off till tomorrow what you can do today.'

While still thirteen or fourteen, William was often allowed to accompany Edward or one of the other drivers on long trips. He could also be quite useful holding ropes in the days of flat-bed lorries, when loads were put on the back, covered with a sheet of tarpaulin and tied down.

'I went once with Edward with a load to North Shields. Edward had never done this trip before, but I'd been twice, with Ken. I said I knew how to get there. But in the middle of Newcastle, we got completely lost. Edward was so furious he gave me a smack. Then he had to go into a police station to ask the way.'

Another time, while William was in the cabin with Edward, they stopped at a transport café and William was sent in to buy twenty Benson and Hedges for Edward. In the shop, William's stutter was so bad he was unable to get the words out. When the assistant pointed to something behind the counter, William simply nodded, accepted what he was given and paid for it, too embarrassed to start again. Edward, as ever, revved up straightaway and zoomed off, holding his hand out for the cigarettes – only to have William give him a packet of pencils. Once again, William got a good slap.

'William's stammer was always far worse than Edward's,' says their sister Anne, 'but he used to joke about it himself. It didn't appear to get him down, not inside the family. He once went on a job with my husband, Ken, to do some lime-spreading on a farm. Ken sent William into the farm house to find out which fields they had to spread. When William came back, Ken asked him which fields they were doing. William said he didn't know. When the farmer had come to the door, it turned out he had a stammer. William had been too embarrassed to say anything to him in case the farmer thought he was taking him off.'

At the age of eighteen, William moved on from tractors to driving a mobile concrete mixer. Not quite as exciting as a heavy-goods vehicle, which legally he could not drive till he was twenty-one, but good fun all the same. It was an Alma four-wheel-drive concrete mixer, which mixed up the sand, cement and gravel on the site, so you could then pour it out into foundations or shuttering or wherever it was required.

When his father got round to creating the Kingstown warehouse, William and his concrete mixer proved invaluable. 'Dad did have a contractor for the concrete floor, but he thought he wasn't doing it right and he got chased off the job. So I took over, along with two drivers. We laid all the concrete ourselves, some 54,000 square feet, working night and day. One of us was always on the night shift as that was when we did the polishing.'

Then bliss came at last for William; he reached twenty-one and could drive a real lorry. He got his HGV licence, class one, one week after his birthday. For the next three years, he was a full-time lorry driver, working for his brother Edward. 'And I loved every moment of it,' says William. 'I liked the solitude. It never bothered me, being on my own. I also liked picking up a geographical knowledge of the whole country. After about a year, I never needed maps any more. I could even get around inside London, no bother.

'I also liked to think I was doing something useful, helping the company. When I'd tipped at the far end, I'd go into their traffic office and hang around, often for an hour or two, to ask if they had any work. If I got a load, I would ring Edward and tell him. All our drivers were taught to do this, to try and pick up new loads.'

William is very proud that he was one of the earliest lorry drivers ever to have had a mobile phone. This was in 1985, he thinks. He'd heard about them and kept on at Edward until he gave in. 'It was a Motorola and cost £1200, yeah a huge amount. And you couldn't use it in certain areas. But it proved so useful, being able to ring Edward back in Carlisle, and get instructions from him. In about six months, all our lorries had one.'

William was on a set but modest salary, being a Stobart with shares in the firm, not on an hourly rate like the rest of the drivers, but he did the same work, had the same routines as the other drivers, which meant he could be away five nights a week, sleeping in his cabin. 'Oh I was very happy driving: best thing I ever did,' he says. 'I started on a DAF 2300, an artic. Then, after six months, I got a DAF 2800. What I really wanted was a Scania. I pestered and pestered Edward till he let me have one, a Scania 112. It cost £27,000, as Edward never stopped reminding me.

'In those days, the early 1980s, lorries would do over 60 m.p.h. You weren't restricted to 56 m.p.h., like today. And there wasn't a great deal of traffic, so you could bash on. It made driving enjoyable – it was still fun.'

From about 1984 onwards, when William had reached the age of twenty-four and had been driving full time for three years, Edward began to tell him he should give it up and come into the office. William always refused. Every time Edward asked, he said no. William doesn't put this down to lack of confidence about his education. 'Oh no, that didn't worry me. I'd worked out my own way of writing by then, if I ever had to, which of course I didn't need to, being a driver.

'No, what worried me was what my job would be. I couldn't see what I'd do – that was the first thing. Secondly, I thought it would just lead to rows with Edward. That's why I always said no.'

Rows between the two brothers were never serious – just brotherly arguments. Edward had always called William 'boy', and continued to do so now, even when he was grown up. He called him 'boy' to his face, as in 'hello boy' or 'do this, boy', or referred to him as 'the boy' when he was talking about him to other people, just as Jack Charlton always referred to his younger brother, Sir Bobby Charlton, as 'our kid'. It might sound affectionate enough but, on the other hand, it can indicate something of the bossy, big-brother syndrome that can often erupt into rows.

One of the worst arguments William can remember occurred some time in 1984, when William was aged twenty-three, still a driver, and Edward was thirty. They had gone into the Kingstown depot one Sunday morning, in order to sort out some problem. 'While we were doing it, I told Edward that, really, he should have sorted it out yesterday, on the Saturday. He should have looked ahead and not let the warehouse people go till it had been done. I was a bit fed up and tired that day anyway, at having to come in. But Edward went mad at me for criticizing him. We started fighting, rolling on the ground.

'Edward had his hands round my neck when he noticed John Bimson coming towards us. He was another haulier, with his premises next door to us. "Don't look up," said Edward to me, "it's John Bimson. Just pretend you've fainted." He was banging my head on the ground at the time, but then he stopped. John Bimson comes up and asks what's going on. Edward says, "Oh nothing, William's just fainting and I'm helping him to recover . . ."'

William never held this incident against Edward – just one of those things that big brothers do to you, then life goes on as before. All the same, it was one reason why William was unwilling to give up the solitude and independence of the road for the close and probably heated encounters with his brother which might well happen, working cheek by jowl with him in an office.

But in 1986, having hired the first two of the three management figures he needed, Edward gave William an ultimatum. 'It happened one Thursday afternoon. Edward and Barrie Thomas told me what they were going to do – and said I had to decide, there and then.'

What they were offering William was the chance to come into the office and run the traffic desk, in charge of all the drivers, planning and organizing their work. If he refused, he could stay as a driver, but they would be forced to go out and hire an outsider, as Edward would no longer be doing that job.

It's one thing to have a row with your big brother, even the odd slap, but quite another to have some total stranger arriving to boss you around, perhaps making your life a misery. So William, aged twenty-five, said, 'OK then, I'll give it a go.'

Edward sat beside William for the first few weeks when he moved out of his driving cabin and onto the traffic desk. It meant organizing the drivers, their jobs, their routes, how and when they had to get there and what they would do afterwards. He was also helped by Geoff Bainbridge, the ex-driver who had moved into the office.

William knew all about the work and the problems from the driver's point of view, having been at the receiving end of the traffic desk for the last three years. He had suffered, so he'd often thought, from people like Edward making unreasonable demands. 'I knew the frustrations. Edward would often say, "Oh, you can soon get there, it's just half an inch on the map." In reality, it could be a hellish place to get to and would take hours.

'Then he'd often suddenly give me a new load, first thing in the morning, and I would moan at him and say, "If only I'd known, I would have slept somewhere else last night and been in the right place for the new load." We'd have a row about it, till he'd say "Just do it. Stop twining."' Twining is Cumbrian for moaning, which William had done his share of as a driver.

Once William started in the office, he could see the problems from the other side, how jobs suddenly came up, customers changed their minds, made new or different demands, things happened that you couldn't control. For the first few weeks, he felt he knew best how to handle things and didn't like Edward breathing down his neck, bossing him around, calling him and treating him like 'the boy'.

'Edward was trying to save me from the mistakes he'd made. He'd learned from them and didn't want me to do the same. But I wanted to do it my way, learn by my own mistakes. I'd been a full-time driver, which he had never been, so I thought I knew it all. We fell out a few times in those early weeks but, in the end, Edward decided to leave me to it, let me do it my way. He then went upstairs to concentrate on other things.

'It did take me a while to settle in, but I like to think that, in six months or so, I was doing it better than Edward had done. This was because he'd been doing all those other things at the same time: invoices, the bank, new customers, as well as the traffic desk. I was able to concentrate wholly on it. In the first few months, the drivers were always saying, "Put Edward on, I'm not doing this, I want to speak to Edward." But, after the six months or so, I won them over.

'I like to think I'm better suited to planning than Edward anyway. He tends to work spontaneously, always has done. He has a gut-reaction to everything, then acts on it. I like to sit down quietly for at least half an hour, think of all the implications, then plan it all out. With the traffic desk, you need that sort of careful planning. If you do it spontaneously, you end up with trucks and drivers all over the shop.

'I was also helped by Barrie if things were getting heated. Barrie was a sensible, cooling influence, but Edward still threw the odd telephone around when he got annoyed with us. You just hoped, when the phones started flying, that the lead was secure. Usually I deserved it, because I'd done something wrong. But, being his brother, I'd answer back, which would upset him.

'I also knew he was just taking his anger out on me, as his brother, because I could take it and understand. When I'd been driving for him, we were always having rows on the phone. He'd hang up on me, or I'd hang up on him.'

During that first year in the office, William didn't find his lack of reading and writing skills much of a handicap. But then Edward had managed it. 'I could always read a bit better than Edward, so that helped.'

But William was always very bad when it came to writing and in the pre-computer age, quite a bit of writing by hand had to be done, even if it was just a brief note, a job sheet on a scrap of paper, ready for each driver when he came in for his next shift.

William developed his own form of spelling, writing down words as he heard them in his head. In the early days, he had to rely on the drivers being able to translate them but, as the firm grew and he acquired his own secretary, someone was always able to learn his language then turn it into more standard English. His was a form of phonetic English, with some regional variations. For example, when instructing a driver that his next job was to go to Daventry, he would write down, 'Tek a lord to Davtree.' Clear enough to everyone in the office even if his old teacher, Mr Bouncer, might not have approved of it.

William's stammer also proved a bit of a handicap when meeting new people. 'As a boy, it hadn't honestly worried me or got me down. It was just embarrassing. It was when I started working, that's when it became difficult. If I was talking to drivers who didn't know me, or arriving at a new place, that was hard. And I always found it hard to introduce myself, tell people my name. But I just had to get on with it.

'Very soon, there were quite a few drivers who'd worked with us for a while who forgot I had any sort of speech impediment. They got used to me.'

After about a year, William's department had made such progress, things were going so well, expanding all the time, that they took on another traffic planner, Rob Beaty, to share the job with William. They each took on twenty drivers to personally look after. 'For the first few weeks,' remembers William, 'there were

The wedding of John Stobart, founding father of the Stobart dynasty, to Adelaide in 1928. John farmed thirty-two acres at Hesket Newmarket and was a Methodist lay preacher. He had two sons by Adelaide: Eddie, born 1929, and Ronnie, born 1936. Adelaide died in 1942 and John later married Ruth.

Eddie Stobart (*back, left*), aged fourteen, next to his brother, Ronnie, and with his father, John, stepmother Ruth and baby brother, Jim. Eddie worked with his father then later branched out on his own as an agricultural contractor and fertilizer spreader.

Caldbeck, Cumberland, heart of Stobart country.

Eddie Stobart's marriage to Nora at Caldbeck Methodist chapel in 1951.

Edward Stobart (*left*), born 1954, second son of Eddie and Nora, with his sister Anne and brother John.

Edward (*left*) at Hesket Newmarket village school, sitting next to school friend William Ridley.

Edward, aged eight, with John and Anne, who is holding baby brother William. Their blazers were not school uniforms but Sunday best, for chapel.

Eddie Stobart and Nora (*centre*) with their four children in 1968. Edward and John stand at the back; William and Anne are seated. Anne was the only child to pass her eleven-plus and go on to grammar school.

Eddie, Senior, created Eddie Stobart Ltd in 1970. He was still a farm contractor but now also had a farm shop in Wigton.

Eddie Stobart Ltd at the Cumberland Show in the early Seventies.

Eddie Stobart Ltd's very first articulated truck, a Scania 110 driving through Hesket with Stan Monkhouse at the wheel.

Lorries at Greystone Road: in 1976 Edward left Hesket, moving into rented premises at Greystone Road, Carlisle. He brought with him eight trucks and twelve staff, and concentrated purely on haulage. This was the beginning of Eddie Stobart Ltd as we know it.

Edward (*centre*) with Bob ('Big Mac') McKinnel, and Neville Jackson, two of the longest-serving drivers.

From the beginning, Edward was obsessed with keeping his trucks clean, and also gave them names, such as Dolly, after Dolly Parton.

Kingstown: in 1984 Edward moved into new premises at Kingstown industrial estate, Carlisle, just beside the M6.

Edward at Kingstown, with brother William (left), pictured after washing vehicles one Saturday.

Edward, with fashionably long hair, at his wedding to Sylvia in 1980. Eddie and Nora are on the right.

William stands proudly with his truck in 1985. In 1986, by which time the firm had thirty vehicles and forty staff, Edward persuaded William to get out of his lorry and into the office and become a management man.

An Eddie Stobart truck in Metal Box livery. In 1987, the firm had a breakthrough when it secured its first contract with Metal Box, Carlisle. (*Right to left*) Edward with Metal Box managers Stuart Allan and Colin Rutherford.

drivers moaning on to Rob, saying, "I want to speak to William, put William on the line," just as they'd done when I arrived . . . .'

BRANCHING OUT

By 1987, the arrival of a proper management team had boosted the firm's turnover to £4.5 million and it had a total of fifty vehicles but, nationally, it was still a small, provincial haulage firm, based at a small industrial estate in Carlisle. This was handy enough for Scottish work but proving more and more awkward for Midlands and Southern work, which was where the bulk of the increase in haulage was generally centred, especially for the breweries and supermarkets. Edward began to look around for some sort of depot in the South; having one, however small, would sound good, make them seem like a national, not a local firm.

Their first depot outside Carlisle was opened at Burnaston in Derbyshire. It was an old warehouse which belonged to BRS. Edward had found it and wanted to buy it, as he considered the site had great potential, but he was only able to take it on a short lease, as the owners had some bigger hopes for it, not revealed to Edward at the time. (Today it's the site of a massive Toyota car plant, which shows that Edward had a good eye for property, even in those days.)

They opened it on 1 April 1987 and it immediately gave the firm warehousing space for servicing their customers further afield. Edward had chosen it deliberately, to be handy for the brewers at Burton-on-Trent. It also meant that, for the first time, the firm was taking on non-Cumbrian staff, recruiting drivers and office workers locally in Derbyshire. Except for the most important job: the boss of the new warehouse, whose role it was to set it up, open it and get it running.

Once again, as with William, Edward decided to promote someone he had known for most of his working life. He chose David Jackson, who had grown up with him, been with the firm from its earliest, toughest days, even if he had no management experience whatsoever. David had been the smiling, cheerful young boy in the yard at Hesket Newmarket, hired by Edward. He had been one of the original two people Edward had taken with him when he opened at Greystone Road in 1976, working as the apprentice mechanic. On reaching the age of twenty-one, David had got his HGV licence and become an Eddie Stobart driver, doing this from 1979 till 1987, by which time he was aged twenty-nine. He had been far longer on the road as a driver than William, so it was quite a surprise to him, and to most other people, when Edward asked him to be depot manager of their first branch.

'I was flattered to be asked, but I was worried, of course, at the thought of having to do things like hire people. I'd never done that before. Then perhaps I'd have to fire them as well. That was a worse thought. But Edward said not to worry: I'd cope. I didn't have any sort of proper training. All I did was sit in the office at Kingstown for two weeks to see how things were done, then I set off.'

The main reason why David accepted the job was that he'd got married and his wife had recently had their first baby. He therefore didn't want to be on the road all the time any more, away for up to five nights a week. It seemed like a good career move, even though it would mean a physical move as well, having to find a house down in Derbyshire and leave rural Cumbria where he and his wife had always lived.

'On the first day,' recollects David, 'we opened at Burnaston, I arrived in the morning to find there'd been a flood in the night. There was goods due to arrive that day, but we couldn't move anything in till we'd made the place dry. It was still raining and the roof was letting in.'

Edward was there, of course, for the grand opening – well, modest opening, as nothing special had been planned. He clambered up to the roof where the rain was letting in, did some quick measurements, then rang Stan Monkhouse in Carlisle and told him to send down some lengths of sheeting, sharpish. When they arrived, they were fixed under the hole in the roof to collect the rain. The sheets soon filled up, of course, and began sagging with the weight of the rainwater, so they had to be drained. Big drums were placed beneath them and the excess water was syphoned off through plastic pipes. David, so he remembers, had to get the syphon system started with his own fair lips, sucking away.

While the depot in Burnaston was still being set up, Edward heard by chance one day that Metal Box in Carlisle were looking for an exclusive haulier. They had asked for tenders from three or four big national firms, and Eddie Stobart Limited was NOT one of them. So much for all Edward's good work in the last few years, and his thrusting new management team. It was a blow to his pride but would be an even bigger blow if a national firm got all of Carlisle's Metal Box work and squeezed out Eddie Stobart Ltd.

By that time, Robsons, the rival haulage firm had totally changed. In 1980, by which time they had two hundred lorries, Stan Robson, then aged seventy-four and not in the best of health, had sold out. United Glass, who were building up their own haulage side, paid £2.1 million for the firm. Over the next few years, there were further changes and the name Robsons, alas, disappeared – a warning to any private family firm that sells itself. You might have spent six decades building up your name, becoming a legend amongst other hauliers and small boys, but it can all disappear, very quickly, once the suits take over.

But Metal Box had decided to go back to the old system of doing an exclusive deal with one haulier – and they clearly didn't fancy Edward's firm. 'They hadn't asked our local rivals either,' says Edward, 'like

Irvings of Longtown, or even Taylors of Worcester who had done a lot of work with them. They were just interested in receiving bids from the big boys, national firms such as BRS [later Exel] and Ryder.

'When I heard, I rang Metal Box myself and got hold of their Distribution Manager. I didn't normally do this sort of thing, phone up people I didn't know. I always shied away from phone calls to new people, but I was so furious we hadn't even been asked to tender, not even considered.

'I got through and asked what exactly the job was. They told me roughly and I said, "That's a piece of cake, we can do that easy." I was asked how big we were and I, well, exaggerated just a bit. I said we had seventy vehicles, rather than fifty. I knew we would soon, so I didn't exaggerate much.

'They were surprised we'd grown so big in the last year. I don't think they'd realized what we had been doing, all the changes we'd made. I said, "But that's nothing, we'll be even bigger next year, now we've got our first depot in the South." They didn't know about that either.

'Anyway, I got out of them that we could tender after all – but we only had three days left to fill in the forms. I said, "No problem. We can do that."' Which, of course, led to panic stations amongst his office staff, up all night for three days, working on the details.

'Edward's sixth sense that something was afoot had proved to be correct,' says Barrie Thomas. 'Their opinion of the ability of local hauliers to operate a contract of £3.5 million was obviously not as confident as our own.

'Edward's timely intervention allowed us the opportunity to quote and so began a process of meetings and reviews with their senior management to try to prove our case. In truth, no one that did not possess the working knowledge of the factory could have ever provided a realistic quotation given the dynamics of a can-making factory and its customers.

'After the review process, we were the favoured option by the local factory management, who trusted Edward and his ability to deliver the goods, literally. However, Metal Box was changing, it was becoming centralized, and the next thing we knew was that a weighty contract arrived, closely followed by a team of high-powered executives led by Harry Wright, one of the senior buyers within the Metal Box group.

'The opinion of Eddie Stobart Senior was that the work was no longer going to be any use: if you had to go through all of this just to get business, then it was time to pack up. Thankfully, Edward realized the value of the business and he and I set out to change the contract to one that we could accept. At heart, Edward is a man of his word, and so a contract is unnecessary; however, he realized that they wanted this contract so he went along with it.

'At the final contract meeting, we were arguing through the various points and I could sense Edward's patience at the process getting more and more frayed.

His interest in the discussion had lapsed after the financial side had been agreed upon and so all he wanted now was to go downstairs and start to plan the extra vehicles that we would need for the work.

'When it came to the point of a lengthy argument over whether or not we should be responsible for upholding the name of Metal Box, as they wanted, or only agree to do nothing that would tarnish the name of Metal Box, as was more reasonable, then I thought Edward would lose it completely. By his body language, he already had lost it. But, thankfully, nothing came out of his mouth.

'Afterwards, when I met one of the Metal Box executives, I was told that they had come to that meeting to try to force us to back out of the contract, but it was our determination to fight every point, including the seemingly minor ones, and not to simply give in that gave them the courage to go through with the contract and award us the work. That was a good lesson for us to learn at that early stage of our growth.'

William recalls that the contract immediately more than doubled their workload. 'Until then, we'd only been getting around twenty loads a day, including our Metal Box work – and none of it was definite. Each day we had to start from scratch looking for work. I'd be ringing Metal Box six or seven times in a morning, asking if they had any work. It would often depend on the mood they were in, if they gave you anything.

'But once we got the Metal Box contract, we shot

up to fifty loads a day. It was a huge step – and all definite work. Metal Box got rid of their own fleet, which I think was about eight or so vehicles. So we did all their Carlisle work from then on.

'Edward had organized it all, done the deal, saying of course we could do it, no problems, but as he'd exaggerated a bit, I suddenly had to find more trucks and more drivers to do all the new work.'

Edward, of course, was thrilled. 'The best thing it gave us was some security, which we'd never had before. It did feel like a really major achievement, our first ever, proper contract.'

The new depot meant the company could transport empty cans down to Burnaston from Metal Box in Carlisle or from Metal Box in Glasgow, where they soon secured other contracts, then store them in their own warehouse till they were needed. When a brewer at Burton urgently needed some more cans, it was impossible to supply them from Carlisle and Glasgow. Thus began a system known in the haulage business as: 'just in time'. Hauliers like Eddie Stobart were able to guarantee certain goods could be delivered within thirty minutes. The company soon also moved on to a more modern form of trailers, complete with metal rollers, whereby loads could be rolled straight off their trucks onto the conveyor belt.

David Jackson recollects those early days at the depot. He started with a depot staff of two, looking after 50,000 square feet of warehouse space. Within two years, vehicles were based on the site, expanding the staff to twenty. 'It was a struggle at first, especially the paperwork. I'd not been good at school and people had always laughed at my spelling. But the worst bit was when the time came when I did have to sack somebody. That gave me sleepless nights.

'I got a bollocking myself one day from Edward. This was about a year after we opened. He'd been to see us with his bank manager, to show him round the warehouse. I was in jeans and a T-shirt, which I still wore at that time. And I was still driving the forklift when I was needed.

'Next day, Edward rang to tell me off. He said I couldn't dress like that anymore, not as the depot manager. So I had to go out and buy myself a suit and a collar and tie.'

This was about the first time that David was aware how Edward had become obsessive about the personal appearance of his staff. David had always been keen on keeping the lorries clean, even from the earliest days, but he, like Edward, had always worn fairly scruffy clothes to work, especially in the days when they both did fairly scruffy jobs.

Another trait David soon noticed in Edward was his reluctance to be known personally, even in a very small pool. 'We'd gone somewhere locally, I can't remember where, just some small social occasion in the area, when Edward happened to be visiting the depot. I introduced Edward to some friend, saying "This is Edward Stobart", as you do. Afterwards, Edward told me off. He said I wasn't to go around introducing him to people when there was no need. It did strike me as strange – but it was just that I liked everybody to know who he was.'

WHAT EDWARD DID UPSTAIRS

By 1990, the turnover of Eddie Stobart Ltd had shot up in three years from £4.5 million to £16.4 million. It now had two hundred vehicles, thus equalling the best that Robson haulage firm had ever done, three depots and 445 staff, 315 of whom were drivers.

The 1990 declared profit was £601,926, the wages bill was now £4.8 million. They also had assorted debts of £5 million – a clue to how they had financed this phenomenal growth. They'd had to borrow to finance the three new depots, which they owned rather than leased this time.

When Edward had created his management team, he made them responsible for the day-to-day running of their areas of operation, all of which he had done by himself until then. The new title he gave himself was rather abstract, not to say airy-fairy. He was now in charge of 'Future Planning and Growth'.

He had obviously delegated well, picking people who, on the surface, might not have appeared to have top qualifications or even any qualifications but whom Edward thought could be trusted to do a good job. It is a gift, to be able to spot and develop people, one that is hard to teach, either by Harvard Business School or Caldew School. Having developed them, it's just as difficult to leave them alone to get on with it.

Edward's career from 1976, when he'd first started up on his own account in Carlisle, might have indicated that he would be incapable of delegating. Until 1986, he had appeared to be a one-man band: an obsessive workaholic who revelled in getting his hands dirty, doing everything, controlling everything, personally slapping people into line. Such people often find it hard to divorce themselves from the front line, that was where their fun was, that was where their strength lay. Rising above the day-to-day grind and exertions, looking into the far distance, thinking and planning long-term, is usually seen as a rather different skill. But, from 1987 onwards, with his team in place, Edward appeared to be able to do this effortlessly.

He himself can't explain in words how it all happened, what skills were required, what secrets, if any, were behind the enormous expansion in such a short time. He has the details in his mind, the blow-by-blow memories of all the major deals, but not the overall qualities or strategies that were needed. 'It just seemed to snowball,' is about all he'll say today about this particular period.

He was, as ever, not sitting back and feeling pleased, admiring what the company had achieved so quickly. Once again, he had set himself new targets. In 1990, one new plan was to open a new depot every six months. The other was to reach the magic number of one thousand vehicles as soon as possible.

In a way, his personality was suited to pushing himself upstairs, on high, on his own, almost in his own world. He had always seen himself as a loner, right from his school days, removed from the others, going his own way, working things out for himself, not requiring the admiration of others, not requiring to be liked or even known, with little interest in social occasions or the social fripperies which go with small-town success.

Edward was lucky, though, in that he turned out to have one particular skill which had been hidden and probably would never have had a chance to be exercised if he had remained a small-town haulier with no depots or warehouses elsewhere. His determination, his passion to grow bigger, meant he had to expand all over the country and, through this, his gift as a property developer became apparent.

The effects of such a gift can be big, not to say enormous when you spot a site which others have missed or overlooked, can see the potential, then work out a way to develop it. That first depot at Burnaston was a good example, but Edward did not profit by it as it was leased. After three years, he bought and developed another site at Burton itself, right on the doorstep of the breweries.

He found he had an eye for properties, for seeing what appeared to be derelict or badly situated sites.

He was able to imagine what they might look like with money spent, when other facilities or amenities were in place, such as motorway extensions or new manufacturing plants.

'I remember going to look at one site with him,' says Colin Rutherford. 'I thought it was very unsuitable; the best thing was to bulldoze the whole lot. But Edward had the perception to see its future, what could be done. He could see things other people couldn't. I don't know where he got it from, this ability.'

Edward probably inherited his gift from his father. Eddie, as a young man, had been a bit of a wheeler-dealer, loved to trade with the local farmers, seeing an opening, doing deals, buying and selling. He didn't maximize this skill, this interest, as he had far more important things in his life. Of his three sons, Edward was the only one with a similar eye, but also with the energy and ambition to put it into practice.

Colin Rutherford also saw another quality in Edward that was vital at this stage in the firm's development, a quality which business people who come up the normal way don't always have. 'The trouble with most management people who have worked in big firms, as I had with Metal Box – or even more so if you come through the public sector – is that you end up with tunnel vision. You do things by the book. You follow your firm's ten commandments, whatever they might be.

'Someone like Edward had only worked for himself.

He always did things his way, ways he couldn't quite explain to others. He just knew. He thought quickly. And he acted quickly.'

Barrie Thomas, the management man brought in to look after the finances, points out that they did take risks. 'At one time, we were very heavily geared-up, to four hundred per cent. This means that for every one pound we were putting into expanding the firm, the banks or the finance houses were putting in four pounds.

'One:one is the ideal proportion. One:two is considered dangerous. We were running one:four which some people would think was mad; wildly risky.

'But it was the atmosphere of the times. There suddenly seemed to be room in the late eighties for the small boys to become big guys. And, of course, Edward's ambition for the firm never wavered. He wanted to go onwards and upwards, all the time.

'Our balance sheet, on paper, was very good. The banks were very keen to see property on the balance sheet so, after that first leased depot, we bought depots. It was easy at that time to raise more money if you already owned some property. But to continue to be taken seriously, you needed to be growing bigger in size all the time. So that was what we did.'

All the same, it's surprising in a way that Barrie was prepared to take any risks, given his background and strict religious beliefs. 'If there had been the slightest sign of any financial or any other irregularity, then I would have left, but I believed, as Edward did, that in business you have to sail right up to the line. You never cross that line; that is the limit. What you try to do is run along it. If you want to make money in business, that's what you do. You don't hang back in the comfort zone.

'In the early years of the growth of the company, we were forced by circumstances to do everything ourselves. When the telephone rang, we did not know whether we had to answer it as a salesman, a lawyer, a financier, a traffic planner or a property developer. In truth, we wore every hat possible because, if there was a pound in the deal, we wanted it – we needed it for growth. So, in those early days we had to be quick on our feet and see any and every opportunity that came our way.

'There was an occasion when Edward and I had prepared a presentation for a customer. We went to meet them and, part-way through the meeting, Edward suddenly realized that the pricing we were offering, which he had worked out himself, was lower than was expected. Quick as a flash, he stopped the meeting and said, "I'm sorry, Barrie has made a mistake with those figures – he has forgotten to include something." So the figures were altered upwards. Unfortunately, I was left looking incompetent and I thanked him for that privilege after the meeting. He looked and smiled and said, "Well I couldn't say that I was wrong could I?"

'Another time, we were invited, so we thought, to British Steel in Ebbw Vale, to a meeting with one of their managers to discuss their plans for the future. Edward and I drove down from Carlisle expecting a relatively easy day as we were to receive a presentation from a customer rather than giving one.

'When we were taken into the meeting room, we were met by a bank of twenty or so faces of senior British Steel managers. Strange, we thought, does it take so many of them to give a presentation to us? However, it quickly transpired that they were under the impression that we were giving a presentation to them about our capabilities to do their work.

'Never one to lose such an opportunity, Edward set out a brief introduction and then turned to me and said, "Now Barrie will tell you our views on the transport market and how we see ourselves fitting into it over the next few years." This was Edward's way of asking me to talk for twenty minutes or so to give him time to work out a transport solution for British Steel. So I spouted forth without preparation and talked for twenty minutes or so without saying anything specific – and then Edward took over and gave a detailed account of a transport proposal tailored to British Steel's needs.

'It would have been easy to have apologized to the meeting and admitted to being unprepared, but would we ever have had the opportunity again to meet with that number of senior British Steel managers? Probably not. The lesson we learned that day was to be always prepared to give a presentation.

'For about ten years, we averaged sixty per cent

annual growth. We were named as one of the top five fastest-growing firms in the middle-market sector.

'It was a good time to do it, with all the money around. We did some excellent deals with vehicle firms like Eden Vehicle Rentals. They had a lot of money which they had invested in vehicles and were keen for us to do good deals with them.

'It was just so exciting; I loved every minute of it. There was so much enthusiasm in the firm, from everyone. At the time, though, we didn't go around thinking, "Aren't we doing well?" We were not really aware of it. We were so busy working on the next project. It was all-consuming, twenty-four hours a day. It was only when people started saying to us, "How have you done it? Where did you get all the money from?" That's when we started looking back and thinking, yes, we have come a long way in a very short time.'

While the company might have been taking a few financial risks, with all the money sploshing around in the economy, Edward was taking none of the rewards personally. All profits were ploughed back into the firm. He wasn't salting anything away for himself for a rainy day in the future. That was a risk in itself, or you could say it was confidence or even arrogance, that the good times would go on.

Colin Rutherford, who worked on the customer and orders side, also remembers things going a bit too fast, when work came in and they couldn't cope as Edward's mind rushed ahead of everyone else's. 'I once caught him out on some figures when he was estimating how much empty space we had in a warehouse, and it turned out he was counting in stuff that hadn't left yet,' says Colin. 'Edward said they had left, but I knew they hadn't. This was typical of him, to be working ahead, as if things had happened when they hadn't.

'It wasn't, of course, that he isn't good at figures. He was just looking at them from his perspective. He came into my office one day when I was working on some new rates. He just glanced at the sheet for a second, looked down the page, and said, "Those two buggers at the bottom are wrong." He'd spotted two mistakes which I hadn't noticed.

'At the time, it didn't feel like moving fast. It's only looking back now, to the nineties, that you see the speed we rose at. We always seemed to be fighting for more work. Things seemed to be slow at times, if anything, waiting for the next development to come on-stream, the next depot, the next fleet of vehicles. There was always a buzz: everyone felt it.'

Colin is honest about working with Edward himself. 'Oh, we had our arguments, falling out over little things, but nothing serious. Afterwards, he never bore grudges. We'd had some disagreement once, then after it was over, he put his arm round my shoulder and said "I love you".' A lad from Hesket Newmarket, saying that to another bloke? Impossible.

It might have been just another Thatcher-style success story, a little firm growing big at a time of economic growth and unrestrained capitalist enterprise. Usually, this would have gone unremarked outside its immediate industry, but for one element in the rise and rise of Eddie Stobart Ltd: how the lorries looked. Almost out of nowhere, unplanned, unforced, Eddie Stobart had acquired an image.

'I was always telling Edward,' says Colin, 'what a good job he had done on the company's image. He didn't know what I was talking about. He hadn't set out to create an image. He'd just done it because he believed in it.'

Colin believes that the whole success of the company depended on two factors. The first is the fairly obvious one, which can be summed up in one word: service – doing for the customer what you say you are going to do, on time, at a good price and efficiently. The other factor is not so obvious. In the media or show business, image is obviously of vital importance, but it also plays a role in the staid, fusty old world of haulage.

'Stobart vehicles were always clean, immaculate and environmentally friendly. That was Edward's own personal obsession. We became known for it. All our customers could see it. They liked the idea of their goods travelling in immaculate lorries, not like the old, dirty days. They liked our drivers and administrative staff being polite and courteous.

'Our lorries were reliable and efficient, and I like to think we gave the best service in the industry but, if pressed, I think I would have to say that it was what

I call our image, even more than service, that created our success. That was the number-one factor.'

This factor was at first only recognized, perhaps even subliminally, inside their own industry. For a long time, the general public was hardly aware of how Eddie Stobart trucks and drivers were in fact different from all the rest. The origins of the Stobart image went back to the early days. When Edward had taken control of the company, he had continued the use of the two primary colours in which Eddie had painted the Guy, his first lorry: Post Office red and Brunswick green. Over the years, the green had grown darker and a yellowy-orange was introduced as the third main colour in the company logo.

Edward, of course, was always the one fussing about the state of his lorries, whether they had been washed or not and, as it grew bigger, he became just as obsessed by the lettering, colour and design of his fleet. When curtain-sided trailers came in, with vinyl curtains replacing canvas tied down with ropes, he had the company's name painted on them in the largest letters possible. This was done to draw attention to the firm – not the attention of the public but of his potential customers. Edward was, naturally, being deliberately naive when denying all knowledge of having an image to Colin, but it was an industry image he was trying to create, not a public one.

The use of female names, which continued even when they reached the magic number of one hundred lorries, was also an early bit of image-making, though it had started out, so Edward insists, as an amusement, a bit of fun. But the change that caught the public eye most, and helped draw attention to the fact that the company had its own special if rather quaint image, was the introduction of uniforms.

Traditionally, the idea of a lorry driver in uniform was laughable. Truck drivers were seen as urban cowboys with tattoos, jeans, long hair; macho motorway men who played country music very loudly. Some of them did have a certain style, and an individual character, though not quite the character you'd want your daughter to marry. But, in reality, most lorry drivers were just plain scruffy: ill-shaven, dirty, tramp-like, not the sort of person you'd want to deliver your precious, clean cargo to a state-of-the-art supermarket, let alone meet your daughter.

It was in 1987 that Edward first started putting his drivers into some sort of uniform with the company name. For the next three years, they wore simple green jackets and battle trousers, more like a boiler suit than a proper suit. Then, in 1990, Edward added shirts, collars and ties, all in the company colours, giving them a complete Eddie Stobart outfit. Very smart, not to say daring.

'It had always annoyed me when I was a driver,' says Edward, 'going into transport caffs and seeing lorry drivers letting themselves down. Not just bad-mouthing the bosses, effing and blinding about their own firms, but looking so dirty and scruffy. They didn't appear as if they were proud of what they were doing. I thought, if only they looked neat and tidy and professional, they might act neat and tidy and professional.

'If you wear some sort of smart uniform, you'll want to have a shave when you get up in the morning, be clean and tidy, in order to look right in your uniform. Good housekeeping is vital, whatever you're doing. If you look smart, you're half-way there to being smart. That was my thinking.'

Only two drivers out of some two hundred refused to wear collars and ties when Edward first introduced them. He imposed them, in fact, as he made them compulsory. The two who refused both left immediately. For the first few months, Eddie Stobart drivers did have to put up with a fair amount of stick and personal abuse. If they went into a transport caff, they were often jeered and mocked by drivers from other firms. What they therefore did was to pop their head in first, look around to see if there were any other Eddie Stobart drivers to sit with. If not, they might try somewhere else, or get a table in a corner. But gradually, as the novelty wore off, so did the ridicule. Within about six months, it was noticed by Edward how several of his rival firms were beginning to put their drivers into some sort of uniform.

Because Edward had made it compulsory, it was then considered a sacking offence to be caught without a uniform on the job. In 1995, one driver was sacked – and immediately sued the firm for unfair dismissal. In his defence, he explained that he had taken his tie off during a heatwave, while his vehicle had broken down and he was waiting for help: pretty good explanation. However, the case did not come to court in the end – the firm settled with him.

Edward's aim in having clean vehicles and smart drivers was to improve the driver's image of himself, and of the company, even if he himself never used the term image-making. (The ties today are in fact clip-on ties, for health and safety reasons, so you are seeing the image of a tie, not a real one.)

By encouraging his drivers to have pride and self-respect, Edward was encouraging them to work harder, that was the unspoken, inarticulated theory behind it all. He was also well aware, without having any image consultant to guide him, that having distinctive livery and lorries would soon make the general public aware of him, not just the industry. 'Folks did begin to think we had far more vehicles than we had,' he admits. Which was handy whenever Edward perhaps exaggerated precisely how big the company had become.

Lorries at that time were proving more and more unpopular with the public as they got bigger, noisier, more frightening. There were campaigns against them and the harmful effects they were said to have and attempts to keep them out of small, rural high streets. The new monster lorries had become known pejoratively as juggernauts – a term first used in this sense by *The Sunday Times* under Harry Evans in the 1970s.

All the more surprising then that people, very often

middle-class folks, the sort who might be expected to be manning anti-road campaigns, should suddenly start falling in love with Eddie Stobart lorries. This was one result of Edward's image-making process that he had definitely not envisaged.

THE BIRTH OF THE FAN CLUB

The company had always received the odd fan letter, ever since they went national. Once their depots started springing up across the country and their distinctive lorries began bashing along the main motorways, people started noticing them.

Edward and William, while young, had themselves loved looking out for interesting, unusually decorated lorries but, not being of a particular literary bent, finding writing of any sort awfully hard work, they were not the types to send off a fan letter.

Within the company, Edward had a rule that all letters, of any kind, had to be answered. 'It was company policy,' says Barrie Thomas. 'When a child writes in, you never know who the father is. He might well be a customer. When a child grows up, you never know what he might end up doing. He might want to work for us, or to deal with us, bring business our way, all because he remembered the nice letter we once sent him.'

Gradually, these odd letters began to turn into a steadier stream, for no apparent reason as far as

Edward could see. Nobody had encouraged them; there had been no public promotion or publicity of any sort. People, off their own bat, just wrote in to ask for details of the lorries, how many were there, makes and types, saying they would look out for them.

A common question in the early letters was: is there really an Eddie Stobart, or is it just a made-up name? People recounted how they reacted to the sight of an Eddie Stobart lorry, what they did in their cars, in the privacy of their own family, or even on their own.

Deborah Rodgers, Edward's young personal assistant, was given the job of answering these letters. Deborah comes from Carlisle and joined the firm in 1987, when she was twenty-three. She'd had dealings with Colin Rutherford in her old job, working at Hazard Haulage, and he had rung her up when he heard she was looking to move. He asked her if she wanted a job at Eddie Stobart Ltd, and she was interviewed and taken on. At the time, the office staff consisted of two other women, one of them working part time.

Deborah was mostly employed typing invoices which, at first, felt a bit of a backward step from her old job, with less variety and responsibility. Stobart's only had fifty vehicles when she joined but, as it grew, she got more responsibility, becoming secretary to Barrie Thomas, then personal assistant to Edward, dealing with his correspondence.

By 1990, as more and more letters from the public came in, Deborah devised a standard letter, replying to the questions most frequently asked. The company had their own calendar by then, but not one intended to be given away to punters, spotters or letter-writers out of the blue: the calendar was for customers. Like most companies, the firm had also acquired various promotional objects to give away to people they dealt with, such as pens with the company's name on. According to Colin Rutherford, when they first started such things, Edward had insisted on all freebies being good quality, not rubbish, even though they were proving quite expensive to produce.

In August 1990, they began *Stobart Express*, a quarterly, four-page in-house magazine – but again it was meant for internal use; for the staff, or regular customers. Young Deborah, still only twenty-six, became the editor.

In his introductory letter on the front page Edward explained that they now had five hundred staff on the payroll, in depots all over England, Scotland and Ireland. This new publication was a way of keeping them all in touch, to tell them about exciting events. The latest was a new contract, worth three million pounds a year, from Impetus Packaging. There was also a story about a charity bike ride at the Carlisle depot and a sponsored football team at the Swindon depot.

On the back page was an interview with William Stobart, Operations Director, which revealed they now had 220 tractors (front of lorries) and 280 trailers, fifty per cent of which were now operating round the clock,

STOBART

Eddie Stobart Ltd
Express Haulage, Storage
and Distribution

Head Office
Brunthill Road, Kingstown Industrial Estate,
Carlisle CA3 0EH
Telephone 0228 37915, Fax 0228 511188

EXPRESS

The magazine for staff and customers of Eddie Stobart Ltd.　　　　**August 1990**

We are really on the move!

WELCOME to the first edition of the Stobart Express!

I hope you like what you see in what is intended to be the first in a regular series of newsletters.

The aim is to tell you all - staff and customers - what is going on at Stobart's and in the industry generally. There's news of contracts won, and all kinds of developments within this firm which has grown into the biggest independent haulier of its kind in the country. But it isn't intended just to be about wagons and contracts. It's going to be about the people who make the firm tick.

We'll be looking at the work of each depot in future editions, and we'll be talking to people in every department about the kind of work they do.

We also want to hear from anyone with news. It doesn't have to be to do with work.

Charity

If you've done something for charity, or won a competition - tell us all about it. Just get in touch with Debbie Rodgers at Carlisle, and your name could make headlines.

We hope the newsletter will be a bit of fun, but it's also an important way of keeping everyone in touch with the heart of the business.

As we've grown over the years, to the point where we have over 500 people on the payroll, operating out of depots from Scotland to the South of England/Ireland it could have been easy to lose touch. We have tried not to let that happen, and the Stobart Express aims to make sure it doesn't happen in the future.

We are all part of the Stobart team, and the way we each do our job affects the rest of the team.

So, let us know your news, and the Stobart Express can keep us all in touch with each other.

Edward Stobart

Read all about the company...

INSIDE this, the first issue of the Stobart Express, we hope you will find plenty of interest.
* On Page 2, the latest contracts make the news.
* On Page 3, There's a competition with a smashing prize. There's background to one of the company's newest ventures, and there's also news of the latest building work at Carlisle.
* Page 4 tells what goes on in the operations nerve centre...and reveals what Swindon's Chris Matthews has in common with Peter Shilton. You'll also find out how to get YOUR news into the Stobart Express!

FLEET Engineer Stan Monkhouse has just welcomed three of the new additions to the expanding Stobart fleet....and there are more to come.

H-reg day, August 1, saw the three Strato 325s above, powered by 10 litre Cummins diesel engines, join the fleet. By the end of the month, a total of 15 brand new trucks will have been added to the Stobart strength, giving a total fleet of around 220.

There has been a major expansion of the fleet already this year, with 60 new trucks brought into the company since last December. In the drive for maximum efficiency, all the latest additions to the fleet carry full air deflection equipment - vital for fuel economy.

Stan Monkhouse, who has been with the company for 30 years, is responsible for advising the directors on the specification of new vehicles.
* Stan is pictured, with driver Neil Slack at the wheel of one of the new vehicles.

Fashionable trends in the cab

In uniform - Tom Redfern from the Glasgow Depot.

THE uniform approach to smartness has just been taken a step further.

All personnel who were previously issued with the Stobart work jacket and trousers are now getting matching shirts and ties to wear every working day.

It's all part of the company's drive to maintain a clean and smart image.

Sheila Woodbridge, personnel administrator, was responsible for the co-ordination of the fashionable move.

She said: "Our drivers are our ambassadors and their image is just as important as our vehicles' image.

"We deal with a lot of major international companies who demand very high standards in their workforce. We have to reflect their image and match those high standards."

The shirts have embroidered pockets and the polyester silk ties carry a Stobart motif. Drivers are issued with eight shirts, and have the choice of long- or short-sleeved version.

Personnel who have been issued with the new clothes must wear them on duty - and so far views have been favourable.

"The drivers are getting a lot of very positive comments," said Sheila Woodbridge.

"It's raised their profile and attracted attention to them, although some felt it would expose them to ridicule at first. Now they seem quite happy with the whole concept."

The next stage of the process is to design a uniform for office staff: talks are currently taking place with manufacturers.

every day of the week. Each was averaging 150,000 miles a year – some even reaching 230,000 miles. The firm had now divided its operations into five regional traffic centres: Carlisle, Burton-on-Trent, Stamford, Knottingley in Yorkshire and Leyland in Lancashire. Each cab had the latest cellphone technology, so that their every movement could be monitored by their individual planner at the traffic centre.

This first edition of *Stobart Express* is now a goldmine of information for true Eddie Stobart fans. They demand the minutiae of every technical advance, wanting to know exactly when certain types of trucks, certain innovations were made – details that Edward and William themselves now find hard to remember, at least in the correct order.

For those whose special study is Eddie Stobart uniform, history of, this first magazine also records that momentous change. On the front page, there is a news story which reports that 'all personnel who were previously issued with the Stobart work-jacket and trousers are now getting matching shirts and ties to wear every working day'. Note that the word 'compulsory' is not used – but a later paragraph makes it clear that personnel issued with the new clothes, 'must wear them on duty'.

Each driver, so the report says, was being issued with eight new shirts which, 'have embroidered pockets and polyester silk ties and carry a Stobart motif. Drivers have a choice of long or short sleeves.' Coming soon, so the last paragraph states, is a uniform for all office staff. 'Talks are currently taking place with manufacturers.'

This new magazine, essentially for house consumption, proved a useful freebie to send out to members of the general public when they happened to write in for information. Debbie was able to pop a copy in the post, along with the little factsheet she had compiled about the firm itself, a sheet which had become longer and bulkier since she'd first created it.

Then, in 1991, they got a letter from a fairly well-known and popular personage, Jools Holland, the musician and television presenter. Jools had been doing an extensive UK tour with his band. On tour, pop people mostly sleep while travelling, recovering from performing, drinking, or whatever else they might have been doing. In the case of Jools and his chums, they occupied a lot of their idle time going up and down motorways by noting the incidence of Eddie Stobart vehicles. It became the tour joke, making references to Eddie Stobart, whoever he may be. They even kept a daily car log of interesting things noted along the way, such as Eddie Stobart lorries.

When the tour was drawing to an end, Jools Holland was looking for something to present to each musician as a memento of their time together. This is common practice in the theatre and film world. After a period of intense pressure and relationships, the star or director – or more likely his personal assistant – devises some amusing present to give to everyone, before they all disband, for ever. It doesn't happen quite so often in the pop-music world, but then Jools Holland is rather couth and civilized, as musical people go.

His then PA, Nicky Keller, wrote to Eddie Stobart Limited, Carlisle, asking if by chance they had an Eddie Stobart wall calendar, or something similar, she could give Jools's musicians to brighten up the rest of their lives. 'Yes, you are quite right,' she wrote, 'they are all indeed mad.' The implication here being that she imagined no one else had ever thought of writing to Eddie Stobart. In a PS, she added, 'What would really make their day would be Eddie Stobart's autograph if you can manage it.'

Almost by return, she was sent some calendars and an Edward Stobart autograph. The latter was quite a coup, as our Edward didn't normally do such things. The delighted Jools Holland wrote back with his own autographed photograph. 'To Eddie Stobart, keep on trucking.'

From then on, when interviewed by various newspapers or magazines, Jools often revealed that he was an Eddie Stobart spotter. When this was mentioned in a *Sunday Times* piece, hundreds of people came forward and admitted that they, too, were Eddie Stobart fans.

This was roughly the moment when Eddie Stobart spotters realized they were not alone. Their personal passion – or so they had thought – was in fact shared by thousands of other potty people out there. People liked the name 'Eddie Stobart' and also appreciated the lorries' distinctive livery.

A real star letter!

To
Eddie Stobart
Keep on drucking
Jools Holland

My employer, Jools Holland (you may recall him from presenting "The Tube" and Juke Box Jury for Channel 4), has recently been on tour throughout the UK with his band. Whilst travelling about the countryside with his Manager and fellow musicians, they have been keeping a daily log in their car of various points of interest that they come across along the way. Also noted in the log are numerous sightings of Eddie Stobart lorries, of which there seems to be a profusion! Yes, you're quite right they are all indeed mad!

Their tour sadly comes to an end shortly and they will be returning to the office here, to deal with mundane things such as paperwork and accounts etc. So, why am I telling you all of this? To brighten up their lives upon their return I would like to present them each with a memento of their tour. I can think of nothing that would be more important to them than an Eddie Stobart wall calendar (or anything similar), that they can gaze at whilst sitting at their desks, reliving the memories of their tour.

So, if there is anything you can send to me, I would be eternally grateful, and you would have thatsatisfying feeling of having brought a glimmer of light into these poor musician's dreary lives.

Nicky Keller
PA to Jools Holland

PS. What would really make their day would be Eddie Stobart's autograph if you can manage it.

We sent a pack of calendars, videos, etc, to Jools, who also sent us the signed picture above, and had another letter back, saying the Stobart calendar now has pride of place on his wall - Edward Stobart.

The attraction of the actual name 'Eddie Stobart' was a surprise, at least to Cumbrians, who didn't find it at all funny or unusual or made-up. In fact, some true Cumbrians were a bit upset to find such a well-known local surname being smiled at. Doubtless the good people of Scunthorpe or Wigan are not amused either when the name of their fair town is taken in vain or jest.

Another recurring enquiry in the early fan letters was about the female names on the lorries, which intrigued everyone who noticed them. They asked who the lorries were named after, were all the lorries similarly named and, if so, could their wife/daughter/girlfriend have her name on an Eddie Stobart truck?

While Jools Holland and his chums had been devising games and recording sightings on their journeys, it turned out that thousands of families with children had been doing much the same. On long journeys, parents were awarding points to their children for every spotting, extra points for a long lorry with a trailer, treble points for reading the female name. As well as passing the time, it taught children to be more observant and also, with a bit of luck, forced them to get out paper and pen and write stuff down.

Making games round spotting lorries was fairly understandable, something frequent motorway travellers can easily relate to. But there was one rather weird manifestation of the early cult of Eddie Stobart, and that was setting the name 'Eddie Stobart' to music. And for some strange reason, people tended to choose the same tune. Without any outside prompting, whole families, or whole car loads, would burst into Handel's 'Hallelujah Chorus'. Instead of singing 'Hallelujah', etc., they sang 'Eh-dee Stob-art, Eh-dee Stobart, Ehdee Stobart, Ehdee Stobart, Eh- dee- Stob-art . . . .' And so on, the whole family taking different parts.

By the end of 1991, Eddie Stobart Ltd discovered that the postage bill alone for sending out fan-mail literature to absolute strangers was £5000. Plus, of course, there was the cost of producing and printing the material, all of which the company was giving away free, for no apparent return, apart from vague goodwill.

What was in it for a lorry company? Why should they be bothered about the goodwill of the general public? It wasn't as if they ever dealt with the public directly at all. They were not like a film company, a famous football club or the BBC, who expect to send out free pictures of their stars to the general public because getting to the general public is what they are all about. Should Edward's company therefore stop replying to unsolicited mail, before the costs got even higher and it took up even more time and labour? Or perhaps they could reduce it to reasonable proportions, making sure it didn't grow any more?

An accountant, if asked such questions, might have said stop now; it's all a waste of money, let's save that £5000 a year. But Eddie Stobart Ltd, in the full flush of their enormous growth spurt of the late eighties and early nineties, was not too bothered about saving piddling amounts, not at this stage in the firm's life. They were more concerned with the next multi-million pound contract, the next hundred lorries to be added to the fleet, the next mega-warehouse to be built, than cutting out any surplus fat or minor expenditures.

On the other hand, it was a bit daft to actually spend money on this service, when they didn't have to. The solution was to keep the service going but to make those who wrote in pay a small sum, purely to cover some of the overheads, such as postage.

Thus, in 1992, the Eddie Stobart fan club was born. They called it that because, well, that was what it was; people had been writing in saying they were fans. From now on, when people wrote in, they were told they had become members of the Eddie Stobart fan club. They also got a car sticker and a regular newsletter. At this stage, in 1992, that was about all that was envisaged; no one for a moment imagined what it would grow into.

So 1992 was a good year for the firm, and climaxed with Eddie Stobart Ltd being voted Haulier of the Year by fellow toilers in the transport industry. But, along with success, was to come something not so welcome, not so good for the company's image.

BAD-MOUTHING

It first started around 1990, after those first four years of incredible growth. Nasty rumours began to circulate about how Eddie Stobart Ltd cut corners, took on contracts at a loss in order to kill off rivals and, worst of all, that it had run up huge debts and was going bust.

Edward took this personally and was exceedingly hurt, not understanding why people were getting at him, picking on him when he had done so much to keep his own head down and out of the limelight. He had always felt, genuinely, that one of his main motivations had been to improve the image of the haulage industry. Now, the gossip factories in the haulage industry itself were creating stories about how bad he was.

The gossip was purely within the trade, restricted to people and firms in the haulage world. In 1990 Eddie Stobart still had no public recognition. Nevertheless, the rumours were dangerous financially, as well as being very annoying. They were also time-consuming for Barrie Thomas, in charge of the firm's financial matters. He constantly suffered the effects of all the rumours in his day-to-day work.

'I got calls from people asking to speak to the receivers. They genuinely believed we had gone bust and the receivers were already in. Then we got calls from people wanting to take over our contracts, cover our loads, as they'd been told on good authority that we could not now fulfil them.

'I think I know who the main culprit was. Yes: another haulier, but I could never prove it. I think it was just one person who started it as a bad-mouthing campaign against us, but it went round the industry.

'It was very stressful as well as hurtful. It undermines your staff, makes it harder to hire new people. And it worries customers if they think you are going bust. For a whole year, it got worse and worse. It was very hard to know what to do.

'I realized, of course, it was all based on jealousy. We had risen so quickly and were now being written about regularly in the trade press. I suppose we brought a bit of the jealousy upon ourselves by being so high-profile. We knew, of course, we were not going bust and that, financially, we were doing very well, but it was hard to prove it. And, once it starts, it's hard to think how you can stop the rumours.'

Jack Semple, now Technical Editor of the highly respected trade publication *Motor Transport*, says he first heard rumours about Eddie Stobart as early as 1986, when he was attending Tipcon, a tipper show in Harrogate. 'People were coming up to me and whispering that

Eddie Stobart had been getting money from some religious extremists but he was now going bust.'

Jack heard similar rumours again in 1991. By this time, Eddie Stobart Ltd was so fed up with the gossip that it took the most unusual step of getting its bank, Midland Bank, to issue a public statement, saying it had every confidence in the firm's finances. Barrie Thomas says it was about the only thing they could think of doing to try to put an end to all the stories.

'I had never heard of such a thing happening before,' says Jack Semple. 'It shows just how worried they must have been. The Midland Bank, or any bank, doesn't normally do such a thing as it could rebound on them.'

At that stage, Jack had not met Edward personally, or visited the firm's HQ, but he had been following its progress closely, as a haulage expert. After the Midland Bank statement, he decided to write a proper piece about the firm. 'I looked at their finances carefully, checked at Companies House, and was confident the firm was financially in good shape.'

Jack went up to Carlisle, brave man that he was, and visited the company's HQ at Kingstown. His six-page feature on Eddie Stobart Ltd appeared in the January 1992 issue of *Truck Magazine*, again another prime source for Stobart students, as it is the first extensive article about the firm in a national publication, albeit a trade one.

In the article, which was under the headline: 'Britain's Fastest-growing Haulier', Jack wrote that

Edward had 'created a £30-million company through spectacular risk-taking . . . invested in the future in a manner no PLC accountant would sanction.' He gave as examples of this the company vehicle livery, washers, and uniforms. Jack also mentioned all the investments in property: 'Having traded through the recession, his firm looks as if it can sustain its break into the big time.'

Jack was particularly amazed by the uniforms which, by now, were being worn by all inside staff, not just drivers. He described the receptionists as, 'looking like air hostesses from one of the better airlines'. Uniforms, so he reported, were currently costing the company £200,000 a year.

Jack's article listed lots of fascinating facts about the state of the firm in 1991. There were eight hundred employees and that year's revenue was forecast to be thirty-one million pounds. As a trade publication, a lot of facts were mostly of interest only to other hauliers. These included the details of the fleet, which was then made up of 330 vehicles, which included 80 drawbars, 250 tractors and 400 semi-trailers. Jack emphasized the large number of drawbars (rigid vehicles with close-coupled trailers), which was considered innovative at the time. Seventeen depots were also listed. Drivers' wages were given as £4.42 an hour for day-work, £5.23 for nights, with all drivers guaranteed fifty hours of work a week.

Jack was clearly surprised to find how the firm was being run: 'Edward holds no board meetings . . . his father Eddie plays no active role in the company'. Jack also wrote of 'Edward's younger brother, William, now the Operations Director, who apparently accepts Edward as the boss'. I hope William was not too upset by that last remark.

Mr Semple also mentioned the firm's charitable work, how it had recently sent two truckloads of goods to help orphanages in Romania, plus a cash gift of £50,000. 'Charitable work is important to Edward Stobart and he encourages his depots to get involved in fund-raising for schools, hospitals and so on. Mr Stobart goes to church, as do his four children.'

Mr Semple's observation in this interview, that Eddie Stobart Ltd was the fastest-growing haulier in Britain, could have looked a bit limp if anything suspect about its finances had eventually emerged. But his statement remained true for the whole of the rest of the nineties as the company progressed ever onwards and upwards.

Looking back today, Jack is quite pleased by the magazine space he devoted to the firm, as it all proved justified. He didn't, of course, include much personal stuff about Edward himself, as he was writing for a specialist publication. 'But I remember being surprised on meeting Edward to find he had a stammer. I didn't know anything about him till then. He turned out to be a little man with a set expression on his face. I wondered what was going on behind that expression: you just couldn't tell. I suppose, now, it was just the old computery brain ticking away.

'What struck me most about him was his basic

vision. He knew exactly what he was doing, where he was going, what he expected from his staff. He had a very clear view and the ability to express it very simply.

'He told me during the interview that haulage was essential to British industry. That could have been bullshit, but I believed him. I could see he had total control, standardized procedure and discipline at every level, right through the company.

'But I suppose, of all the things he was doing, it was the standard of cleanliness which surprised me most of all. Most hauliers were still living in 1950's conditions; they either had scruffy offices with peeling paint or were crouching in Portakabins. Few had uniforms for any of their staff. Most other hauliers thought it was excessive, when Eddie Stobart first appeared with collars and ties, but, of course, many soon followed.'

Jack Semple's article was one of the elements that helped bring the bad-mouthing to an end, much to the relief of Barrie Thomas. 'I suppose it lasted, as far as we were aware, for about two years. We didn't lose money by it, in that no customers did actually leave, but we lost a lot of valuable time in denying it. During that period, I had to get our accounts completed as quickly as possible each year, then let our main contractors see copies, just to prove how well we were doing.

'The rumours about some religious cult being behind us went on for a bit longer. Wherever I went in the industry, someone would always ask if it was true about the Mormons.' It is understandable where this might have come from. Once the company had any sort of profile, it came out about Eddie, the founder of it all, being a keen and passionate Methodist. Edward always acknowledged his own Christian beliefs, as did Barrie Thomas and others in the firm, such as David Jackson, manager of the first depot. Lorry firms are not normally known for their religious beliefs, hence their rivals finding it easy to get the gossip mills working.

Edward himself, during this period of rumour, even contemplated something that he had always been against, which would have gone contrary to all the simple principles on which he had built up the firm. Into his head came the awful thought: why not hire a spin doctor? Not that he used that actual phrase, as it was not quite current, but Edward's thinking was much the same. It might be useful to get a firm which specialized in financial public relations to work on their image in the right quarters.

'We did interview two financial companies and discussed with them how we could raise our profile amongst City people. But, just as we were thinking seriously about hiring one of them, the fan club started. The fan club had sprung up out of the blue, but it began to give us a much bigger profile – without us having to do anything. We soon saw there was no need to pay anyone to do anything on our behalf.'

There were two other factors that brought the

rumours finally to an end. One was the company's continual rise throughout the whole of the nineties, in size of fleet, turnover and staff. It became clear to all that no firm could have kept going at such a rate, increasing by fifty per cent each year, if there was anything dodgy going on.

With the company's explosion in size came something else: power. Some of those rival firms, presumably including the ones that had enjoyed the bad-mouthing, had at one time been much the same size as Eddie Stobart. Now they began to fall well behind. It meant that they were often becoming dependent on Eddie Stobart for sub-contracting work, for crumbs from their table. You don't rubbish someone you are keeping in with – not aloud, anyway.

At the same time, even the company's deadliest rivals had to admit that Eddie Stobart Ltd was giving their industry the sort of profile it had never had before, so they smiled through gritted teeth and waited to see what the firm would do next.

MONEY MATTERS

There comes a stage in the story of any rags-to-riches success when you think you might perhaps have missed something, a sleight of hand that hides the reason behind enormous growth. One moment Edward had fifty lorries and was turning over £4.5 million and, a few years later, he had a thousand lorries and a turnover of £150 million.

Even in Cumbria, there are still people who wonder how he did it. Perhaps most of all in Cumbria, as they know too well the little village he came from, the modest beginnings, the lack of any real capital in the Stobart family. Not Mormons, of course, but perhaps some sort of Methodist mafia had been at work? The Quakers in the nineteenth century always helped each other, with Quaker banks lending money to Quaker biscuit-makers or the Quaker railway. Could the Methodists have somehow informally helped Edward behind the scenes? Edward doesn't even bother to laugh at the idea, and begins instead to explain how he pulled everything off financially.

'I bought my first two lorries when I was still at Hesket, working for my father. They were two DAFs, brand new. I can still remember the registration numbers, as I can with all the early trucks. The two DAFs cost £20,000 each. I paid twenty per cent down and the rest was on hire-purchase, spread over three years. I took these two DAFs with me when I moved to Greystone Road, still paying them off.

'I remember at the end of that first year, when my father's accountant came to do the books, he said he thought £1300 a month was far too much to be paying out for the two trucks. He had a right go at me, and so did my father. They said you're not doing so well, you know, not much money's coming in, so you shouldn't have such big HP payments. It was my biggest outgoing, so if anything went wrong I would be in trouble.

'I thought what they were saying was rubbish, but they went on and on about it. I was just beginning on my own, so when I next bought some vehicles, I bought several second-hand ones. What a mistake! They cost a fortune in maintenance and breakdowns. They proved more expensive in the end than paying HP.

'Next time, I just ignored what they said and bought six new DAFs. Because I was buying six, I got a brilliant deal. I paid only £17,000 each, instead of £24,000, and I only had to pay ten per cent down. I got them from the DAF dealer in Carlisle and they organized the finance, through DAF Finance. They weren't directly connected, but they specialized in DAF lorries.

'The running costs were nothing. I worked them day and night and never lost a day due to maintenance. When you own a vehicle, you have to pay to tow it home if it breaks down, pay for the repairs and, while it's off the road, you can let the customer down. With a new vehicle, they have to sort it for you or replace it.

'I did all the sums and it confirmed to me that an HP agreement was cheaper. And, of course, you don't have cash tied up; it means you can keep on growing.

'That was a turning point for me. From then on, I never bought a second-hand lorry ever again. I still don't. And I never pay cash – and still don't. If you pay cash, you stop your growth.'

In the eighties, interest rates went up as high as sixteen per cent, which made HP more expensive than it had been, but Edward still continued to use this method. All he did now was spread the payments over four or five years, as opposed to three, to keep the payments low.

Since 1997, Edward has given up the majority of HP arrangements on vehicles and started a new arrangement: trucks are now on contract-hire for three years, which includes full repair and maintenance. The annual payments are similar to HP but it means that, after three years, he doesn't have an old lorry to sell – it always took time and effort to sell old vehicles. What it therefore means today is that seventy-five per cent of Eddie Stobart's thousand trucks are not technically owned by Eddie Stobart.

The reason for contract-hiring was brought about partly by changes in accountancy and taxation systems. It helps to keep the value of a company down, and its tax liabilities, by not owning vehicles. Many companies now do the same. The size of his firm's fleet has enabled Edward to arrange highly favourable contract-hire deals direct from motor manufacturers. 'If the Government changes the rules, and leased vehicles get classed as being owned by you, then we might have to change again and go back to HP. But my basic rule would still be the same: paying cash up-front is never cost-effective.'

The other way of raising or getting access to money to finance growth, apart from using HP firms for new vehicles, has been through the bank. In the early years, like most people, Edward went cap-in-hand to his local high-street bank and said, 'Please, Sir, if you will, Sir, can I have some money?' His cap was always pretty dirty during the early years in Carlisle, so the banks often looked down on him and his plans. 'Oh I did try to have a wash, before going to the bank,' says Edward, 'but it's true I didn't wear a suit. I was still driving vehicles, so I had to be ready at any moment to take a load somewhere.

'I'd go with my dad in the early years, let him do all the talking. Sometimes I thought he talked too much. When we came out, I'd say, "Dad, why did you tell them all that? There was no need to tell them we hadn't actually got a certain contract all signed."

'I wasn't saying he should tell lies. Just give simple,

honest answers to their questions. No need to tell them things they didn't need to know – just put the best light on things, paint the best picture, always appear optimistic. But my dad would go on and on, chatting, telling them everything. Sometimes it wouldn't work and we didn't get the money.'

Although Edward doesn't feel that the banks displayed social or class prejudice, there was another problem, as he saw it. This problem was often their lack of common sense. 'They couldn't see the obvious possibilities or understand that, in the end, it was us who were paying their wages. They should have seen that this guy in front of them had so far always done what he'd said he'd do. That should have been enough for them to take a risk on the next stage. Some managers were capable of taking risks. Others wouldn't.

'I'd agree I might not be making much profit out of running ten vehicles, but I explained I would do better by running twelve. I knew it, it was clear to me: that's the way haulage costs work, but often they couldn't understand it. So I wouldn't get the overdraft I needed to pay the deposit down on two new vehicles.'

Edward did, of course, get his trucks in the end, if not always as quickly as he wanted. But, when his firm moved on to property as opposed to vehicles, Edward was fortunate in that the climate of the time was more in his favour. 'It so happened that the Midland Bank had brought in a new scheme to help firms if they were buying property. It wasn't the norm until then, not for firms like ours.'

Once Edward's firm had acquired a bit of a track record, the financial suits started suggesting methods of raising cash. 'They'd tell me about these people: venture something . . . venture capitalists, who would find investors for me who would buy shares and that. Every time it came up, I said no – they were offering too little. They always wanted to buy shares on the cheap. But, mainly, it was because they'd want control, stop me doing certain things, make me have meetings, papers, all that discussion stuff. I couldn't be doing with any of that.'

So Edward continued with bank overdrafts plus HP deals on vehicles but, when he started geographical expansion, setting up depots away from Carlisle, he was entering a bigger league. 'I wanted to buy our first depot, but could only lease it. When the lease ended, I did buy the next one, at Burton-on-Trent. It cost one million pounds and I got a bank loan for seven years. I always try to keep loans short.'

Buying the Warrington site in 1991 was something of a saga, still talked about by Eddie Stobart people who were there at the time. Edward had been looking for a new site for some time, preferably in Yorkshire, but hadn't found anything suitable. One day he and William had to go to a meeting at Haydock with Spillers, then and now one of their biggest customers. It was a normal, three-monthly meeting to discuss the contract.

While staying overnight at the Haydock Hotel, they woke up to find William's car had been stolen. They lost most of that day, talking with the police, waiting around. The car was found over in Liverpool, in a scrapyard, so they drove in Edward's car to pick it up. When they got there, they found the steering lock had been broken. So they decided to leave it there and drive back to Carlisle.

Near Warrington, the brothers passed an industrial site with a notice outside saying it was for sale. Edward stopped the car at the gates to the site, but they couldn't see much as the rain was bucketing down.

'The only building I could see seemed to be made of asbestos,' says Edward, 'so I thought that would have to come down. The gates were locked, so we couldn't get in. All we knew about it was what was said on the billboard: 17.8 acres for sale, with a phone number.

'I rang Barrie in Carlisle, gave him the number, told him to ring and find out the price. I don't like ringing people – I'm not good at it. We sat in the car, out of the rain, and Barrie eventually rang back. He said, "It's sold." I said, "I didn't ask you to find out if it was sold or not – I said find out the price." He said, "It's sold. The price doesn't matter." I said, "Ring them back, get the price, just do what I ask you."

'So we sat and waited again, while the rain still came down. Eventually, he rang back. He'd found out what the original asking price had been: £1.4 million. I said, "Ring and offer them that." He said, "It's sold, there's no point." I said, "Ring them."

'So we sat and waited once again. He is good, Barrie,

on the phone – I will say that, good at getting information. He'd found out it was in the hands of solicitors but, as I'd suspected, they hadn't got their asking price. So I told Barrie to put our offer on paper, then we drove back to Carlisle.'

This was much to William's relief. He'd got pretty fed up, sitting in the car in the rain with Edward for several hours, thinking the whole thing was mad. He'd not said much, as Edward had made it clear it was all his fault they'd ended up there, wherever there was, by allowing his car to be stolen.

'It was touch-and-go for three days,' says Edward, 'till our offer was accepted, subject to planning permission. I still hadn't been inside the site, till we bought it. I hadn't even got out of the car; it was too clarty [muddy].'

This was the site that Colin Rutherford, when he saw it, said was awful, a terrible mistake. So what attracted Edward to it? 'It was just four miles from the M6 and two miles from the M62: a perfect location. I reckoned that, even if we had to knock it all down and start again, it would still be a good investment. In the end, we didn't have to knock everything down. We managed to rebuild some of it, but we still spent £3.6 million on it, just to get it the way we wanted.'

In 1997, Edward sold the site to a pension fund for just over eleven million pounds, over twice what it had cost him altogether, thus making a profit of over six million pounds on the deal. He then leased it back from the pension fund, on a long lease.

When Edward eventually came to buy a Yorkshire site, that, too, happened by chance. Someone told him about a plastic-bottle factory in Yorkshire, which had its stores scattered around fifteen different warehouses – yet nearby was a large empty site for sale.

Edward did nothing about it, it was just a piece of information lodged in his brain, till one day he had to go to Manchester to appear in court on a driving charge, for doing 60 m.p.h. in a 50 m.p.h. area. He was going to plead guilty, but was also going to plead for leniency due to his circumstances at that time. Nevertheless, he was still expecting he'd be fined and would lose his licence.

Edward's exceptional circumstances were not his work. His marriage to Sylvia had recently broken down and he needed to be able to visit his four children and take them on outings. To his surprise, the magistrate accepted this; all he got was a fine of £40. 'She then asked me how I'd like to pay, and I said cash. She said she meant over what length of time would I like to pay. I said, "Cash. I'll pay cash now."' By this time, Edward was, on paper, a multi-millionaire, with his name all over the motorways. However, by having kept such a low personal profile for all those years, his face was not known and no local paper had picked up on the court case involving E. Stobart.

Because Edward had unexpectedly kept his licence and didn't have to take the train back to Carlisle, he had time on his hands, so he decided to drive home via Yorkshire. 'When I got there, I could see a notice on a site, saying thirty-three acres for sale. I rang Carlisle and told Richard Butcher, our Commercial Director, to get on to the agents. It turned out they were asking for sealed bids and today was the last day. There was no time to do any searches, and I didn't know what sort of price they might have in mind. I sat in the car, looked at the site, worked out what I thought it was worth, per acre. We sent down a messenger that day with a sealed bid of £2.8 million. No, I hadn't spoken at that stage to the bottle factory. They didn't know what my plan was.

'Our offer was accepted. I then went to see the bottle-factory people: announced I'd bought this site right beside their factory and was going to build a big warehouse on it. Would they be interested in using it?

'They were very surprised. One of them said I held all the cards, which I did. But it was their fault – they'd sat on their backsides when it was staring them in the face. I did offer them a good deal, a brand-new warehouse of 400,000 square feet. And they agreed to rent it. I've now sold it, to a fund, and leased it back. This was to generate profit and cash for further development. I kept ten acres undeveloped, which I'll use sometime for something . . . .'

As well as having lorries and depots, a haulage company needs some good contracts. Edward today can get a bit upset if anyone in the trade suggests that the original Metal Box contract, so vital to them then, was in any way a piece of luck, or dependent perhaps on the Carlisle connections, or that Metal Box were in any sense doing them a favour. 'All that happened was that we priced better than others. In business, no one gives you something for nowt.'

Once that first Metal Box contract had been won in Carlisle, Eddie Stobart Ltd went on to win contracts from other Metal Box factories all over the UK. But, far more important to its growth than carrying empty cans, was transporting pet food. Spillers, now known as Friskies Petcare, is still its biggest single customer.

In the early years, the company took a lot of empty cans from Metal Box in Carlisle up to the Spillers factory in Barrhead, near Glasgow. Each time it delivered, Edward enquired about the chance of any work the other way, taking the filled cans from the factory to the warehouse used by Spillers in Wisbech, East Anglia. This was being done at the time by BRS, which held an exclusive contract with Spillers for transport from its Scottish plants. Edward pestered Spillers for three years, sometimes once a day, but only ever got the odd load, no regular work, no contract.

Then Edward managed to get the contract with a smaller Spillers factory at Maryport, on the west Cumberland coast, to take its loads to Wisbech, a contract which had been held by another Carlisle firm, John Watts.

'It wasn't a very good job, going to Wisbech,' so Edward remembers. 'There was a lot of hanging around at the warehouse – sometimes five to ten hours. You couldn't do much about it, or pick up other loads. There wasn't the work available round there. But we still thought BRS was making a pathetic job of it.'

At long last, Edward was given the chance to tender against BRS for the Spillers work out of the distribution centre at Wisbech. 'I didn't know what my rivals were bidding. I just worked out my own price, per mile, and put a bid in blind. And I got it. It was only later, I heard on the grapevine that my bid had been much lower than theirs. No, I wasn't too upset – I didn't regret it. I had done my sums and knew we'd still make a profit. It was worth it to get a good contract with Spillers. I have never deliberately put in a loss-making bid, just to get the work, even if it's sometimes turned out that way. What happens is that you think a certain job is so vital that you have to remember it's got to be profit-making.'

Edward believes that a good contract does not just consist of profits. The most important thing in any contract is the personal chemistry. 'Chemistry' might be an odd word to use for a haulage contract but Edward knows exactly what he means. 'Managements have got to get on, to fit together. It can happen that you have different views on business, how it all should be run. If it doesn't feel good, if you are having to spend too much time explaining things or arguing, then it's as well just to give it up. Often, firms insist on things being done a certain way, or they will use fancy jargon, which doesn't suit our style. We parted from Rockware Glass because our attitudes were different: the chemistry was wrong. I'm not blaming them, but I was relieved when it finished. The two management teams just didn't click.'

Edward's mention of fancy jargon is interesting. His background of having only ever worked in his own firm, almost in a vacuum for many years, combined with his basic personality, has made him rather resistant to anything at all smacking of the fanciful. Even in an apparently old-fashioned industry such as haulage, lots of new ideas have come in over the last decade, exciting concepts, codes of conduct, quality controls, mission statements, many of them taken from American business schools. Plus, of course, some very impressive graphs and flow-charts.

'It was worse a few years ago,' says Edward. 'I was being asked all the time when I was in for a job what my Total Quality Statement was. I'd say: "To run clean lorries, with smart drivers, who arrive on time at your factory." What more is there to say? They would then go on about BS 5750. I now can't remember what that meant.

'Once they start following all these fancy textbooks, they make things so complicated and also very rigid. They like to have things in black and white. But it rarely works out that way. Mostly, we are all working in a grey area. We have to work it out as we go along.'

The company lost one good contract in 1996, with a British plasterboard firm – not over fancy jargon this time, or even over a clash of chemistry. It was to do with them working for another firm they didn't approve of. 'It was for a German plasterboard firm,' says Edward, 'one of their rivals. They got upset when we tendered for work with them. They said, "You're doing a good job for us, we get on well, but if you work for them, that's it."

'We got the German contract and lost the British Gypsum one. But there was no cash benefit for us, either way. The new contract with the German firm was about the same as the British firm. We just couldn't be told how to run our business.

'We do constantly work for firms who are rivals – for Britvic soft drinks as well as Coca-Cola. All packaging firms are, in a sense, rivals, whether they're glass firms, can firms, carton firms. They are competing in the same packaging and container market. The German plasterboard job was the first time anyone had tried to stop us working for a rival. If we let that sort of thing happen, we'd lose most of our work.'

One of Edward's more important new contracts in the non-food and drink market came in 1998 when his company secured a contract with the *Mirror* newspaper group. This was to deliver all its papers and magazines in the south of England – a contract worth five million pounds a year.

'We had tried to tender before, then the opportunity came up again. It's an easy one to do, in theory. You don't have the seasonal shifts in the volume. It's seven days a week, all the year round. All you have to do is not be late. No one wants yesterday's newspaper today.'

One of the company's new contracts is with the NAAFI, the government forces supplier. Each week, Eddie Stobart Ltd transports foodstuffs and consumer goods from the NAAFI's main UK distribution centre at Preston to over sixty British military locations in Germany. There is a regular 743-mile run from Preston, which goes through Belgium and Holland to Fallingbostel in North Germany.

The haulage division of the company is also still prepared to do small, one-off jobs, depending on what they are. One very small but awfully clean job it has had for the last three years is transporting domestic items for Prince Charles. When he moves with his family and entourage, from his home at Highgrove to Balmoral or Sandringham or other royal palaces and homes, he usually gets an Eddie Stobart lorry to carry his gear. This might mean personal stuff belonging to Prince William and Prince Harry, or plants and crockery if Prince Charles expects to do a lot of entertaining.

The job came out of the blue in 1998. The company was asked to give a quote, as with any other job, which was then accepted. An ordinary Eddie Stobart lorry turns up to collect the load, though it is always a 'box' lorry, one with proper sides, not plastic curtains.

Apart from the *Mirror* newspaper contract and minor royal duties, the firm continues to be heavily reliant on the soft-drinks, food and packaging-related industries. This can be seen from a list of its major customers for one month at random, April 2000. This covered conveying empty or full bottles, cans, cartons, packaging or materials needed for the food- (including pet food) and drinks-related industries.

The top ten, in order, were Friskies, the pet-food firm, followed by Britvic Soft Drinks, Coca-Cola Schweppes, Robert McBride, Gerber Foods Soft Drinks, Mirror Group, CarnaudMetalbox PLC, Botcherby, Gerber Foods International, Schmalbach-Lubeca Pet Containers Ltd and Knauf.

The top three, each worth over £600,000 a month, were all in the food and drink field. Out of the top ten, only three were non-food and drink related: Robert McBride (household goods), Knauf (plaster board) and the *Mirror* (newspapers). CarnaudMetalbox PLC is what the old Metal Box company is called today and Botcherby is in Carlisle, so some of the company's oldest contracts have been retained.

The food-and-drink industry has greatly expanded in the last two decades, with the growth of fast foods, the increase in supermarkets and the popularity of eating out. But, in the Western world, the rise in pet-food consumption has been even greater. This is why, in recent years, the major food companies, such as Nestlé – the world's biggest, have been paying billions to acquire the leading pet-food firms. The dog and cat population of the Western world has been growing at four per cent annually, roughly twice the rate of humans, which has been one reason for the increase in pet foods. The other is that dogs and cats rarely eat out. Eddie Stobart Ltd has been fortunate, or smart, to have concentrated on an area where the demand for haulage has grown enormously and is still growing.

Throughout this build-up in business, continually going for expansion, Eddie Stobart Ltd didn't grow bigger by doing what many successful firms do to increase their size quickly: they never took over anyone else. Takeovers have always been as common in haulage as elsewhere. Robsons of Carlisle, during their rise, took over smaller firms, until they themselves were taken over. Even when BRS, the nationalized firm, was eventually split up, Eddie Stobart Ltd never bought any of the bits. Edward only went after their customers.

One reason was that the company never had sufficient money, or access to money, to mount any takeover bids. It was already fully extended in financing more vehicles and more depots. Another reason was Edward's philosophy. He had always liked the company to grow organically, in its own way, with its own people.

Only once so far has this unwritten rule been broken and this was for a specific reason. In 1997, Eddie Stobart Ltd bought a small firm called Janerite, based in Stoke-on-Trent. It had only some twenty vehicles, hardly worth taking over when, at the time, Eddie Stobart had six hundred vehicles. But what Janerite had was a government contract. It was for the Ministry of Defence, transporting military supplies to Eastern Europe. Until then, Eddie Stobart had never done any government work.

Janerite had only one year of a three-year contract

left when it was bought – and, when the year was up, it wasn't renewed. So that wasn't so smart. But, around the same time, the war in Kosovo broke out and the Government needed more transport, so new contracts were on offer. Eddie Stobart tendered and got one of the new ones. 'So it worked okay,' says Edward. 'Kosovo turned out to be fortunate for us, if not for them.'

The takeover of Janerite also proved difficult from a management point of view. Eddie Stobart Ltd was happy enough with the vehicles it had bought and the drivers, but it didn't get on with the management team that came with the firm. Three-quarters of them were let go. 'In the end, all firms are about people. That's what you are buying: people. But you don't really know what they're like till you've bought them. That was the only time I've ever bought a firm. Because of the management problems, I vowed never to do it again.'

So that's how it's done. From buying a DAF truck on the never-never for a few hundred pounds a month, to doing multi-million-pound property deals, all in twenty years: simple really.

But we haven't come to the really big one yet; the site that is today the pride and joy of the whole Eddie Stobart empire. It is situated just off the M1 near Daventry – or Davtree, as William might spell it . . . .

DAVENTRY

Daventry is big. Daventry is awesome. Daventry is on a scale too grand for little human eyes to fully comprehend. Eddie Stobart's Daventry sites cover some sixty acres; about the area needed for some twenty Wembley stadiums – the old stadium, of course.

Each of the purpose-built warehouses is nearly sixty feet high inside. You look up and up at rows and rows of stuff, neatly stacked, and can't see the top, nor can you see the end of the rows. You wonder where it's all coming from or going to. From the middle, you can't quite see that each warehouse has sixteen loading docks, all purring away. You wonder who's in charge, if anyone, as all you can hear is a low computer hum or an electric buzz from the sophisticated handling machinery. The technology itself appears to be doing all the work, twenty-four hours a day, seven days a week.

Eddie Stobart has 820,000 square feet of warehousing space at Daventry, on three adjacent plots, which now comprise the biggest single part of its empire. Carlisle, where it all began, has 350,000 square feet;

Warrington has 510,000; Workington has 500,000. So Daventry now dwarfs them all. It represents an investment in excess of forty million pounds.

The Daventry site is just a mile from the M1 at Junction 18, near its convergence with the M6. Tilt your head to the left as you drive north up the M1, but mind how you go, and you'll catch a glimpse of the familiar green, red and gold letters of the Eddie Stobart logo. London is eighty miles south, down the motorway; Birmingham is just forty miles further north. Pretty handy, therefore, for England's main conurbations.

But Daventry's prime attraction, and why so many other haulage and transport and warehouse firms have followed Eddie Stobart Ltd there in the last few years, is because of DIRFT, a rather confusing acronym that stands for Daventry International Rail Freight Terminal. DIRFT has now replaced the white cliffs of Dover as the doorstep to Europe. With the opening of the Channel Tunnel, and all the new and wonderful rail connections – a lot of them still to come – this location was chosen to be the spot whence Europe would begin and end, freight-wise.

Eddie Stobart's part of it was opened by the Princess Royal in 1997. It was very apt that the site was blessed by Her Highness because, according to newspaper reports, she let slip during the opening that, in another life, she would have liked to have been a lorry driver. Indeed, her Private Secretary confirms that she has got an HGV licence and, 'much enjoys driving HGVs'.

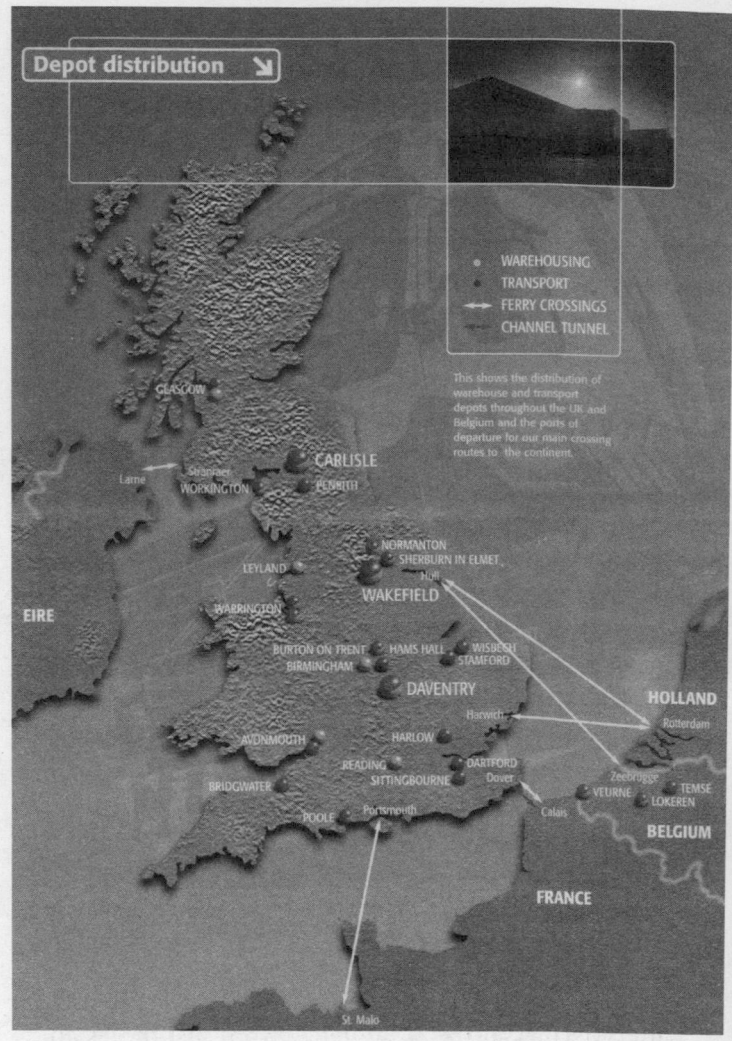

Depot distribution

WAREHOUSING
TRANSPORT
FERRY CROSSINGS
CHANNEL TUNNEL

This shows the distribution of warehouse and transport depots throughout the UK and Belgium and the ports of departure for our main crossing routes to the continent.

GLASGOW

Larne Stranraer
WORKINGTON

CARLISLE
PENRITH

LEYLAND

WARRINGTON

EIRE

NORMANTON
SHERBURN IN ELMET
Hull
WAKEFIELD

BURTON ON TRENT   HAMS HALL   WISBECH
BIRMINGHAM   STAMFORD

DAVENTRY

Harwich

HOLLAND
Rotterdam

AVONMOUTH

HARLOW

READING   DARTFORD
SITTINGBOURNE   Dover

Zeebrugge
VEURNE   TEMSE
LOKEREN

BRIDGWATER

POOLE   Portsmouth

Calais

BELGIUM

FRANCE

St. Malo

194

BUCKINGHAM PALACE   23 March 2001

Dear Mr Davies,

      Thank you for your letter of 19 March, concerning material for your biography of Eddie Stobart.

      As far as your queries are concerned, I have no idea whether the quotes you mentioned were actually said by the Princess as I was not present. She has however had an HGV licence for many years and much enjoys driving HGVs.

      I am sorry not to be of more help.

Yours sincerely

Colonel Timothy Earl, OBE
Private Secretary to
HRH The Princess Royal

Hunter Davies, Esq

Today, although Edward's HQ is still in Carlisle, he now spends around two days a week at Daventry. Driving down from Carlisle to Daventry can be hellish, with hold-ups all the way, yet Edward just drives an ordinary car, no Ferrari with a personalized number-plate. In fact, he has no idea of his car's numberplate, 'It's funny, I can remember all our registration numbers from the seventies, but none of them today, not even my own car.'

The trouble with owning a personalized number-plate, so Edward says, is that, when he parks it in a public place like a car park or hotel, there's always somebody who will work it out and then come up to him and say, 'Hello, Mr Stobart.' Edward gets embar-rassed, so he no longer drives a personalized car.

His administration offices at Daventry are in a highly modern glass building, more like a hotel than a lorry park, floors gleaming, walls immaculate, design tasteful, cool foliage. It has a swish reception desk and, beyond it, in an even vaster reception area, there once stood, in all its glimmering glory, an Eddie Stobart lorry. A real live lorry – not a model – about the size and length of a small row of terraced houses. It was a twelve-wheeler Volvo articulated truck, with trailer behind, and was called Tina.

Edward was pleased by the Daventry deal, but it had been a complicated one. Since 1995, his company had leased a fourteen-acre site. They had wanted more land on which to build, so had bought twenty-four acres, which had cost them over £7.5 million. 'We did our own rough designs, of what we wanted, and got a builder, Bowmer and Kirkland of Derby, to build it for us. They did an excellent job: it was finished in twelve months. The building work cost over twelve million pounds.

'The day it was all finished, I sold it to a pension fund and made a substantial profit on the deal. Before we'd even started building, I had done that deal. I'd also arranged a lease for twenty years for us to run the buildings and site.

'It was all new territory for Barrie and me, doing two complicated deals back-to-back. At each stage, I was always positive, saying either we won't do this, or we will do that. I always had something in my mind I was trying to achieve. Barrie was the one who understood what I was getting at. He made it all work. He was a good number two.

'We never spoke to any financial advisors or any experts in the City; we did it ourselves. At one stage, we had the bank loan of £7.5 million and nothing else agreed. But it all worked out. We came out of it with a profit and a brilliant site: the best in the country. It put us in a different league. Now, when people come and see us here, all the warehouses, all the offices, they can see we are not just a lorry firm.

'I like the fact that our name can be seen from the motorway. It upset me today, driving down from Carlisle, every time I found myself behind a lorry with no proper markings. Imagine not taking the chance to get their name known?

'I do like the property side, the planning of it all, the deals. And I love doing it on our own: city investors or shareholders would just hold you back. They'd tell you not to take risks, they'd slow you down and cause endless aggravation. The minute you let other people's money in, that's the time you take a backward step. That's my thinking, any road up . . . .

'But I'm not doing it for the money. That doesn't really come into it. I'm doing it for the business, and the people who work in it. That's what it's all for. The normal golfer doesn't take out an HP agreement on his golf clubs, does he? That's because it's his hobby. This is my hobby. I don't look upon it as a job.'

THE FAN CLUB TODAY

From its humble origins in 1992, the Eddie Stobart fan club has grown to enormous proportions. Members began to ask if there were toy models of Eddie Stobart vehicles that they could buy. Edward and Deborah his PA, thought about this and talked to Corgi and other model-makers about how it was normally done. Edward decided not to hand over the distribution and sale of Eddie Stobart replicas to an outside firm, as is often the case. Instead, he paid Corgi to make them, and his company did the selling themselves, to members of the club.

From the moment the company launched the first set of model lorries, they sold out. The next ones also sold out, as did some more expensive, limited editions. By the end of the first couple of years, the Eddie Stobart fan club had 10,000 members and a growing list of Eddie Stobart products.

No adverts had been placed; no business plan devised; no publicity campaign had been used. Like the firm itself, the fan club grew without any mission statements, company messages, public pledges – all very popular under PM John Major.

Edward himself was apprehensive about the growing awareness of his name which, in his private life, he had done so much to hide behind. Not quite his own name, of course, as most people did not know, and still don't know, that 'Eddie' refers to his father.

Edward avoided all personal publicity, even when it was good. As the firm had grown bigger, better known, with more and more depots all over the country, national and local charities were continually asking for donations or help. 'Edward was very willing to do what he could,' says Barrie Thomas. 'And we contributed a lot to charities or hospitals, but he'd never go anywhere himself. He'd send me or someone else along to hand over the cheque or turn up at the event, so we'd get our photo in the local paper. He didn't want to be seen.'

It wasn't Edward's aversion to personal publicity. He couldn't quite decide whether this sudden public awareness of his company was genuine or just a passing fashion. 'I remember the first time I was told that a fan had arrived at the depot at Kingstown. It was a Saturday morning, and I was in the office. Someone said that a bloke had driven up all the way from the Midlands with his family to look at our lorries. He was asking to see me. I didn't want to go out – I didn't want to meet some stranger. I couldn't believe it anyway, thinking the bloke might be a bit, you know, funny, or it might be some old driver with a tattoo and a CB radio. Anyway, I got talked into going out and saying hello to him – and he turned out to be a bank manager! He was a perfectly respectable, normal person; not at all what I had imagined.'

From being a word-of-mouth affair, the fan club was next taken up by radio presenters – again, without the firm doing any publicity. 'People like Bruno Brooks, Terry Wogan, Steve Wright started making references to us,' says Barrie. 'From then, it just exploded.' A lot of these references were meant to be satirical, half mocking the existence of a fan club whose members were in love with lorries, but the effect was much the same: people flocked to join.

The Eddie Stobart fan club today has 25,000 paid-up members and gets 500 new members every month. The annual fee is now ten pounds, but for that you get a fan-club badge and a sticker, a quarterly magazine, an Eddie Stobart calendar at Christmas, special offers on certain items, ten per cent off all prices in the club shop and, perhaps most important of all, an Eddie Stobart Fleet Manual and Spotter Guide.

The Fleet Manual and Spotter Guide are essential for true fans who want a list of all the current Eddie Stobart vehicles, complete with their female names, registration numbers, fleet numbers, vehicle makes and liveries. This is not just great bedside reading, but invaluable if you are on the road and you or your loved ones want to record your sightings. In the manual, there is a space after each vehicle for you to tick once you've spotted it and write in the place where you did the spotting and when.

GAMES PEOPLE PLAY

Jools Holland

I THINK the best games should help pass the time, like on long motorway journeys. I decided we needed something to keep our spirits up when we're on tour, which is a lot of the time — we did 80 dates around the country last year. So I introduced a game called Stobart Spotting, which I want to see take off as a national game. Stobart lorries are so distinctive — they are green with red and gold lettering, the drivers all wear ties and they're known, I've since discovered, as the Knights of the Road. And because it's the biggest haulage firm in the country, they crop up all over the place but, strangely enough, particularly on the A1 and the M56 and, less often, in the West Country. I reckon I personally had about 300 sightings last year. In fact I challenge anybody to go up the A1 and not see one. It's like when you buy a Ford Sierra you notice that everyone else has got one.

One thing I've realised with games is that it is very important to make the rules up yourself. Whenever you spot a Stobart lorry you shout "Stobart". Your sighting then has to be confirmed by one of the other people in the car and you can then claim a pound. There is also the unconfirmed sighting, like

when the driver claims he's seen one while everyone else is asleep. You don't get any money for that. Obviously, your winnings go up and down because you have to pay out for other people's sightings, but you can make £5 on a journey. When you go past a depot there might be 20 Stobarts there and some people try to claim £20, but that is obviously fraudulent and I make up the rules. After we started playing this game, we actually rang up Edward Stobart and told him about it. He sent us pens and calendars and everything. So now we've said that any Stobart driver who spots us has to wave and flash the lights and get a T-shirt or something, to make it a reciprocal thing. The thing I enjoy most about it is that you are travelling with people you have known for years and yet you don't trust them in the slightest. Anyone will cheat you. You become like a photographer after that great picture; you're ever alert for a Stobart and always ready to shout "Stobart", wait for the mumbled confirmation and claim your money. It's a game for all the family. My former mother-in-law did claim to have never seen a Stobart, but she obviously wasn't looking correctly, so I sent her a video of Stobart lorries to learn how to identify one. ●

Interview by Simon Morgan Warr

The fan club comes under the title Eddie Stobart Promotions Ltd and is still run from Carlisle, not Daventry, which is only right and proper. Carlisle is the Camelot of the Eddie Stobart legend, where the myths started, where the once-and-future king still lives.

Deborah Rodgers is still technically in charge of the club but, as Edward's PA, she has a great deal of other things to concern herself with. The club therefore now has a large staff, who do the day-to-day running of it while reporting to Deborah on major issues, who in turn reports to Edward.

The current manager of the promotions department

is Linda Barbara Shore. Today, she has a staff of thirteen, including three who work in the Eddie Stobart shop in the middle of Carlisle. The shop, which opened in 1997, was a very exciting development, not to say mouth-watering for all fans – a shop totally devoted to Eddie Stobart fan-club merchandising. It's in Castle Street, right opposite the Cathedral – you can't miss it.

At Kingstown, two miles away, the entrance to Linda's department also has a showcase of current Eddie Stobart goodies, handy for spotters when they have been on a tour of the site. Prices of the model trucks range from £1.25 to £140 for special limited editions. Since 1992, there have, of course, been a lot of models, many of them editions now long sold out, some of which now change hands for huge prices, having become collector's items. The record, so far, for an Eddie Stobart toy truck is around £700 – which originally, just a few years before, had been on sale in a limited edition at £99.95.

At the moment, Linda is rather pleased by one new item in the range: Eddie Stobart tapestry. You buy the basic material, the threads and needles and frame, follow the instructions, and bingo: you have your very own Eddie Stobart tapestry, suitable for framing, with about sixty hours of fun along the way.

The line in Eddie Stobart clothes is now almost as extensive as the toys. It includes Eddie Stobart fleeces, for children as well as adults, T-shirts, jackets, scarves; all of them in the Eddie Stobart colours of green, red and gold, just like the lorries. Selling really well, too, are some boxer-shorts for men, covered in little Eddie Stobart trucks.

Eddie Stobart teddy bears have been steady sellers for some years and there are now ten in the range. It's a bit hard to see the connection between these and Eddie Stobart lorries, although 'Teddy' is, of course, short for Edward. Even more unconnected is Eddie Stobart tea. This is described in the catalogue as 'Specialist tea, blended to bring express refreshment'. Perhaps the idea is that, having spotted an Eddie on the motorway, you brew yourself an Eddie cuppa, then give your Eddie teddy a quick cuddle.

The catalogue is thick and glossy and rather self-importantly calls itself 'The Collection', as if it's the

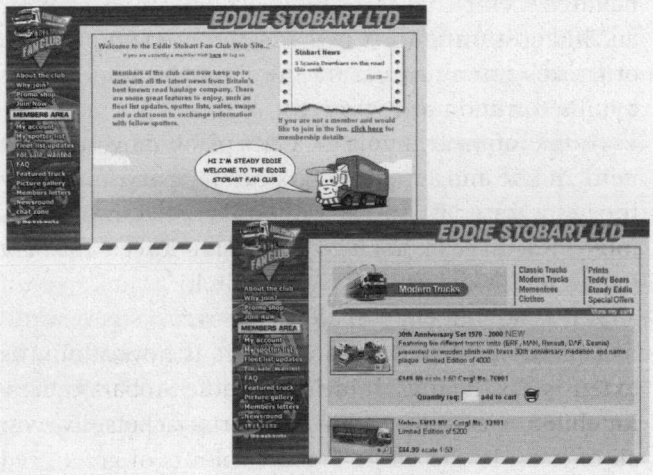

latest from Yves St Laurent or Gucci. But it is pretty impressive, as merchandising catalogues go – well up to the standard of the one produced by Tottenham Hotspur FC, if not quite as extensive as Manchester United's. And the thinking, too, is the same: football fans love their clubs, just as Eddie Stobart fans love theirs. So why not give them a chance to display their love and admiration, even if – to outsiders and non-believers – the goods on offer might appear rather remote from the objects of their affection?

A good proportion of the merchandising is aimed at children. Apart from the teddy bears, there are pens, mugs, balloons, puzzles, colouring books and story books. The books feature a cartoon character, Steady Eddie, and are very reasonably priced at £2.99. There are even plans for the character to be turned into a children's video.

The most up-market items in the catalogue, aimed at the discerning adult, are the limited-edition prints by: 'Renowned motoring artist Alan Fearnley, featuring some of your favourite Eddie Stobart vehicles at work, home and abroad. Each print is signed and numbered by the artist and is a unique record of Britain's most famous road-haulage company.' There are nine in the set, priced at fifty pounds each.

If it's moving pictures of Stobart trucks you want, then what you need is a copy of the sixty-minute Eddie Stobart video, price £12.99. It cost the company £150,000 to make in 1995 and it's sold steadily ever since.

Linda has to turn down ideas for new lines all the time, as being not suitable or not practical. She's been thinking hard about whether to do Eddie Stobart duvets, wondering how many might be sold. When it comes to model trucks, they can reckon on around ten thousand of every new line being sold almost at once. The duvet might be too big and expensive to attract large orders, though.

Altogether, the fan club and its merchandising have a turnover of £1,500,000 a year, which is more than many companies make on their core activity. It does make a modest profit, although that is still not its main aim. The object is to respond to fans, fly the flag. The company probably could make more money out of it, but doesn't want to, as so many of the fans are families with children. The actual fan club itself runs at a loss – mainly because of the cost of postage – but it is subsidized by the profit on the merchandising.

There is still no national advertising for the fan club, no newspaper promotions, no special offers for the general public. You have to find out about it yourself, either from friends or by writing in, though anyone can walk in off the street and into the Carlisle shop to buy the goodies.

The unpaid for, unsolicited publicity still goes on. DJ Steve Wright recently told Radio Two listeners that the original Eddie Stobart was called Eddie de Stobart and that he arrived in England centuries ago, from France, on a horse and cart. In the *Daily Mail*, Peter

McKay has also made some references to Eddie Stobart. It still is seen as an in-joke, an amusement that makes people smile.

Joanne Wharton is the fan-club secretary. She often takes small parties of fan-club members on a forty-five-minute tour of the HQ. These visits happen on most days. You don't have to be a member of the fan club to get to see an Eddie Stobart depot, but most are. You can, in theory, just turn up, but the company prefers it if you make an advance booking; that way, you will be given a proper, guided tour.

The tour includes going around the whole site, visiting the warehouses, having a look inside the operations rooms, watching the traffic planners and enjoying a cup of tea in the staff canteen but, of course, the biggest thrill for most visitors is the chance to have a ride in an Eddie lorry. This ride is not necessarily around the depot, but might be a half-hour trip down the motorway. They also don't use a special, superannuated driver for this task, kept to amuse the fans. Joanne simply grabs a working driver who, during his own break, agrees to show off his lorry.

'That's always the highlight,' explains Joanne. 'You should see their faces. They just can't believe it when they climb up and get inside the cabin. Some are so overwhelmed, they can't speak.'

The two most commonly asked questions are: 'What's behind the curtains?', meaning what loads are being carried, and 'Is Eddie in today?' Joanne usually says he's away on business, knowing Edward's shyness about meeting people, but, now and again, he will make a quick appearance and sign an autograph.

The average age of fans is between forty and fifty-five years old. They tend to be people who travel a lot, such as reps, or people with weekend cottages and noisy children. They have quite a few vicars, police officers and solicitors in the fan club, for reasons Joanne cannot explain. The fans also come from all over the country, and abroad. Joanne recently showed

HOUSE OF COMMONS
LONDON SW1A 0AA

LEADER OF THE OPPOSITION

Q&A FOR EDDIE STOBART BIOGRAPHY

1 **Had you heard of Eddie Stobart, before your visit?**
   Yes, of course – Eddie Stobart is a real British success story. He is a great model of
   our country's entrepreneurial spirit.

2 **Do you spot their lorries or are aware of them on the roads?**
   As I travel across Britain all the time, I do see many of the green and gold Eddie
   Stobart trucks on the roads. In fact, since I went to visit the lorry named after Ffion,
   we have been very pleased to see that lorry on the road.

3 **What did you think of them having a lorry called Ffion?**
   I greatly enjoyed my visit to Daventry to see the lorry named after Ffion, and I
   certainly can't think of a better name!

4 **What do you think generally about the firm, their clean lorries, their drivers'
   uniform, their fan club and the female names?**
   It is all these things that have given Eddie Stobart the cult status that his company
   has developed across the country.

5 **They have had a hard year, like all haulage firms, with the heavy fuel, license
   and other costs. Any plans to help the industry, should you win the next
   election?**
   I know that the price of fuel remains the most pressing concern for the haulage
   industry. We have the most expensive fuel in Europe, and I want to cut the price of
   fuel for all road users.

   We will also be able to reduce vehicle excise duty, which has increased hugely
   under Labour, by introducing our BRIT disc. That would be a charge on all
   commercial vehicles that use Britain's roads, including foreign lorries.

   The VED set on a 40 tonne lorry in the UK is about seven times higher than it is in
   France. So it is no wonder that Labour's anti-haulage policies have driven tens of
   thousands out of work as foreign companies find they can operate at a competitive
   advantage.

The Rt Hon William Hague MP

April 2001

round a family who had come from New Zealand, especially to see the Eddie Stobart HQ.

One member of the fan club's staff, Julie Silivestros, is in charge of lorry names. Her job is to keep a log of all the requests from fan-club members who write in asking to have their special female names immortalized on an Eddie Stobart lorry.

The thousand lorries currently in the Eddie Stobart fleet have a wide variety of names. Some of them rather exotic, such as China, Tananya, Kinta, Zoya. Some are first and second names, such as Excilie Elizabeth, Michelle Kathleen, Habibi Megan, Harriet Violet. They have all, of course, got to be different, so having an unusual name does help your chances. But the fleet is constantly being replenished, old lorries being taken out of service, along with their names, and new ones being introduced. So, even if you are a plain old Mary or Margaret, Val or Victoria, do not despair: your time could come when an old lorry departs.

Around twenty people each week contact Julie with their favourite female name but, naturally, she can't promise anything. She tells each person they will be informed, if and when their name comes up. One of the lucky names to come up in 1998 was Ffion. She was fortunate in having an unusual Christian name, not to mention an unusual husband. Her dear hubby, William Hague, was present at the christening, while on a 'fact-finding' visit to the Daventry depot. So was Edward, for once. And he was photographed, even smiling, along with the then Leader of the Tory Party, as they were both captured admiring Ffion – the lorry of course, not the lady.

Later, I wrote to Mr Hague about his visit, and his views on Eddie Stobart and haulage in general. He graciously replied with some very interesting answers. It was, perhaps, a shame for haulage that he never made it to Prime Minister.

THE FANS

Every Thursday, a group of the more fanatical Eddie Stobart fans meet up at the Daventry depot. In the summer, or when the weather's reasonable, there might be twelve or fifteen of them. In winter and bad weather, there could be only four or five.

Amongst them is usually Alf Cooper. On his 'Thursday Club' day, as he calls it, he gets up at 5 a.m. in his four-bedroomed, detached house in a quiet street in Chelmsford, Essex. He leaves his house at about 6 a.m., drives for two hours, reaches the depot by 8 a.m. and goes into the car park. There, he meets some of his chums, his fellow followers, and stays with them at the depot all day long, till 8 p.m. 'Oh, you have to,' he explains, 'Lorries are coming in all the time, from all over. You don't want to miss any.'

He does have a short break for refreshments. For this, he and the other fans are allowed to use the Eddie Stobart canteen, quite a thrill in itself. 'Oh they're very good that way.'

Alf is aged seventy seven, and is a retired bank officer. He worked in the City of London, in a French bank, and rose to the height of an Authorized Signature. His late wife, Joan, also worked in a bank. 'In 1997,' says Alf, 'my wife and I went on a coach trip with Shearings to Scotland. On the coach, we amused ourselves by counting the Eddie Stobarts. Not the registration numbers, just how many we could see. We had to stay overnight in Carlisle and we realized that was where the firm came from. Then we heard they'd just opened a shop, a couple of weeks previously, so my wife and I went along. At the back of the shop, they had forms for the fan club. We didn't know till then there was a club, but we decided to join. We didn't actually bother much with the club during the next year. But then my wife died, at Christmas 1998. After that, I threw myself into Eddie Stobart.

'It gives me something to do, you see. We never had any children, I live all on my own, so I can just do what I fancy. Last year, I drove 25,000 miles lorry-spotting. I've been to every Eddie Stobart depot all over the country. I'm always made welcome wherever I go. They were a bit sticky at Warrington for a while, about entry to the site. Nothing to do with the fans – just security problems. But they're okay now.

'My favourite Eddie Stobart depot? Oh well, if you're forcing me, I think I'll have to say Daventry. It's better now than Carlisle. Though Carlisle is very nice. The girls in Carlisle are very friendly.'

So far, Alf has spotted and recorded his spottings of almost all the current thousand Eddie Stobart lorries.

He now only has fifteen to go. 'And they're mostly shunters – you know, they spend their time inside the depots, shunting stuff about.'

When Alf saw himself coming to an end to his Eddies, he was presented with a bit of a problem, till more Eddies come on-stream. He's solved it by spotting other lorries from other companies, as he does enjoy spotting lorries so much. One of his favourite firms is James Irlam, another private haulage firm, of course. No true lorry spotter will have much interest in those boring vehicles owned by the PLC's with their meaningless initials.

'There's a rumour amongst lorry spotters,' whispers Alf, 'that Eddie secretly has shares in James Irlam. There was a time when James Irlam wasn't doing very well, then, suddenly, they were – on the lines of Eddie Stobart. The gossip was Edward had bought forty-nine per cent, but was keeping it quiet. He's a sleeping partner, you see. I don't know whether it's true or not.' Edward denies the rumour, but the gossip amuses him.

Alf, after a hard day's spotting, driving hundreds of miles, hanging around an Eddie Stobart depot all day, likes nothing more than to get home and settle down in front of his computer. Thanks to his banking background, Alf is a whizz with modern technology. He'll then spend the evening spotting on the net.

He recommends a website club called Lorry Spotting, which lists and gives the latest information on thirty independent lorry firms. None is as big as Eddie, or as glamorous as Eddie, but Alf enjoys finding out about these smaller companies, getting to know their logos and liveries, following their fortunes. He particularly likes John Raymond, a Welsh lorry firm, Dodds Transport and also MacFarlanes of Leeds. 'MacFarlanes have got a very striking yellow-and-green livery. You should look out for it.'

Alf's biggest thrill as a lorry-spotter occurred in 1999, when a lorry was named after his late wife, Joan Doreen. 'After she died, I put her name on the list. I didn't expect her name to come up for years and years, if at all. I know how long the list is. But the girls at Carlisle, they were very kind. They're always good to me.

'And I'll tell you something interesting about Joan Doreen, the lorry. I went to visit her at Warrington, to take her photograph, and the driver gave me a ride in her. And do you know, what a coincidence, it turned out that the driver's wife had not only worked in the same bank as my wife – he had actually known her! Wasn't that remarkable? So he now drives Joan Doreen around, knowing exactly who she was named after. Isn't that lovely?'

Two of the other Thursday-Club regulars are Ena and John Poulton from Gloucester. They are also in their seventies, each retired. He was in security, she worked for the local electricity board, and they have two grown-up sons.

It was John who first became an Eddie Stobart fan, five years ago. They were driving from Gloucester to

Perth, to visit Ena's relations, and, on the way there, they started spotting Eddies. 'It was just something to do,' says John, 'to pass the time. We stopped for a break at the Gretna service station and there at the back were some Eddie Stobart fan club forms. Just some stencilled sheets. So I joined.'

John then visited a few depots, taking Ena with him. She felt a bit spare, not quite having as much interest in ticking off lorry names as her husband, so she decided that she would take photographs of the lorries. She had never been interested in photography before, didn't even have a camera, but she bought herself a Minolta for £100. Today, she has eight hundred photos of Eddie Stobart lorries.

Ena keeps the pictures at home in five large albums. At one time, she arranged them in the order she had taken them. Now she has them filed under their registration numbers. 'Oh, it took me some time to arrange them that way, but I'm on top of it now, thank goodness.

'I usually take the lorry as it comes through the gate, front-on. I did used to take side views, now I just stick to front views. You have to be ever so careful as you can get reflections on the windscreen. If I get a bit of a sun spot, then I scrap that photo.

'I prefer the Volvos to the Scanias. You can't see the woman's name on the Scanias, that's why. I'm always having terrible trouble whenever it's a Scania. There's less space on the bit below the windscreen because they have the words "Scania" in such big writing. With the Volvo, they leave more space to fit in the woman's name.'

Ena's own name hasn't quite been immortalized yet on a truck of her own. 'I did have, after a fashion. My full first name is Georgina, Ena for short. And there used to be a Georgina, not named after me, but I tracked it down and photographed it. It was at Kingsland Grange, Warrington. It's now been pensioned off. They do bring back old names, so I've got my name down. I don't expect any luck for years yet, but fingers crossed.'

Unlike Alf, John and Ena are totally loyal to Eddie Stobart, and are non-promiscuous in their lorry-spotting, considering no other lorry firms. 'Most people probably think we're mad, but we find it good fun. Our only problem is that, living in Gloucester, it takes us a long time to get to many of the depots. On a Sunday, we can drive four hundred miles, just going out Eddie-spotting.'

For their golden wedding anniversary last year, John and Ena treated themselves to a day out. They went to the Daventry depot, naturally. 'We got a trip on a truck and had a lovely day. No, we didn't tell people it was our golden wedding. John is very reserved. He doesn't like a fuss made . . . .'

One of the vicars in the Eddie Stobart fan club is the Rev. Michael Smith, rector of Linch and Milland in West Sussex. He first became aware of Eddie Stobart some four years ago, when he and his wife used to drive regularly to Nottingham, where their daughter was a student. 'It broke up the interminable trundles,' he says, 'trying to spot his lorries – without, of course, compromising our driving. But, I have to say, it was my wife who was the driving force – to coin a phrase – in us joining the fan club.'

His wife is known as Elizabeth to most people outside the family but, to her husband and children, she is Excilie, her real Christian name. It's French in origin, and can never be pronounced by most English people.

'I never knew there was a fan club,' she says, 'till I heard it mentioned on the radio one day – by Ed Stewart, I think it was. Or it might have been a quiz question. Anyway, when I heard it mentioned, I wrote off and got the forms and we joined.'

Their children think it rather strange that their parents, in their middle years, should suddenly have become anoraks. Mrs Smith is more of the spotter, ticking off the Eddies every time they spot one. The Rev. Smith takes a more philosophical view of the whole Eddie phenomenon. 'They did break the mould, by being so neat and tidy, with their uniforms and their livery. This may be subjective, but I sense more and more lorries, from other firms, are now being painted red and green. Don't you think?

'It reminds me of the pre-nationalization years on the trains. The individual rail companies took such a pride in their own liveries and how their trains looked. The workers were proud of the service they gave, the job they did.

'When I was a lad, there were such standards in

society. People were not known by what job they did but how they did it. Not by how much they earned, but the quality of the service they gave. We seem to have lost those values today. The only way we judge people now is by how much they are paid. We've quite lost that sense of pride in doing an ordinary job.

'I can understand Eddie Stobart's thinking in having his drivers so smart. Psychologists will say that you have to make people think the right way for them to make the right actions. But the reverse can happen. You can bring about the right actions, in this case making them dress smart and have clean lorries, and the result is that they think the right way. They become proud of their work, of the service they give.

'There's a lot of truth in that saying, "Fake it till you make it," it can work. We are all animals after all. That's why the Army has always insisted on uniforms and discipline and team effort. People will then respond, become smarter in themselves.

'I am intrigued by what he has done, especially when you consider there is no Eddie Stobart product. All he is offering is a service. And there is no advertising – even the Royal Mail spends money on advertising. It proves the old rule that, if you make the best widgets in the world, people will come to your door. You don't have to go to them. Yes, I think Eddie has done a good job: I applaud him.'

And Eddie Stobart Ltd has applauded the Rev. Smith and his wife by giving them the ultimate accolade: a lorry named Elizabeth Excilie. 'Isn't it exciting?' says Excilie. 'I haven't seen it yet, I'm not even sure which depot it's at. All we've had so far is the notification. As soon as we get more details, we'll make a trip to see it.'

When Excilie first submitted her name, she was told that she would have a better chance than most. If she had really been called plain old Elizabeth, she might have had a long wait. So, after all these years of having people stumble or get confused by her unusual Christian name, it's now paid off.

SPIN-OFFS

Any success story carries in its wake other successes. There are ancillary people and organizations who have been influenced by, or who have managed to feed upon, the host plant. They have found a little niche, or provide a special service, that would not otherwise have been there, but for the rise of the main attraction.

The effects and ripples can be small and purely passing. Few will remember now that, in 1995, a group called The Wurzels recorded a song called 'I Want to be an Eddie Stobart Driver'. Quite catchy. Quite amusing. But hardly played today.

It was written by Andrew Titcombe, who comes from Wigton in Cumbria. He had previously written 'Looking Good', a song to celebrate Carlisle United getting into the First Division in 1974. Andrew has done various jobs in his life, including dealing in old records. 'I was on my way back from a record fair, on the M1 coming home, when I noticed all the Eddie Stobart lorries. The bloke I was with said, "Why don't you write a song about them?" So I got a friend from Silloth – Tim Barker – to write the words.'

I WANT TO BE AN EDDIE STOBART DRIVER

I WANT TO BE AN EDDIE STOBART DRIVER
BEHIND THE WHEEL IS WHERE I WANT TO BE
OH LET ME BE AN EDDIE STOBART DRIVER,
THE FINEST FIRM IN HAULAGE HISTORY

EVERYWHERE YOU GO YOU'LL SPOT THE EDDIE SPOTTERS
STOBART IS THE NAME THEY WANT TO SEE
ALL THE OTHER TRUCKS AND TRAILERS
ARE COUNTED OUT AS FAILURES
SO EDDIE IS THE ONLY MAN FOR ME

I WANT TO BE AN EDDIE STOBART DRIVER
NOWADAYS WE ALL SING EDDIE'S PRAISE
OH LET ME BE AN EDDIE STOBART DRIVER
COS EDDIE STOBART RULES THE MOTORWAYS

I WANT TO HEAR THE CHILDREN
CHEER LIKE THEY CHEER EDDIE,
WHEN HE OVERTAKES US FROM AFAR
WITH HIS FAN CLUB EXPANDING
HE LEAVES THE OTHERS STANDING
I'D LOVE TO BE A STOBART SUPERSTAR

I WANT TO BE AN EDDIE STOBART DRIVER
BEHIND THE WHEEL IS WHERE I WANT TO BE
OH LET ME BE AN EDDIE STOBART DRIVER
THE FINEST FIRM IN HAULAGE HISTORY

TELL YOU JUST HOW FAR I'LL
GO ON UP THE CARLISLE
TELL YOU WHAT I'LL DO WHEN I ARRIVE
I'LL WALK RIGHT UP TO EDDIE
AND TELL HIM THAT I'M READY
JUST PUT ME ON THE ROAD AND LET ME DRIVE

I WANT TO BE AN EDDIE STOBART DRIVER
THAT'S EXACTLY WHAT I WANT TO BE
AND IF I CAN'T BE AN EDDIE STOBART DRIVER
I'M GOING HOME TO BURN MY HGV.
(I'M GOING HOME TO BURN MY HGV.)

Andrew organized a demo tape, though he wasn't very pleased by the way the singer on the demo sang it. 'He put on a Wurzels voice, which I didn't like at the time. I said, "This is art!" But it did seem to suit the song, so I wrote to The Wurzels.'

The Wurzels, as all pop-pickers well know, had a number-one hit in the 1970s with 'Combine Harvester' and also got to number three with 'I am a Cider Drinker'. They said they liked the song and agreed to record it.

'We did it up in Cumbria,' Andrew recollects, 'in a little studio in Abbeytown. Yeah, hard to believe, if you've ever been to Abbeytown. I put it out on my own little indie label, Loose Records.

'It was a minor hit and got in the Top 100. It was very exciting – well, for a small indie firm from Wigton. It was played on The Big Breakfast Show, Chris Evans's Radio programme, the Terry Wogan show and was used on BBC TV's *Top Gear*.

'We sold, in all, about two thousand copies. We never made any money from it, but it was enormous fun. The Wurzels played it at various gigs, dressed as Eddie Stobart drivers. It's long been deleted, which means it's become a collector's item. EMI are about to repromote some old Wurzel numbers, so I'm hoping it might help to revive our song . . . .'

Other businesses that have provided equipment or services for Eddie Stobart Ltd have had longer-lasting rewards. When Corgi was first approached to make toy trucks, it started by producing 5000 models in 1992. Today, it produces 500,000 models a year.

'I had heard of Eddie Stobart Ltd when Edward first contacted me,' says Colin Summerbell, Sales Director of Corgi Classics, 'but, at the time, we didn't put the

The Wurzels performing their excellent song, 'I want to be an Eddie Stobart Driver', which got to number 96 in the charts in 1995.

Eddie Stobart Ltd has no PR department and has never advertised but, in 1995, did sponsor a section of the lights at Blackpool Illuminations.

Eddie Stobart vehicles have featured in weddings, films, charity events, and showbusiness occasions, such as this line-up of pantomime stars.

Edward (*second left*) about to depart with (*left to right*) Rob Beaty, David Faulder and Steve Egglestone on an aid trip to Romania in 1991.

The Kingstown depot, which has 350,000 square feet, is just one of twenty-seven Eddie Stobart Ltd depots today, but it is still the company's HQ.

The Princess Royal and Edward at the opening of Eddie Stobart Ltd's Daventry depot in 1997. There, the company has 820,000 square feet of warehouse space on three adjacent sites, representing an investment of £40 million.

Eddie Stobart Ltd celebrated its twenty-fifth anniversary at the Dorchester Hotel, London, in 1995 – by which time it had 500 vehicles, 1600 staff and a turnover of £50 million.

Edward celebrates at the Dorchester with Jools Holland, one of the earliest Eddie Stobart spotters.

More celebrations, this time including the truck Twiggy and driver Jonathan Barker. Her name was the first that Edward ever put on one of his lorries.

Barrie Thomas, who joined the firm in 1986, later becoming Legal and Commercial Director.

David Jackson, a boy mechanic at Hesket Newmarket, a driver in Carlisle, then manager of the firm's second depot.

Colin Rutherford, one of the new management team of 1986, who helped transform the company's fortunes.

Norman Bell's retirement in 1990, photographed outside the Kingstown offices.

Linda Shore, promotions manager. Her department runs the 25,000-strong fan club, the merchandise and the Eddie Stobart shop in Carlisle, and turns over £1.5 million annually.

Billy Dowell, an Eddie Stobart driver. All drivers must wear a collar and tie.

Carlisle United celebrate winning the Auto Windscreens Shield at Wembley in 1997 in their 'deckchair' shirts, sponsored by Eddie Stobart Ltd.

William Stobart today. He and brother Edward are the sole owners of Eddie Stobart Ltd, the biggest private haulage firm in the UK.

Eddie and Nora Stobart today, at home in Dalston, Carlisle. Eddie retired from active involvement with the firm in the 1980s.

Edward with William Hague, then leader of the Tory Party, admiring a truck named after his fragrant wife, Ffion, in 1998.

Edward receiving the 'Haulier of the Year' award, 1992, from Transport Minister John McGregor.

Edward at Daventry with his personal assistant, Deborah Rodgers, who has been at his side since 1987. In 2001, the firm had 1000 lorries, a staff of 2200 and a turnover of £150 million.

name of real lorry firms on our model trucks. They usually had names like Cadbury's or Mars or Seven-Up, names children would recognize.

'Edward said he wanted a model with the firm's name on for the fan club and also for promotional reasons, to give away to motorway service stations to stick on their counter, so people would see the name Eddie Stobart.

'He got rid of them all, then he asked us to do a better one. He said the first one was a bit crude. He wanted more detail, a better finish. I said the tooling would be very expensive, but he said he'd pay for it. He pushed us into it, really. But we did do a better model, and didn't charge him for the tooling. That sold out as well. We've just gone on from there. Edward is tough on price, but he and William are excellent to deal with: sincere, genuine, enthusiastic.

'One of the early models we did, which cost £29.99 just five years ago, is now changing hands for £250. We've just done a limited set which will sell at £150. That's the most expensive so far.'

Corgi still produces all the Eddie Stobart die-cast models sold through the fan club, but they also sell Eddie Stobart models to the general retail market as well, paying a royalty for the licence. Altogether, model toys bearing the Eddie Stobart livery are now worth £3.5 million a year in retail sales.

'We produce seventy per cent of the country's die-cast models,' says Colin, 'and I would say that Eddie Stobart is now the best-selling line. I can see it continuing, just as long as Edward keeps his lorries on the road and they are all clean and the drivers smart.

'One reason is the breadth of the appeal. I'm always amused to see a Mercedes on the road with an "I'm an Eddie Stobart Spotter" sticker in the back window, followed by a beat-up Mini with the same sticker. Adults of all classes buy the models, along with children and collectors. That's the secret.'

Another company to have benefited from the unique look of Eddie Stobart Ltd is Dickies, the clothing manufacturer. The uniforms for Eddie Stobart staff are all made by Dickies, a firm in rural Somerset which specializes in work clothes. The firm began over one hundred years ago in Midsomer Norton, but is now American-owned. Its first Eddie Stobart order came in February 1989, when it was asked to supply some work trousers for the lorry drivers.

'There were a few problems at first,' says Richard Chilcott, the Managing Director. 'Normally, we had been supplying work trousers for people in factories who stood by a bench all day and didn't move. But, when the Stobart drivers climbed up into their cabs, their trousers would often split. One leg would go up and in before the other, which resulted in a rip. We solved it by putting more material in the crutch. No, I wouldn't say we made them baggier – just roomier. We now call the style the "Stobart trousers". We also put in more belt loops at the back, so that when drivers

Ladies single breasted jacket
Dark green textured fabric with engraved buttons.
55% Polyester / 45% Wool
Dry clean only Ⓟ

Ladies skirt
Black skirt fully lined with back vent. The wearing of hosiery with black skirts is compulsory.
55% Polyester / 45% Wool
Dry clean only Ⓟ

Ladies cardigan
Dark green cardigan in wool mix with green and gold buttons.
50% Acrylic / 50% Wool

Ladies round T-top blouse
Short sleeved blouse in 100% Poly crepe-de-chine fabric.

Ladies pleated Summer skirt
Full length permanent pleat skirt in 100% Poly crepe-de-chine fabric. Hosiery optional with Summer skirt.
We recommend crepe-de-chine garments are washed and hung to dry on clothes hangers to reduce creasing.

Note: Hand wash only, do not iron.

Ladies revers blouse
Short sleeve blouse in 100% Poly crepe-de-chine fabric with shirt tail hem.

Shoes
Shoes are not provided but must be black court shoes (or similar styles).

are bending over or getting out of their cabs, you don't see any unsightly expanse of, er, skin.'

Dickies was naturally thrilled when Edward decided to move on from work trousers to the full uniform. The firm got the order, which it still has, to supply everything, from ties to jackets.

Then, in 1997, came more excitement when Dickies gained the contract to dress all staff in uniform, including office workers and planners not seen by the general public. 'We had long discussions with Deborah about it, then we went up to Carlisle and did a presentation to Mr Edward and Mr William. We showed them the full range – on mannequin models, not real models. They were then tried on various members of the staff before they agreed on the final uniform.

'We are so proud to supply clothes to Eddie Stobart. We see them as prestigious clients. They help to impress other firms, because everyone knows how clean and smart their drivers are.'

In 1989, when Dickies first started working for Stobart's, its annual turnover was £4.6 million pounds and it had 180 staff. Now, its turnover is £25 million pounds and the staff number 210.

One of the company's more recently acquired contracts is for Safeway, making its staff uniform. This is worth some £2 million pounds, about ten times the size of the Stobart orders, but Dickies would still hate to lose its Stobart contract. 'They are absolute gentlemen,' says Mr Chilcott, 'If you give a good service, tell the truth, then there's never any aggravation or nastiness, not like some modern-day business firms we have to deal with . . . .

'But they are very particular. We always keep a dyebatch in store, in case trousers get ripped and have to be replaced. If they don't match exactly the colour of the shirt, Mr Edward won't have them.' There is now such a colour as Eddie Stobart Green. Both Dickies and ICI, who makes up the paint for the lorries, refer to it as such.

While several hauliers have copied the example of Stobart's, Mr Chilcott says the majority of transport firms have not. 'Yet it's so logical to have a uniform: not just for cleanliness and protection, which back in 1989 was a factor, if not so much now, but for team spirit. When staff wear a uniform, they breathe together. There is a sense of belonging. And in the case of Stobart's, they have a sense of belonging to the best.'

Another case study of a company that has benefited from Eddie Stobart's success is Boalloy of Congleton, Cheshire. It was founded in 1946 and is the bodywork firm that Edward first used back in 1976, when he wanted to convert some of his trucks and have the very latest curtains on his trailers. In 1976, the firm had around 200 employees. Today, it has 650 employees with premises in Glasgow, Preston and Stowbridge as well as Congleton. Its turnover in the year 2000 was £45 million.

Boalloy's Managing Director for the last nine years has been Gerry Brown, and he was involved in a management buy-out of the firm in 1992; previously, it had been part of a public company. Gerry says there is no doubt that his firm's success has been directly related to Eddie Stobart Ltd. 'He still is about our biggest single customer. We do all his trailers. On average, he provides between £2.5–£3 million of work for us every year. But, as a reference point, he has been even more valuable to us.

'His vehicles are fabulous – no, they really are. It was such a marvellous concept to paint them the way he did, and have his drivers in uniform. Everyone now knows his vehicles, and admires them, so it reflects on us. It's brought us a lot of work from other firms, such as Irlam's. We do their lorries as well now.

'You couldn't meet two nicer people to do business with than Edward and William. They are so disarming, so straight, so considerate, and always pay on time. I can't speak highly enough of them . . . .'

Gerry explains that the lorry curtains used on Stobart trailers were his firm's idea. 'Boalloy invented them. We have a world patent on them which we took out in 1969. But it was Edward coming along which put them on the map. There are now variations on the market, made by other people. We call ours Tautliners – that's the product we provide, the trailer complete with our tensioned side-curtains. You can pull them taut, hence the name. We make ours of PVC coated in a polyester weave.'

Boalloy also does all the painting of the lettering on the sides of the Stobart trailers. It has three painters working full-time every day, painting the words 'Eddie Stobart Ltd', getting through forty new trailers every calendar month. It was done totally free-hand at one time, when it was script lettering. If you looked carefully, you could always spot a slight difference between each lorry. When Boalloy moved on to capital letters, it was able to use a stencil. Now the letters are computer created and sticky stencils get cut and stuck on, but the paint itself is still applied by hand.

While the painters at Boalloy are craftsmen rather than artists, there is one real artist who has done well out of Eddie Stobart: Alan Fearnley, who was commissioned to paint a set of Eddie Stobart lorries. Prints of nine of the paintings are sold through the fan club (a tenth was used on an Eddie Stobart calendar). Alan Fearnley is aged fifty-eight and comes from Yorkshire. He has worked as a freelance artist for the last thirty years, specializing in transport subjects. He's always been interested in mechanical things and particularly likes vintage cars: he paints them and also drives one, a 1935 Lagonda.

Alan has been chairman of the Guild of Railway Artists and a member of the Guild of Aviation Artists. There's also a Guild of Motoring Artists, but he's not in that. He estimates there are two hundred artists who specialize in painting transport scenes – about forty of whom make a full-time living from it.

It was in Monaco, in 1993, that the first contact was made between Alan and Eddie Stobart. Edward was a guest of Ford for the Grand Prix, although it is unusual for him to accept any corporate hospitality. Alan was showing an exhibition of his motor-racing paintings in a local hotel, the Hôtel de Paris, his fifth one-man show in Monaco.

'Someone took me to the exhibition,' says Edward,

'and I bought one of the paintings. It cost £5000 and it showed Damon Hill winning his first Grand Prix, with Senna behind him.' It wasn't like Edward to buy a piece of art, but the subject had always interested him. As a boy, his hero, of course, had been Stirling Moss.

'I didn't know the artist was English,' continues Edward, 'till someone told me, and that he came from Yorkshire. I later made contact with him and asked if he'd be interested in doing paintings of some of our lorries.'

Alan had heard of Eddie Stobart lorries, and had been noticing them in an idle way on motorway journeys, but says he was astounded when Edward Stobart approached him about painting some. Old racing cars have always had a certain aesthetic and artistic beauty, as have old steam engines, and even aeroplanes, and they are all popular subjects with artists, but lorries have rarely made it on to canvas.

'I'd never ever painted a lorry before,' explains Alan, 'so it was, let's say, a bit of a challenge. With vintage cars or racing cars, I don't just do portraits. I always put them in a setting, in a landscape, try to create an atmosphere, tell a bit of a story. So I wanted to do that with his lorries. But it was hard to think of suitable ones.'

Alan came up with ideas for ten settings and submitted them to Edward. 'He agreed to them all, with a few minor suggestions.' In one of them, entitled 'Journey's End', it showed a large truck being washed. Edward suggested there should be some of his workers

in the painting, in uniform of course, which Alan
agreed was a good idea.

The other paintings, all of which have nicely evoca-
tive titles, include: 'The Lone Trucker', which shows
an Eddie Stobart lorry on an empty road passing a
fir tree with mountains behind; 'Night Time in Paris'
depicts a gleaming Eddie going down the Champs-
Elysée, the centre of attention; 'Winter' has a truck
going under a motorway sign in snow; 'Romania' is
very rural, with a horse and cart and sheep and
shepherds; 'Lake District' is a very pretty, chocolate-
box painting, showing an Eddie driving along what
looks like the shore of Ullswater; 'Northbound' is an
Eddie Stobart freight train on rails, not road this time;
'Leaving Dover' has the white cliffs behind; 'Fleeting
Encounter' shows two Eddies, passing each other on
a motorway, going in different directions: very moody.

All the paintings have an atmosphere, suggest little
stories, make small points, repay closer examination.
Some even have a 'Stag at Bay' grandeur about them.
One or two of the scenes lead one to suspect some
slight artistic licence, as if the lorries had been moved
by Alan's imagination into certain settings, such as
'Night Time in Paris'. Alan admits this painting wasn't
painted from real life: he made it up, but it could have
happened. The setting of 'The Lone Trucker', beside
the fir tree, was also imagined. Alan did go to the Lake
District, and the setting is Ullswater, but, no, that lorry
wasn't actually there at the time. He plonked it in
later. But most of the other paintings, Alan says, were

JOURNEY'S END

THE LONE TRUCKER

NIGHT TIME IN PARIS

WINTER

ROMANIA

LAKE DISTRICT

NORTHBOUND

LEAVING DOVER

£50.00 each

Actual size 700mm x 466mm

A superb collection of limited edition prints by renowned motoring artist Alan Fearnley featuring some of your favourite Eddie Stobart vehicles at work, at home and abroad.
These limited edition prints represent excellent value to collectors of Eddie Stobart memorabilia.

Each print is signed and numbered by the artist and is a unique record of Britain's most famous road haulage company.

FLEETING ENCOUNTER

PRINTS

Published by Eddie Stobart Promotions Ltd, Kra 8500 Road, Kingstown Industrial Estate, Carlisle, Cumbria, CA3 0EF. Tel: (01228) 584408 Fax: (01228) 514452
No part of this publication may be reproduced in part or whole without the express permission of the publisher.

based on his first-hand observations, going to a scene and taking photographs. 'For the one I call "Winter", I did drive up and down the M1 with my camera fixed on the dashboard, looking out for Eddies and taking photographs.'

Alan's favourite is 'The Lone Trucker'. 'I think I got a good atmosphere into that, caught the feeling of being a lone trucker in a lone truck. Which of course most of the drivers are, most of the time. I felt that worked well.'

The work on Alan's ten paintings was spread over four years, so he got to know Edward quite well. 'I was very surprised when I first met him – I expected some go-getting powerhouse, because of what he has achieved. He turned out to be quite ordinary, and I mean that in the nicest sense of the word. He is an ordinary person, which makes his achievements even more astounding.'

Alan has remained a fan of Eddie Stobart, and enjoys reading all the fan-club magazines and literature. 'It is a special company.' For his ten paintings, Alan received £5000 for each – his normal fee for such paintings. So not a bad little earner, though, alas, no other haulage firm has so far asked Alan to do paintings of their lorries.

Someone who was already a Stobart fan has managed to turn Eddie Stobart spotting into a job. In 1992, John Martin, who lives in north Devon, was working in the medical-equipment design world and found himself doing a lot of motorway driving. He began spotting Eddies for his own amusement. When he got home, he made little notes on all the trucks he had seen. When computers came in, he decided to create a database of all Eddie Stobart lorries.

In 1998, John launched an Eddie Stobart website, so that fans could download from the Internet all the details he had discovered about Eddie Stobart. 'From then on, it just escalated. People wanted to know about other lorry firms as well, such as James Irlam.'

John's website is now called Lorry Spotting and it lists details of over thirty firms apart from Eddie Stobart. 'There's a waiting list of haulage firms wanting to be included, but I only want those with nice livery and well-looked-after lorries. I turn them down if I think their firm is a complete and utter shed – that's a trucking term for someone whose lorry is a total mess, all rusty and crummy.'

John still lives in Devon, but now has a staff of three and eight separate phone lines. He charges fans £17 to get access to his website. The rise of Lorry Spotting has amazed him. He says he has MP's and brain surgeons as well as vicars on his list of subscribers. 'It's all very strange. There's something in human nature which means if you give certain people a list, they will immediately start ticking items off. I don't know why, they just do. They probably can't explain it themselves. Lorry spotting has become the thinking man's train spotting.'

Not only has John created a little business, thanks

to Eddie Stobart, but he's got himself a little job as PR for one of their rival firms, James Irlam, and also looks after their fan club. 'Eddie Stobart and James Irlam are the top end of the market. They like to think all their drivers are professional people. We call the drivers at the lower end of the market steering-wheel attendants . . . .'

James Irlam and Sons Ltd have been the haulage firm most influenced by the rise of Eddie Stobart. They have used their idea of a fan club, as well as a great deal beside. Edward himself is a great fan of Irlam's and sees them as a friendly rival. 'We share a lot of the same customers,' says Edward. 'I think they look up to us as the leader, the one to compete with. But there's no worries. I think they're still a bit frightened of us. We'll remain the leader in the private field as long as I'm still here. But they do remind me of us when we were their size, very hungry, setting the same good standards.'

Edward is unsure how big the rival firm is, how many vehicles it has. 'David Irlam will probably say 600, which is what I'd probably have said as well at their stage. I don't exactly know, but I'd guess 250 today . . . .'

David Irlam, the present head of the firm, is much the same age as Edward, and has a similar background. The firm was begun by his grandfather, the late James Irlam, in 1949 in Cheshire, delivering fertilizers. It was his son, Ken, who moved into lorries, but on a small scale. It was only in 1980, by which time they still only had three trucks and five staff, that his son David, plus his three brothers, started building up the firm. David, now Managing Director, left school early, as Edward did. He, too, was hardly there for his last year. 'Put it this way. If there was work to be done, I did that instead of going to school.'

By 1985, the firm was still quite small, with just nine lorries and fifteen staff. Their growth spurt came in the 1990s. 'I was first aware of Eddie Stobart in about 1990. I used to see his trucks on the M6, always very clean. It was the cleanliness that struck me. When you're in the same business, you notice things other people wouldn't see.'

While Eddie romped ahead, in size of fleet, and volume of turnover, James Irlam also expanded, but not quite as dramatically. He introduced uniforms for his drivers, following Eddie Stobart, and also began naming all his trucks, not after women but after British towns and villages. His red-and-yellow trucks are kept as clean and distinctive as Stobart's.

'I always said I would never have a fan club. That would be too much like copying, but people began to ring us up all the time, wanting to see round our lorries, asking why we didn't have a fan club like Stobart. So we gave in. We thought it was time it wasn't just a one-horse race.'

Today, the James Irlam fan club has 3700 members – and still growing. The firm itself has a turnover of £40 million, 650 staff and 320 lorries. So Edward wasn't too far wrong guessing 250 vehicles but, of course, it's still nothing like his own size of fleet. 'Edward says he's got 1000 lorries?' says David Irlam. 'Are you sure he's not counting in the Corgi toys . . . .'

Irlam's is still a family firm, owned by the four Irlam brothers. Their father is still alive, but is not involved in the day-to-day business any more. 'He's sixty-six,' says David, 'and he plays the organ every week in the local Methodist chapel, just as he did when he was sixteen.' David still counts himself a Methodist but, like Edward, he doesn't go much to church these days. 'It's a generation thing, I suppose.'

Considering they began about the same time, from a similar background, David can explain why Eddie Stobart has today got so far ahead of his company and is now about three times its size. 'It's very simple. Edward has taken more risks. We have only five depots, for example, while Stobart's have a lot more. But we own all ours. We don't do sale and leaseback. That's why we've expanded more slowly.

'I've always looked for long-term growth, not quick growth. I tend to think in terms of having some good pensions in the years ahead for me and my brothers, plus a secure family firm for the next generation to take over. I have a son called James Irlam: he's only eleven now, but I'm hoping him and some of the others in his generation will run it in the future.

'Edward has always been quick to go for any business available. We don't do that. Only if the price is right: we don't have any loss leaders. 'Edward also goes for areas I wouldn't try to get business in. I don't do Scotland for example. There's a lot of little haulage firms up there anyway and it's hard to get in, unless you wear a kilt. But the main reason is that it's hard to get a return load from places like Ayr. If you analyse it, there's more going into Scotland than coming out. So I won't touch Scotland. I think you'll lose money there in the end. And I don't do out-of-the-way places in England, like Devon or Yarmouth. But Edward is always willing to take a risk – and, so far, it's paid off.

'He also works on lower margins than us. When you work on three per cent, it just takes a bad spell and you're making no profit. I've always been cautious, never taking on work for work's sake.

'But I do admire what Edward's done. He's been excellent for the industry. It always had a scruffy image, till he came along. I know he's been bad-mouthed, and so have we, accused of under-cutting people, or getting our capital from religious cults. Oh, we've had those nasty rumours as well.

'The people who dislike Eddie Stobart don't know the company. I deal with Edward a lot as we share contracts. I admire both Edward and William as people, not just as hauliers. I'm proud to be considered in their league.

'I don't think he's quite as shy or hates publicity as much as he makes out. He has done some clever marketing; it hasn't all been an accident. But he's like me. It's not the money that gives you a kick. It's people saying nice things about your lorries, admiring your clean site, saying how efficient your service is. That's the best buzz. Not the money.'

UP THE MANAGEMENT MEN

One of the features of Eddie Stobart Ltd, right from the early days, was that workers got a chance of promotion, if they fancied it, if they were thought suitable. Lack of education or paper qualifications were never seen as a handicap – otherwise, Edward and William would never have got where they are.

The two very earliest workers of all, David Jackson and Stan Monkhouse, are still with the company. They went from Hesket Newmarket to Greystone Road in 1976, and both wear suits today, although they have had varying success and enjoyment as management men.

For David Jackson, the honour of being Manager of the depot, at Burnaston, turned out to be more pain than pleasure. After three years, he returned to Carlisle, still as a management man, but in the less stressful job of training drivers. 'I bottled it really,' says David. 'Being the Depot Manager got me down in the end. It was sacking people – that was what I found hard to do: it gave me sleepless nights.'

In 1998, David was promoted to Driving Training Manager for the group. He moved to Daventry and acquired a house locally with his wife and family. He found his new role a challenge, due to ever-tightening health-and-safety regulations, plus he had what he today calls some kind of mid-life crisis. He therefore, in 1999, left the firm for about a year, to work locally with a friend.

David returned to the fold in 2001, at Daventry again, on the fleet maintenance side. 'I love being here, looking out at the vast warehouses and the hundreds and hundreds of lorries; it makes me quite emotional. I'm always thinking back to Greystone Road, when we first moved in and we had to slash up against the wall as we didn't have a toilet.'

Stan Monkhouse is the longest-serving employee of Eddie Stobart Ltd. He joined Eddie in 1960, as a tractor driver, when young Edward was still at primary school. He still remembers, when he was Eddie's driver, how Edward and William would do odd jobs around the yard. Because both boys had speech problems, they had to have the name 'Eddie Stobart' written down for them on a bit of paper when they were sent into Carlisle to pick up parts.

From being in charge of lorry maintenance at Greystone Road, Stan eventually became Fleet Director with a staff of twenty-five. He still has that title today, and is still based in Carlisle. Nowadays, with most trucks being on contract-hire, not owned, there are not the same maintenance problems for Stan to deal with. Instead, he concerns himself with the legal and licensing problems of the fleet.

Stan says he didn't find it too hard, moving up to management. 'Luckily I've never had to sack people. That's always been done by someone else. I've always enjoyed keeping records, so that was a big help. And when you get older, you've seen it all, you've learned how to cope.

'I've enjoyed all my forty years, even those early years, spreading slag for father Eddie: not the nicest of jobs. The year 2000 was a hard year, but I can remember much harder years, like the times when drivers had to be laid off in January and February as we had no work.'

Stan, now aged sixty, with four grown-up children, still lives in Hesket Newmarket. He and his wife have a little guest house in the village. It should do well in the years to come, when Eddie Stobart fan club members start making pilgrimages to where it all began. As surely they must.

Colin Rutherford, the ex-Metal Box Transport Manager, who was one of Edward's three new management appointments in 1986, got a new lease of life and health when he joined the firm. He stayed with them through the glory years, until retiring for good in 1995, aged sixty-five. He still lives near Carlisle and keeps in touch with Edward and his old colleagues. Everywhere he goes, he says people always want to know about what it was like, working for Eddie Stobart.

Barrie Thomas, who also arrived in 1986 as the manager in charge of finance, retired from the company in August 1998, at the comparatively young age of forty-four. Part of the reason was that, following a suspected heart attack, he was advised by his doctor to slow down.

During those twelve years, he had been on the inside as the company grew from a small, provincial lorry firm into a nationally known company. He had been promoted first to Company Secretary and then to Legal and Commercial Director. He was even given a seat on the group board – one of only three directors, the other two being Edward and William. Not that there were many proper board meetings during his years. 'It was usually a matter of Edward ringing me while he was on the motorway and saying, "Does this feel right?"'

Barrie was also given some shares and share options, the only non-family person to be so honoured. The theory was that, in years to come, should they ever sell, or be taken over, Barrie would be able to cash in his shares and thereby be rewarded for his part in the company's success. But, in 1998, Barrie gave back his shares, without any financial benefit. 'If they'd sold the firm while I was working for them, then I would have been justified in taking the money. But, as I no longer worked for them, I felt it was only right to hand back the shares. After all, I'd been given them as a present.'

Barrie's other reason for leaving when he did, apart from on medical advice, was to devote himself to God. Like Eddie Stobart, Senior, he always felt there was more to life than working. He had already become a pastor in the Church of the Nazarene, which has roots in Methodism and Wesleyanism. On his retirement, Barrie decided to do a degree in theology at Manchester University. This currently takes up two days a week of his time and, by the end of 2002, he will have graduated and become an ordained minister.

He enjoyed all his years with the firm and admits the strain in his final years was probably because he was trying to do too much, combining his church work with his Eddie Stobart directorship. He still lives in Carlisle and has three children. Two are still at school while the oldest works for Eddie Stobart Promotions.

'All companies evolve, move from stage to stage,' says Barrie. 'I remember the big excitement when we reached 100 vehicles. That was an important stage and it meant a slightly different structure and style of management. And, as we went on, more changes were necessary.

'In the early days, we hired people who could do everything. When the phone rang, whoever answered it had to be the person who was wanted. Today, now the company is so big, Edward needs specialist people who know a lot about a little area of expertise. He no longer needs people who can do everything.

'Looking back, I don't think we grew too quickly, but it's true that when you are expanding at a great rate, as we were, you have your eye on the next deal. You might be working on a contract for, say, one million pounds, therefore you don't bother with things that might save you £20,000. The benefit of growth is more important at the time than strict financial control.

'But, of course, there comes a time when you have to spend time on the details. I've been out of the business for three years now, but I am sure that this is what Edward's been doing. As he always had to. That's the stage he reached. Now he'll shoot forward again.

'What's happened to the firm is that they have risen to a point where they are on their own; they are in a category of one. Yes, there's still a huge gap in size between Eddie Stobart and the PLCs but, at the same time, there is a big gap between them and their nearest competitor behind them. They can afford to stand still for a while and consolidate. They will go forward, because Edward will not be happy otherwise. He could lose interest, unless he has a challenge . . . .'

One of the highlights of Barrie's time at the firm was the company's twenty-fifth anniversary celebrations in 1995. Edward decided to do it in style, spare no expense, and so hired the ballroom at the Dorchester Hotel in London and laid on a lavish, black-tie dinner for over three hundred guests. There was entertainment from Cannon and Ball, music from Jools Holland and his group, while Steve Rider, the sports commentator, was the compere and introduced the speakers.

But perhaps the high point of the evening was when the curtains were pulled back at the end of the

ballroom to reveal . . . an Eddie Stobart lorry. Not just
the front part, but a whole Eddie, the truck and the
trailer. Everyone wondered how had they done it, how
had they got such a monster into the hotel, down the
corridors and into the ballroom. In truth, it was partly
a fiddle, a clever piece of trompe l'oeil. The front part
was real enough, a genuine artic. with a proper cab,
but Volvo had specially pared it down, adapted it so
it could be taken into the hotel and assembled. The
trailer was false, a stage setting, made of wood and
cardboard, but beautifully painted in the well-known
Stobart livery. Even those who went up and pressed
their noses against it, and worked out how it had been
done, had to admit it was a triumph.

In most ways, 1995 was a triumph for the firm all
round. Not just twenty-five years up but, that year,
they broke the 500 vehicles mark and topped £50 mil-

lion a year in turnover. The next five years were just as successful, with the fleet number doubling in size but, when the year 2000 came round, along with their thirtieth anniversary, it was, for many reasons, not quite the right time to be triumphant.

PROBLEMS, PROBLEMS

In 1999, Eddie Stobart went into Europe. It was a brave venture for an independent firm, still with its headquarters in a small northern provincial town, with no European partners, no European connections or experiences. During that year, Edward spent on average two days a week in Belgium. By the end of the year, they had opened two depots in Belgium, had created a presence in Greece, and were running 125 vehicles in Europe, with fifty staff.

A good beginning, for a small firm. Which is what they are. In fact a rather small firm, in global or even European terms. In Europe, lorry firm Norbert Dentressangle has 2,800 vehicles, and Willi Betz has 3,800, but they are not as independent as Eddie Stobart, having either government involvement or are associated with major international firms like Renault and Mercedes.

In Britain, Eddie Stobart, despite having become by far the best-known name in haulage, is also a relatively small company. Depending on how you do the rankings, basing it on employees, size of turnover, on UK or world-wide size, Eddie Stobart comes in about tenth in the British distribution league (see appendix). But all those above him are PLCs, or parts of other groups. When it comes to private, independent haulage firms, then Eddie Stobart is number one.

The world distribution leader, at present, is a surprising one: Deutsche Post. Not exactly a fair comparison, as the company still runs the German mail service, so has a lot of post vans. However, in recent years, it has also been gobbling up distribution firms all over the globe. It owns fifty per cent of Securicor and has large stakes in DHL and Lufthansa. In 2001, its worldwide sales were expected to top £16 billion, which rather puts Eddie Stobart, with its £150-million turnover, in the shade.

In Britain, Exel is now the number-one distribution company, and is also second in the world to Deutsche Post. In 2000, Exel merged with MSAS Global Logistics

Left:
Mrs P.A. Donovan of Cardiff spotted this vehicle in Patras, Greece, on 5th June.

Right:
Mrs P. Champ of Rickmansworth, Herts., spotted this truck in Venice on 22nd June. Probably waiting for a gondola!

to create a firm with 50,000 employees in 1300 locations around the world. Its worldwide turnover is £3.5 billion and its customers include two-thirds of the world's largest non-financial companies.

In distribution, size matters. The big firms, the PLCs, like to do business with other big firms and PLCs. They are not bothered by public recognition or affection in the same way as general, knock-about, take-anything, go-anywhere hauliers. They have secured long-term contracts with the people who really matter, doing a lot more for them than just simple distribution. They don't care that people don't know their names, most of which consist of meaningless initials, or can't spot their vehicles which usually carry the name of the customer not the carrier. Exel has over 4000 vehicles in the UK, many of which are working full time under the banner of BP or Marks & Spencer, with whom they have global contracts. Eddie Stobart does a bit of this when shifting the *Mirror* about, the vehicles sporting the '*Mirror*' not 'Eddie Stobart'.

While Edward might be doing well in haulage, plus warehousing, he is a long way from the big league. Moving into Belgium was only a first, small step onto the global stage. After a fashion, he was trying to compete with firms which, by their very nature, are already global.

It was also an expensive step, for by the end of the year 2000, it was clear that, for the first time in the firm's history, the haulage side would not make a profit. For the previous ten years, it had increased in size, turnover and profits from 30–50 per cent every year.

Belgium was only a small part of it and some impact was to be expected, with all the set-up costs. There were several other reasons, however, for the slowing down in company growth and profits. The increasing cost of fuel and road licences played a major part. Then, in the summer of 2000, there was a fuel blockade and demonstrations against the fuel tax, which kept most lorries and many private cars off the road for up to two weeks. In Eddie Stobart's case, it represented a loss in revenue of £250,000 a day.

'I could understand the frustrations, but I'm against blockades personally,' says Edward. 'You shouldn't make the general public suffer for your problem. I think it should be the supermarkets who get blockaded, not the oil depots. If you hit the supermarket chains, by filling their car parks with giant lorries so people can't get in or out, making it clear you just can't cope any longer, then the supermarkets would quickly come in on your side and get something done. The supermarkets are the really powerful people in our business.'

The Road Haulage Association produced figures in 2000 to show that VAT and excise duty in Britain amounted to seventy-three per cent of every litre – the highest rate in the whole of Europe. In Britain, a litre of diesel cost 83p compared with 62p in Denmark, 56p in Italy and France, 53p in Germany, 52p in Ireland, 44p in Spain, 37p in Portugal and 18p in Russia.

The average forty-tonne truck holds 14,000 litres of fuel, enough to take it 2300 miles. In Britain, a thousand-litre tank was costing £830 to fill, compared with the average across Europe of £490. Fuel represents thirty-six per cent of a haulier's running costs. Yet road traffic shows no sign of diminishing, despite the high costs. Rail freight just can't compete for speed and efficiency. In 1998, eighty-one per cent of all domestic freight went by road: a figure expected to increase every year for at least the next ten years.

There is cheaper diesel available to farmers, known as red diesel, but it is not available for road haulage. Nor do big lorries, or big firms with lots of lorries, get any discount for bulk. An Eddie Stobart lorry is paying the same price for diesel at the pump as any ordinary motorist who uses diesel. In 2000, diesel cost them £500,000 more per month than it did in 1999, yet they were running the same number of trucks. Road tax also cost an extra £200,000 a month in 2000 than in 1999.

'Making money gets harder all the time,' says Edward. 'We have yearly agreements with our customers not to put costs up, but then things happen outside our control: fuel goes up again, taxes increase, the licence system changes, there are sudden strikes here or in France, which bring everything to a halt.

'At Budget-time, if fuel goes up by 10p, we can usually pass that on. Everyone agrees and understands. But when you wake up one day and find there's an extra 2p on petrol, for no apparent reason, then we have to live with it. You can't keep going back to customers every time there's a small rise. The margins are very thin. We are now working on a profit of only three per cent of turnover, so if anything goes wrong which we didn't expect, we can easily end with no profit.'

Edward did threaten, during 2000, to move all his operations out of the UK, to give up being a British-based firm and register as a European company. This was at a time when the Road Fund Licence for British registered lorries was £4750, fifty per cent higher than in Europe. It did come down to £3950, for a forty-tonne truck, but it was still about thirty-five per cent higher. It therefore would have made sense had Edward registered his lorries abroad, thereby of course depriving the British government of millions of pounds in income.

'It was just a threat,' says Edward, 'I just wanted to point out the anomalies – I was never thinking of moving the firm abroad. But what's happened today is that all the big firms we are now competing against are conglomerates of some sort; global companies with branches worldwide. They can easily move their business around to take advantage of lower costs or lower taxes in any particular country. We can't.'

Another reason for the poor year, as far as profits were concerned, was traffic. All haulage firms, and all of us who drive, have had to put up with that problem for decades, just as we've had to live with rising fuel prices and road licences, but congestion on the road has led to two problems for all haulage companies.

Firstly, it slows everything down. It makes journeys take longer, petrol costs rise, fewer loads can be carried, income is lost, profit disappears. The traffic planners at Daventry, which, on the face of it, was such a perfect situation in so many ways, now know that, at certain times of the day, if a load is setting off down the motorway from Junction 18, they have to add on an extra hour on its timetable. An extra hour soon cuts into profits when you are working on only three per cent.

But the worst result of the horrendous traffic on all our motorways is that, at long last, the drivers have had enough: they can't take it any more. For the first time in living memory, an acute driver shortage began to become apparent during 2000. Older drivers might still enjoy it, but young ones are no longer tempted.

It is now seen as the biggest single problem in haulage today. It hit Eddie Stobart later than most other firms, thanks partly to the firm's good name and partly to being traditionally northern-based, where work has always been harder to find. It meant that, for most of the 1990s, their staff turnover was minimal, around six per cent. In the year 2000, it jumped to ten per cent in the North – but twenty per cent in the Midlands and South, where most of their work now takes place.

The obvious way to recruit more and better drivers would be to pay them more – but when working on a very narrow profit margin or, in 2000, none at all, this can hardly be done. There is also the anomaly in the haulage business that, while profits are low, there is still over-capacity. Thousands of owner-drivers, desperate for work, will work on the slimmest possible margins just to stay alive. This keeps the profits down and the wages low in an industry which, like the hotel and restaurant business, has traditionally always been poorly paid.

In 2001, Eddie Stobart drivers were getting around £6 an hour, more for night-time and weekend work. It was a sixteen per cent increase on the previous year, and was considered good for the industry, but was not attractive enough to lure new drivers. 'It is the lack of young drivers – that's the problem,' says Edward. 'We don't get the sort who have enthusiasm for it, who see it as exciting. Oh, it did used to be seen that way. The conditions for drivers were considered pretty attractive when all the new driving aids came in: fully automatic; state-of-the-art, warm, comfortable cabs; their own sleeping quarters.

'The trucks are very comfortable and pleasant to drive, but the traffic has ruined it. The hold-ups spoil everything. So much time gets lost, so much aggravation on the road. And it gets worse when you do arrive there. The supermarkets have got bigger, the loads have got bigger, but the parking lots have got smaller. You are booked in for a certain slot to unload. If you are fifteen minutes late, that's it, you've lost it. It's probably been the traffic's fault, but the driver gets a bollocking. He can't park outside the store, so he has to go and wait somewhere for hours. Oh, it makes it very stressful for drivers.'

The only way to pay drivers more is if they earn more money for the company. One way they could do this is by driving twenty-five more miles on every shift, but they can't do that because of the traffic and also because of speed restrictions on all lorries.

Despite the low pay and tough conditions, an over-capacity of lorries and drivers still exists. There are currently 400,000 trucks in the UK, with a total of 110,000 different operators. Edward is unsure why this situation persists. 'I don't know, unless they come into the business because they've heard about us. They see the nice depots we've got, think we must be doing well, so they hang on. Being owner-drivers, they don't have the overheads we have.'

The result of the poor year meant that, for the first time in twenty years, some belt-tightening took place at Edward's firm. During the year 2000, two depots were closed at Bristol and Stamford, and nearly a hundred workers lost their jobs. Edward says the reasons for closing the two depots were customer-driven: warehouses were moved, systems changed, so they had to respond. At the same time, two new depots were opened, at Hams Hall near Birmingham and Dartford, Kent, so they ended the year with the same number of depots (twenty-eight) as before.

Perhaps the most important thing that happened to the company during the year, more than the tempor-ary blip in profits, was an extensive management overhaul. The last major one had been in 1986, when Edward brought in his brother William plus Barrie Thomas and Colin Rutherford.

Edward felt it was time for some new blood. Perhaps he himself had taken his eye off the ball a bit, spending all that time in Belgium, or perhaps the management had grown a bit tired and out of touch. During that year, they had a several-million-pound contract that went wrong and they had to get out of it.

'Some people did not develop as the firm developed,' admits Edward. 'You have to be ruthless to be loyal; you can't get too close to people if they are not performing. If certain people are causing problems, then it's worth sacrificing a few people for the sake of the other 2500. That's what had to be done.

'I didn't do it earlier because the firm was getting bigger every year. We were just growing so fast, doing so well. Now has been the time to sit back and look at the things that went wrong, at people who haven't worked out, examine the real reasons why the year didn't do so well.' Edward again found himself looking at new management, to include a new Finance Director to play a key role within the business.

'We are not in any financial difficulties,' Edward emphasizes. 'The warehouse side, the fan club and the promotions side, they all made a good profit. Our property division also had a good year. We made a good profit on one deal, but that's not included in the annual accounts. Overall, the group itself made no profit in 2000. On the haulage side, they made a loss, thanks to rising costs.' Despite the setbacks, by the end of that year, with his new management team in place, Edward was ready for whatever lay ahead.

UP THE WORKERS

So what is it actually like to sit in an Eddie Stobart truck, with a real driver, down a real motorway – the fantasy of all true spotters? I arranged to meet a driver at the Daventry depot, hoping he'd take me on an M1 jaunt. But, first of all, I went into the Planning Department, the command base for all the Daventry-based drivers, whence they get their orders and are told what to do next and where. Inside, it is a bit like a war room, with computer screens flashing and instructions being barked into microphones.

Rowland Hobley, usually known as Roly, is one of the Planners who works there. He used to be a driver himself, so he knows how they think, how they react, how they drive. He also used to be in the Army and still has a military bearing, an efficient manner and very highly polished shoes.

He comes from Rugby, left school at sixteen and went into the Royal Engineers, becoming a Class-One Instructor, teaching people to drive lorries. In the Gulf War, he got injured, falling off a lorry and breaking both his legs. It took him eighteen months to recover.

He came out aged thirty-three, worried that being a soldier was affecting his marriage. He took a job as an agency driver, doing local runs. It didn't save his marriage so, when a full-time driving job came up in 1994 with Eddie Stobart, he took it.

The basic hourly wage in 1994 was £4.15. By working all the hours on offer, Roly considered his income was reasonable compared with many of his friends. For two years he was on an articulated vehicle – a tractor and trailer, forty feet long. Then for two years he drove a draw-bar, a lorry unit which draws a trailer, stretching to sixty feet in length.

With the artic, Roly's sleeping quarters were behind the driving wheel, so were very handy to get into. With the draw-bar, his sleeping quarters, or pod, was above the cab, which was a bit awkward at first to clamber into, but he soon got used to it.

In each case, he had his own vehicle all the time, so he was able to customize it to his own requirements and pleasure. They all come with a mattress, but you have to supply your own sheets or duvet and pillows. In his quarters, Roly installed his own built-in wardrobe, CD-player, mobile phone, two-ring gas cooker and grill, TV and fridge. What luxury. In Central London, it could cost you £100,000 for a one-room studio flat with all that.

'Yes, it was nice,' remembers Roly, 'especially when I had to wait anywhere to unload or pick up. It meant, while I waited around, I could just switch on and brew up. If I had a long wait, I could make myself a proper meal and watch television.'

He called himself a tramper, which means he slept in his vehicle four to five nights a week. This must not be confused with the word tramp, meaning a scruffy person, of which, alas, there are still some in the industry. 'Yes, even with all today's mod cons, you still get scruffy drivers.'

His normal shift consisted of three days of fifteen hours, followed by two days of thirteen hours. In his fifteen-hour day, he started at six and finished at nine in the evening, as long as he did not drive continuously for more than four-and-a-half hours at a time.

Although this sounds extremely arduous, Roly wasn't phased by it. 'Oh, it's not so bad, if you're doing 56 m.p.h. and it's a good road. It's when there's a traffic hold up, that's what ruins the job. We have a tachograph, in a sealed unit, which records each vehicle's speed, so you can't fiddle it.'

He enjoyed the camaraderie of the overnight stops, when he would meet up somewhere in a lorry park or lay-by with other Eddie Stobart drivers, have a few beers, perhaps invite a friend in to watch his TV. He also enjoyed talking to his fellow drivers on his CB radio as he was driving along.

'It could be very boring one day, then very rewarding the next. The worst thing is not the traffic but the waiting to unload or collect. You can be made to wait one hour or eight hours. And all the time you're being hassled. The customer is ringing the office to ask where you are, or telling you which bay to head for, or where to wait. Then your Planner is ringing to find out what's gone wrong, giving you the next job when you haven't finished the first. I used to sit for hours at Tesco, waiting for my bay to come up.

'The traffic, of course, is terrible. Some drivers used to long for a job to the north of Scotland, just to get away from it all, drive on an empty road, rather than fight through the London jams. I always liked London. It might be hellish, but it was never boring.

'The road I hated worst of all was the ring road round Birmingham, the M54, from the junction with the M6, Junction 10, to Junction 4 where it meets the M42. That was a lot worse than the M25. There was no escape. At least on the M25, if you can see what's happening ahead, you can get off and try other ways.'

After four years of heavy-duty, five-days-a-week driving, Roly's second marriage began to be in some danger, so he jumped at the chance to become a Planner. That way, he would at least get home every night.

Today, he looks after thirty or so drivers. Beside him, in the large, open Planning Room are about another fifty workers. Around a quarter of them are women. Most of the older men are ex-drivers, but there are also a lot of young men, fresh out of college. The older ones know all about driving. The younger ones come in knowing all about modern technology. Each Planner has his or her own battery of screens and computers and telephones.

Roly's drivers are now on a basic wage of £5.50–£6.40 an hour. 'Reasonable, when you think about it. No disrespect, but you don't need a lot of qualifications to be a lorry driver. If you work the maximum, from Monday to Saturday afternoon, taking the required breaks, you can put in seventy-two hours a week. But let's say you want your Saturdays off, so you just do sixty-eight hours. That comes to £435. Then you get £16 a night overnight allowance, that's another £80 a week, tax free. You also get £2.50 a day for meals. So you are making over £500 a week. It's not bad for 2001, is it, considering? The thing about working for Eddie Stobart Ltd is that you can be sure of these hours. You can rely on getting a decent wage, if you want to work.'

Roly's biggest problem each day, as a Planner, is finding a driver who will have the least distance to travel to his next point of collection. On his screen, there is an ever-present list of jobs to be done, given to all Planners by Customer Control. It changes all the time, grows and decreases, but is always there. A Planner has to be quick to grab the job that will best suit one of his own drivers, so he therefore has to know where each of his drivers is, at what stage and when he might be clear for the next job. Above him, there are Team Leaders, who make sure the Planners are fitting drivers to the most suitable jobs. Then there is Central Control, which makes sure all the Planners reach certain targets. 'Their job is to push us to the limits. Our job is to push our drivers to their limits.' Sounds pretty stressful all round.

Roly works from 6 a.m.–6 p.m., with a one-hour break. He does this for four days, then has four days off. For this he gets just under £20,000 a year. He thinks this is fair enough.

'I get just fifteen days paid holiday a year as, technically, I only work half the year. But if you think about it, I'm making £20,000 a year by working only five months and fifteen days a year. I don't have many friends who earn that for working half the year. I could do more if I wanted overtime. But that's enough for me. It means I get home each evening and I do have a decent social life.'

He doesn't miss the camaraderie of the road. In the Planning Room, he says there is quite a bit of banter and chitchat, though they all look tremendously serious, crouching over their screens, very professional in their Eddie Stobart uniforms. The men wear crisp, white shirts with the E.S. logo and company tie, the women wear E.S. blouses.

While Roly chats to me, he continues to work, watching his screen or breaking off to speak on the phone or radio to sort out problems. Someone at Milton Keynes has a flat tyre. A driver in Belgium has lost the details of his next job. A driver on the M6 is confused about whether he is going to Denisco at Faversham or Denisco at Evesham. Very easy to confuse those two places, says Roly: if a driver writes down his next job on a scrap of paper, he often can't read his handwriting. Or perhaps someone elsewhere in the chain has mixed up Faversham for Evesham. Get it wrong, as one driver had done recently, and it's a wasted seventy-six-mile drive.

'If a delivery load is worth £200 to us, it can end up costing four times that, if you think of all the things that can go wrong. Let's say for example we arrive late with a load of rice pudding. A lot of it will therefore miss its sell-by date and have to be dumped. Oh, time is money, when you're in haulage.'

Roly is one of those Planners, being situated at Daventry, who has to cope each day with the horrors of the M1, knowing that from 6–9 a.m. each weekday, and in the evening rush hour, he has to add an hour on every journey between Junction 10 on the M1 and the M25 interchange.

But, on the whole, Roly still enjoys his job. He doesn't mind wearing the company uniform: after all, he did so for years in the Army. He likes his colleagues. 'And it's a nice, comfortable office in which to work. Air-conditioned in summer. Warm in winter. The canteen's good. We've got fitted carpets on the floor and I have my own fitted locker with my own key.'

So how bad is it these days, for the workers at the coal face? I went to find the driver with whom I'd finally step inside an Eddie Stobart lorry. Billy Dowell had just arrived at the Daventry depot. I was a bit disappointed to see he was driving only the front part of his lorry, the articulated bit. It was big enough, handsome enough, Eddie Stobart liveried enough, and I could clearly see it was a Scania, registered in Europe, and its name was Margaret Helen, but it was like the front of a pantomime horse without the body, the head of a whale without the tail, hardly the full Monty

267

of a modern lorry. I didn't want to say anything, being well brought up. Presumably, Billy was aware he was trailerless, that he hadn't lost it on the M1.

Over a snack lunch provided by the staff restaurant, Billy explained that he'd just dumped his trailer in Birmingham and was now on the way to France, where he'd pick up another trailer. I could come with him all the way if I liked. I felt that a lift down the M1 would be quite sufficient.

Billy is fifty-one, comes from Carlisle and is now one of the long-serving Eddie Stobart drivers. His father was a lorry driver and, as a boy, it was all young Billy ever wanted to do. He had to wait till he was twenty-one to get his HGV licence so, till then, he did the next best thing which was to become an apprentice mechanic, working on lorries. At twenty-one, he joined Robsons Transport in Carlisle, where his dad was working. Young Billy drove Border Bandit. His dad's lorry was called Border Phantom.

Billy did mainly long-distance work, delivering Milo from the Nestlé factory at Dalston to all over the country. 'I didn't like it at first, even though I'd dreamt about it for so long. I remember setting off for Blythe one Sunday evening and thinking "What am I doing? Twenty-one years old, yet here I am, about to spend the whole week away from all my mates and girls."'

So, after two years, he gave up long distance and took a local job as a tipper-driver at Harrison's lime works, which gave him more time for courting. After he'd got married, he went back to long distance, working for Proudfoots who specialized in fresh fruit. 'I'd travel overnight to be at Covent Garden first thing to load up, which we did by hand, in those days.'

He then became an owner-driver, getting enough money together for a deposit on a Fiat lorry, for which he had to pay £570 a month. It was as an owner-driver that he first started working for Edward at Greystone Road. Edward gave him work when he could. As an owner-driver, no one had any responsibility for Billy when times were bad. Which they often were. 'I can remember in 1979, during the recession, days would pass with no work at all. Me and Edward would sit by the phone, just waiting. An exciting day would be three phone calls.

'But, even then, Edward struck me as a thinker. He had only six lorries when I first worked for him, yet he was thinking of selling them to buy six brand-new ones. He said that, when the recession was over and work started coming in, he'd need lorries that were reliable. I couldn't understand his thinking. I thought he was daft when he went ahead and bought them. But he was right. It paid off in the end.'

Unfortunately, it didn't for Billy. He worked for Edward until 1985, still as an owner-driver, then had to pack it in. 'I was declared bankrupt. I needed at least £1000 a week income to cover the payments on my lorry, the petrol and overheads, and leave myself something to support my wife and family, but some weeks, nothing was coming in at all.

'In the bankruptcy court, my debts were declared

at £13,000 and my assets at £9000. So, really, I went bust for just over £3000. The judge said he gave me credit for not having spent all the assets. I half wished I'd had, as I got treated just the same . . . .'

Billy then went back to being an employed driver, which he has done ever since. He did have a short spell in Stobart's traffic office, but gave it up to go back to driving, as he much prefers being outside. The day I met him, he had risen at 5 a.m. in Carlisle and had driven himself to the Kingstown depot where, at 5.45 a.m., he had picked up his lorry, already loaded with pet food, and had set off for the Friskies depot at Hams Hall, Birmingham.

He was now on his way to Portsmouth, where he would catch the night ferry to St Malo. From there, he would drive to Fontenay le Comte, near La Rochelle, and pick up a trailer stacked with two other trailer beds. He would then take them to the Boalloy works in Cheshire where they would be converted, customized and painted for the Eddie Stobart fleet. 'Sounds very romantic,' I said, 'catching the night ferry to St Malo.' 'Not when you've done it every week for the last five months,' Billy replied.

Around a thousand new trailers had been bought for the fleet and all had to be brought over from France. Billy's weekly trip takes him three days. 'It's nice being abroad, not so nice being away from home at night.' The rest of the week, he normally spends going to Scotland, which means he usually gets home to Carlisle on those days.

We set off after lunch. Normally, Billy works his way round via Daventry, heading for Southampton, but he agreed to take in a bit of the M1, so I could experience its full horrors. Climbing into his artic wasn't as easy as it looked; so much for my thoughts about it being puny. The metal steps are quite sheer, rising some six feet and, when you get inside, and on to the seat, you are about eight feet above ground level. The view is great, over and beyond all the pygmy private cars.

Billy's driving cab felt very spacious. Between me in the passenger seat and Billy at the wheel, there was room for a small but tasteful rug. We both sat on excellent seats, luxury finishing, in grey and black leather.

In front of Billy was a rounded console, more like an airline pilot's controls than a car's, with about twenty different, impressive-looking knobs and buttons. Above it were three storage places. Billy explained which was the radio and tape cassette (there for his personal pleasure and easy-listening) and which was the two-way radio (for work, connected to his Planner in Kingstown and, also, if needed, to any Eddie Stobart depot anywhere). Then there was his own private mobile phone on a stand, for him to ring home or the world at large.

Other facilities included cruise control, heated wing mirrors and something called a 'white-smoke limit switch'. When Billy's engine is idling in a confined space, he can switch it on and reduce exhaust emissions so that nobody nearby gets itchy eyes.

Behind us were double bunks, the width of the truck. I'd always assumed there was just one, but most Stobart lorries have two, in case they are travelling with another driver. At the end of the lower bunk is a little wardrobe space. Each bunk has a reading light, an alarm clock and a heater which can be controlled while lying down: jolly cosy.

Billy has not customized his cab, as Roly used to do. The only extra he has personally added is a kettle and cool-bag. He used to take his own TV but, these days, he hardly spends more than one night a week sleeping in his truck. On his French trips, he sleeps on the ferry itself. Once on board, his truck is locked away and it is illegal for him to go near it.

Together, we left the depot and headed for the M1, Junction 18, with Billy going through his gears as we negotiated two roundabouts. He has power steering but not automatic gears. He prefers gears as he likes to be in control. His Scania has eight gears, some other trucks have up to eighteen.

The view was excellent, even on the M1, even in very busy traffic. And it all felt very comfortable. The seats are air-cushioned, so rise and fall to fit the driver's body. They're also heated, for early morning cold starts.

'Drivers in the old days always ended up with dodgy backs. My dad today has disc trouble, after forty-five years as a lorry driver. When I started, the seats were metal, very hard, with a rigid back. You were always being thrown all over the cab. I took my dad for a ride the other day, to North Wales when I was on a job. He couldn't get over how comfortable the cabs are today, all the facilities. He thinks, of course, we've all gone soft . . . .'

The sun had come out while we'd been having lunch and had heated up the cabin, which has a very large area of glass, so I was soon feeling pretty warm. Billy had switched off all the heating not long after we'd left the depot, but it still seemed to be getting hotter. I asked if he had air-conditioning, but his Scania hasn't: that's about his only complaint. I could open the window if I liked, get some air. I said certainly not; I didn't want to hear the M1 traffic – it was bad enough looking at it.

It was remarkably quiet in the cab, quieter than in a normal car, but it did feel a bit shaky, with a swaying, side-to-side motion. Billy said this happened when the unit didn't have a trailer behind it; any bit of wind tended to catch it. Fully loaded, it didn't sway. All the same, it did feel very safe. In fact, I felt invincible, sitting so high, surrounded by so much solid metal, cruising at a steady, sensible speed. If any car messed with us, they'd definitely come off second best.

I noticed several drivers, while whizzing past, smiling and trying to turn their heads to spot the name of Billy's lorry. We passed three other Stobart lorries on the other side, going north. Billy gave them a wave, but said he didn't know any of them; there are just so many of them now.

While driving, Billy normally has on the radio for

BBC Radio 2. 'With age, that's the sort of music and chat I like, but I might tune in to Radio 4 for the *World at One*.' He used to have a CB radio, and could chat to other drivers on the road, but gave it up; he quite likes his own company. 'I talk to myself a lot. I sometimes have arguments, which of course I always win . . . .'

In Billy's brown leather hold-all, which lay behind me on his bunk, he had his overnight things, including two clean shirts – Eddie Stobart regulation ones, of course. 'I was taken aback when the uniform first came in. Having to wear a tie, that was the sticking point. I called Edward worse than scandalous for bringing it in. It did cause us a bit of abuse. You'd go into a transport caff and they'd mutter things: "Here's one of them bloody lot." They'd ask you daft questions. "Have you got to wear that tie all the time then?" "Not in bed," I'd reply. I'm used to it now; I quite like wearing it.'

Like all drivers, Billy gets issued with six shirts, two jumpers, two trousers, two ties, one rally jacket, one waterproof jacket, one hard hat, one pair of working gloves, one pair of working boots. 'I also take my own boiler-suit with me. It's to keep my uniform clean, just in case I have any dirty jobs. But that's rare. The days of having to tie down ropes and sheets are gone at Eddie Stobart's.

'I'm proud to work for Eddie Stobart. He has raised standards. I know other firms say he's a cost-cutter but, in thirty years of driving, I'd say he's no more a cost-cutter than anyone else.

'Some people knock the fan club. When they see the spotters hanging around the depot, they say "Get a life." I don't – I'm interested in trucks myself, so I can understand them. They're doing no harm. I enjoy it when I get spotted, when people come up and admire my truck, saying I look smart.

'I was recently going over Beattock, on the way to Glasgow, and had to go onto the weighbridge. There was a woman from the ministry there and she checks your tachograph and also what's called the ministry plate. When I opened it up for her, she said, "At least I can see it, which I usually can't for dirt. Typical Eddie Stobart vehicle, keeping it so clean." I was really pleased by that.

'I was on holiday with my wife in Greece last year. We got talking by the pool to some other couples, as you do, and they were fascinated when they learned I was an Eddie Stobart driver – couldn't stop asking me questions. They knew all about the women's names and wanted to know what my truck was called.

'I did get to name one myself once. It was called Lucy Hannah. I named it after my two grandmothers. This was a few years ago – I was just lucky that they hadn't got a Lucy Hannah.

'I've been to a wedding in my truck, and I've been in a film. Hold on a minute. See that Ford Granada ahead? Look how it's slowed down, for no apparent reason. I bet I can tell why . . . I bet he's on his mobile . . . .'

As we caught up, I strained my eyes and Billy was right. The driver was making a call. It was only when he finished that he zoomed ahead again. 'They slow down without thinking, because they take their foot off the pedal when they make a call. Sometimes they start swerving as well, so you have to take care.'

We'd been driving in the slow lane all the time. No hold-ups so far, no traffic jams, just gliding along at a steady 50 m.p.h. Billy only moves into the middle lane to overtake something really slow. Inside his lorry, there was a feeling of space and security and comfort and an absence of tension, despite the goings-on outside.

Lorry drivers like Billy seem able to remain calm and resigned. Otherwise, I suppose, they would never survive. 'I can often come back from a long day and Linda, my wife, knows not to talk to me for at least half an hour. I'll have a shower and a drink and chill out, then I'll be ready to talk.' By drink, Billy means a Coke. He neither smokes nor drinks alcohol. There is always a big plastic bottle of diet Coke on his side of the cabin, in a special holder.

The wedding he went to with his truck was for a member of the fan club who was getting married at Gretna Green – very handy for the depot at Kingstown. As a surprise, the groom had arranged to have a lorry named after his wife, Karen. In fact, he'd arranged the wedding round it.

'What a surprise she got when I turned up outside

the church in my lorry – and then she saw it was called Karen. She got in and I drove her to the hotel for the wedding reception. It was a great day. No, Eddie Stobart doesn't charge for that sort of thing. They always like to help fan-club members, if they can.'

Billy's film appearance took place at Castle Douglas, also in Scotland. 'I was just told one day by my Planner to be at Castle Douglas auction market at 9 a.m. I said, "What's the load?" He said, "No load. You're in a film."

'When I got there, I was given a two-way radio and told to wait till they were ready for me. I waited three hours, but I didn't mind – I watched what was going on. The film people had got the town centre closed off. Then, at 12 p.m., a voice on the radio said "Right, Mr Stobart, it's your turn."

'I had to drive round the town and drop this girl hitchhiker off at a certain place. I was supposed to have picked her up and dropped her off in Wales, but they were filming it in Scotland. I did it in three takes, which wasn't bad, was it?

'It was a British film called *Hold Back the Night* and it had Sheila Hancock in it. I've tried to find out about it, but no one seems to have heard of it. Funnily enough, there was a mention of it in the *Daily Mail* last week. They had a list called something like "Top Ten Turkeys", British films which had got lottery money and all failed. My only chance for real fame in life – and my film bombed!'

Transport of delight

It was a case of 'get me to the register office on time', when Lesley Shaw got married.

And, to make sure the blushing bride arrived promptly, groom Rob Jordan hit on the idea of using the most reliable form of transport – a Stobart vehicle.

Rob, a former lorry driver, decided on the eve of the wedding to ask the Carlisle depot to provide the unusual 'wedding car' for the trip to Gretna register office...and we were delighted to oblige.

Driver Brian Wilson and warehouse administrator Sarah Wilton even acted as witnesses for the happy couple (pictured), who rode up from Birmingham on Rob's motorbike for the ceremony.

High flyers Mark and Rachael get a real Eddie Stobart send off...

Airtours pilot Mark Burtonwood and his bride Rachael Jones received a very special card on their wedding day.

Best man, and fellow pilot Lee Bennet, wrote to ask if we could send Stobart fan Mark a special card on his wedding day. Our artist couldn't resist coming up with a cartoon featuring a swooping jet and a Stobart truck, which was duly signed by Edward Stobart as a unique memento of their special day.

Memo to all Stobart drivers... If you see a Boeing 737 flying low, and keeping pace with your vehicle, slow down, it's only Mark trying to get your fleet number!

In real life, Billy never accepts hitchhikers. 'You can't be sure today who you might be picking up.' In the old days, he often did, such as soldiers from Catterick, taking them across to Cumbria.

Most weeks, Billy puts in from 60–65 hours. After tax, his take-home pay is usually just over £300. He also gets his meal and overnight allowance. In the UK, an overnight is £18 but it's £27 for abroad, so his French work pays better. 'And I think you get treated better abroad. The car parks don't charge night-parking, which they mostly do in Britain now. In our motorway service stations, there's so few facilities. You can't have a shower, the way you can in France. If you want a wash and shave here, you have to strip down to your waist in the public lavatories. Which isn't very brilliant.

'French food is better and cheaper as well. You can get a four-course meal at a French Routier for £5. Here, you can pay £5 just for a plate of fish and chips. Abroad, drivers don't do any dirty work. No loading at all; they're chauffeurs, really. We don't do as much as we used to, but I still often have to open the curtains and help unload stuff.

'In Britain, you also have to expect poor treatment from the supermarkets. They try to wind you up. "You'll probably be here all day, driver," so somebody with a clip board will tell you. You get wiser with age and don't rise to it. I'll say, "That's okay, there's another day tomorrow." Or I'll say, "That's fine, I'll just have a sleep, you wake me when you want us." That usually fettles them. It's funny how often they then come back in half an hour.

'They do it because they expect an outburst from you. I did used to get angry with them, when I was younger. Perhaps I should have an outburst more often. They say it's good for your ticker, to let off steam, but I don't these days. Driving does get easier with age. You've seen it all, don't get as worked up. The young drivers can't take it; they just want an easy 9–5 job, get home every night.

'I like the freedom of it, being in charge of my own lorry, all on my own. You do have more contact today, now they can get you on the blower all the time, changing your orders. I've had a few set-tos with the odd Planner, shouting back. But, basically, you are still out on your own, making your own decisions – I like that. I do enjoy my own company, it doesn't worry me being alone. Part of everyone is a loner.

'Yes, of course, the traffic has got far worse. Often, on a road like this, all you're doing is driving from one traffic jam to the next. They blame us of course, the lorry drivers. But I don't: I blame the cars. There's just so many of them today, far more than there's ever been. Just think how many folks you know who are two-car families today. Well then.

'Driving's got more complicated as well, all the new, technical stuff, all the laws, all the paperwork. As a professional, I don't allow myself to get stressed by it all. It's the young who kick against it and pack it in. I love going to Scotland, or the West Country, out in the open countryside. You get good views, see the seasons changing. I had a grand run for many years once a week up to Oban. I did like that.

'There is a satisfaction in driving. People think it's just a matter of going from A to B. It's more than that. You are responsible for an expensive lorry and a valuable load and have to get it there in time and safely. When you've done it, you do feel a sense of achievement. I'll see it out, till I retire . . .'

Before I left Billy and his lorry, I asked what his routine would be tonight. The first stage of his trip, to Portsmouth, would take him about two-and-a-half hours. He was making good time so should be there well before 8.30 p.m., when the ferry departed.

He'd drive on, check everything, lock up, then go and find his cabin. If, by chance, there was another

Stobart driver on board, and he'd know if there was by then, they'd share a cabin and have a meal together.

After his meal, he would retire to his cabin and read for about an hour – he finds a bit of reading usually helps him to nod off. This time he was reading a book about Henry VIII and his six wives. He has been sea-sick on a rough crossing in the past, so was hoping for a calm night. In the morning, he would have a croissant and coffee, then hang around the deck, till arrival. He would not be allowed near his lorry until they docked. Then he'd be off, heading for La Rochelle.

His trailer would be ready and loaded for him. The two new trailer beds would be stacked, one on top of the other, like a car-transport carrier. All he would have to do is couple it and strap them together. On arriving back at the ferry, he would check for any illegal passengers, any refugees who might somehow have smuggled themselves on board. Not much chance, as on these trips his trailer has open sides and everything can be seen. But he would check under-neath his vehicle as well, just in case. Then, back in England, he would do his drop-off in Cheshire and then head back to Carlisle. Before the circuit began once again.

Billy and his wife have two sons, both in their twen-ties. Neither wants to be a lorry driver and neither has any interest in lorries or haulage. They prefer to work with computers. 'I'm pleased, in a way. I achieved my ambition in life: I wanted to do the same job as my father. And I did. But I'd like my sons to come up with their own ambitions, then achieve them. I suppose it's because I'd like a better life for them.'

THE FIRM TODAY – AND ITS FUTURE

There are today four divisions, four separate departments in the Eddie Stobart Group which, altogether, employ 2600 staff and have a turnover of £150 million. It was only the haulage side that had a poor time in 2000, but this is still the largest division. Eddie Stobart Ltd, which is the British haulage side, had a turnover of £100 million. The European haulage side, which is called Eddie Stobart International Ltd, was responsible for another £12 million a year.

While haulage accounts for two divisions, the third division is storage, meaning the use of Eddie Stobart UK warehouses. That brings in £20 million a year. The fourth division is called Process Management, and is currently worth £10 million a year.

This began around 1990, when the company was having problems with Metal Box in Carlisle, which was unable to load Eddie Stobart lorries twenty-four hours a day. 'They said they didn't have the staff or facilities for night-time work,' says Edward. 'So I said, "I'll send in my own men, at our expense, to do it." It was vital for us to keep up the flow of our deliveries.'

They sent thirty of their staff into Metal Box, to load up their lorries. This was followed by sending in fork-lift trucks and various other machines, till they had taken over the whole loading system.

Today, there are Eddie Stobart staff working in factories and warehouses all over the country, inside the premises of other firms. 'We now charge for this,' says Edward, 'not a huge amount, but it helps our business generally. We even sell Process Management to firms we don't even deal with, such as Pirelli.' It's a new and growing area for the company, all because they thought laterally, in order to solve a particular problem.

Eddie Stobart Ltd still hasn't got a press officer or an advertising department. Most firms of its size have an in-house spokesman, who answers calls, and a PR consultant who organizes campaigns and product launches, or who just gives expensive advice.

If you ring up, you won't get Edward, who still shies away from all phone calls from strangers, but you might get Deborah Rodgers, his PA. She works from Kingstown, which now covers an area of over thirty acres, having endlessly grown and expanded since father Eddie built the first warehouse there in 1980. Like Daventry, it runs twenty-four hours a day, seven days a week, with the same facilities, departments and warehouses. It doesn't, however, have its own barber's shop, which Daventry has, where drivers and other staff can get a haircut at greatly reduced prices; Edward does like to see his staff looking trim and smart.

It's interesting to hear the receptionists at Kingstown answering the phones. Sometimes they answer, saying Eddie 'Stow-bart', with two long syllables, and sometimes they say 'Sto'butt', with a short and a long syllable, which is how most people in Cumbria pronounce it. Apparently, the different pronunciation depends on who they are talking to: when dealing with non-Cumbrians, they usually say 'Stow-bart'. If it's a local call, then they'll say 'Sto'butt'. Both Edward and Deborah will more often say 'Stow-bart' these days, national pronunciation having become the norm.

As the firm's unofficial spokesperson, Deborah deals with all media enquiries, from TV companies wanting an Eddie Stobart lorry to appear at a certain time on a certain stretch of motorway, to giving out statements and quotes when Eddie Stobart Ltd, or the haulage industry generally, is in the news, such as at times of fuel or road crises.

'I've had to learn from experience how to handle such things,' Deborah explains, 'to see what it is they're after, where they're coming from. They do get a story into their head and don't listen to you. They deliberately bark up the wrong tree, because, otherwise, they would lose a story.

'For example, during the last fuel crisis, when our lorries were off the road during the blockade and we were losing a lot of income, they wanted to run a story saying that Eddie Stobart now made more money from toy lorries than running the real lorries. I could see where they were coming from, and it was an amusing story, but it wasn't the true picture – the toys are just a very small sideline. But they wrote it nonetheless, giving the impression it was true, that it was our major earner. It then goes into the cuttings archives and gets quoted for ever.'

Like Edward, Deborah has had to pick up her expertise and wisdom as she's gone along, with no one to teach her or train her. You can see how it started, the widening of her role, giving her the sort of duties she would never have acquired in a normal firm. Edward still doesn't like answering the phone or ringing people up unless he knows them really well. He depends on those he already knows, regardless of their qualifications, and is willing to trust and promote them, give or take the odd stern word. Deborah has had her share of being shouted at over the years.

Amongst her other duties, Deborah looks after the firm's charitable work, which Edward is very keen on. The company has a trust called the Woodlands Trust which, in 1999, gave away £350,000, putting it in the top twenty of all firms in the north of England who contribute to charity.

But Deborah's main job, apart from looking after Edward, has been the promotions side of the business, meaning the fan club and the merchandising. This is the bit she's enjoyed most. 'The growth of the fan club has been amazing. I still get surprised by the national attention it receives. When the club first started getting mentioned on local radio, BBC North-East did a little piece about it. They interviewed people in the street in Carlisle about the Eddie Stobart fan club. What was interesting was how many people in Carlisle hadn't even heard of Eddie Stobart.'

Deborah didn't know much about the firm either, when she first joined in 1987, nor did she often meet Edward during her first couple of years. 'He seemed very shy. We didn't have a lot of conversation, even when I started working for him and shared the same office.'

Now Deborah knows a lot about him, when to keep quiet, when not to say things, when to bring up certain topics. She is a calm, efficient, steadying influence, one of those people in the firm whom Edward depends on to give an honest opinion if perhaps he is getting carried away. Not, of course, that he will necessarily take much notice. 'I like to drive without brakes,' so Edward says. 'Others are there to slow me down.'

Deborah has a good idea of what Edward's strengths are. 'His eye for detail, that is very strong. And he's a good organizer: when he's involved in something, he's on top of every aspect. Sometimes he will go on a bit much, asking me all the time if something's been done, if I've understood, till I want to say "OK, Edward, we've got the message!" But, at the same time, he is a very good delegator. He can let people just get on with things, if he trusts them.' As for any weaknesses Edward may have, Deborah only names one. 'Impatience, I suppose. He always wants things done yesterday.'

Edward has no other personal staff, no assistants, no chauffeur. Unlike most captains of industry, he doesn't arrive trailing clouds of glory or assorted minions. Sir Richard Branson is laid-back, as we all know, and wears pullovers not suits, asking to be addressed by all his staff as Richard. Yet even he floats about with an entourage, rarely seen without his press advisor nearby, or an assistant in the background.

Edward often appears a rather isolated figure, almost in his own world, while Eddie Stobart Ltd, the company, whizzes away under its own steam in the background. Edward agrees with this impression: 'I let them get on with it. There would have to be something seriously wrong for them to come and tell me. It would then be an admission of some sort of failure, that they'd let themselves down by not being able to cope.'

Edward has no side, no pretentions, no airs and graces. At work, he is always in a neat, dark suit and sparkling white shirt, looking rather stiff, embarrassed and uncomfortable. He says he doesn't actually like wearing a suit, but it has to be worn as long as he is at work.

On meeting Edward, his stammer is noticeable at first, as he hesitates over certain words and sentences. However, once he gets into the flow of things, he becomes more fluent, especially when it comes to contracts, business and property deals. He is not so fluent, however, when it comes to personal information or anything that smacks of philosophy, of business wisdom. Edward doesn't do deep: he just does – a doer not a talker. 'I'm the thinker in the firm, the developer of new ideas.'

What he is currently thinking about is Europe, closely followed by ideas on property. He has recently spotted a new bit of land which could make another warehouse. 'I can always see the profit in property. It gets harder to see the profit in trucks. I think our future growth will be in Europe. It's where we can expand. I don't think we can grow much bigger in Britain, not in haulage.

'The really big haulage firms, Exel and TDG, have got the big contracts tied up. They've got Boots, W.H. Smiths, Kelloggs, Heinz, Marks & Spencer: all the big companies we have never worked for. Originally, we were too small to be asked to tender. Now, when we could, they have got complicated contracts which would be hard for us to break up. I think, of course, they've done a lot of these deals just to keep us out. Most of them are tied in with property, leaseholds, warehouses, distribution systems – all of which would be very difficult to unravel. They would be hard to get rid of, and expensive, like getting rid of a wife . . . .'

Despite it being a tough business, Edward has no regrets about having chosen haulage rather than property or warehouses. 'No, that's where we've come from. That's what got us where we are today. I can't see us getting out of haulage. But we'll get into other areas as well.'

Edward says he often finds himself thinking back these days to the early years, to people who helped him along the way. 'Norman Bell, our first driver at Hesket, was like a second father to me. He would never miss a day's work: if his vehicle required maintenance, this had to be carried out at night and Norman would stand over you to make sure it was fit for work the next day. He was so honest and loyal and very hard working – I learned so many practical things from him. He was no good on theory but was passionate about things like washing down your vehicle. He also taught me how to get out of bed in the morning.

'Then there was Clive Richardson. He was more of a friend, as he was only slightly older than me. He was also one of our drivers at Hesket. But he wanted to do long-distance work, which we didn't have at the time. So he left, but he was always to come back, when we grew and got more work. But, tragically, he died in his twenties, after a brain tumour, and never returned.

'I could mention so many other names from the early days, who helped start the business off. Without such people, the business would not be what it is today. We're all in this together. That's how it's been in the past and will be in the future.'

One of Edward's general aims for the future is something he claims he's always tried to do: improve the nature and standing of the haulage industry. Over the next five years, in the UK as well as in Europe, he hopes efficiency will continue to improve and haulage generally will have an even better name.

As for his own company, ever since the name of his firm entered the national consciousness, Edward says he's been thinking about how to take advantage of it. 'We don't manufacture anything. And I don't know anything about manufacturing. All we offer is a service, yet we've got a name which is recognized everywhere now. I keep thinking could we stick that name onto something else, on a product perhaps? If so, on what? And would it sell?

'Virgin has used its good name to stick it on other things, such as Virgin Cola. We could have Eddie Stobart Cola, couldn't we? It would get recognition but it would be a pretty daft thing to do as it would mean competing against our own customers, like Coke and Pepsi. So I wouldn't do that would I?'

Edward has therefore decided that, should they transplant their name elsewhere, it will have to be on something where his present customers are not involved. So that rules out food and drink and even pet food. Eddie Stobart dog biscuits would surely have gone down well, at least with the fan club.

One idea he's been thinking about is a chain of small transport hotels. They would be very smart and clean, just like Eddie Stobart vehicles and drivers, and they'd be highly efficient and well organized, just like Eddie Stobart Ltd. They would be providing a service, not a product, which is the business they are already in. Edward has strong views on hotels, having stayed in so many over the last fifteen years as he's gone round the country. And his main view is: he hates them. He's found few he really likes. So that might help him to create a new sort of hotel.

'But I'm still thinking about it. I'd want to do it out of surplus cash, out of our back pocket, when we have say four or five million to spare, then we could set up our first hotel. I don't want to borrow to get it started. I want to do it all by ourselves. If it works, we'll own and control it all, just like this firm. If it doesn't work, then we haven't lost much.

'At this moment we don't have the spare cash and, anyway, I'm concentrating my energies on the new management structure, getting that running properly. After that, we'll see. But I am keen to try something new in the near future.'

As for the longer-term future of the firm, Edward has no intention, at present, of changing the ownership of the firm in any way, by bringing in new capital or new shareholders. He expects himself and William to remain as the sole owners.

'Once I get to over fifty or so, well, I might have to think about it. There are no obvious family members at present in the next generation who might take over. So, yes, I might then have to think of selling some shares, bring in new people, new capital for investment. Or we could go public. I don't know what I'll do. I haven't decided yet. Except to decide I don't need to make any decision for the next five years.'

EXPERT WITNESSES

Eddie Stobart Ltd has been watched by the general public for the last ten years with a rather amateur, affectionate and, at times, soppy and romantic eye. There are, however, those inside the industry who have been observing progress for the last twenty years with a rather colder, beadier stare. They have their own professional, informed views on how the company got to its present position and where they think it could or might go in the future.

One such industry insider is Jack Semple, Technical Editor of *Motor Transport* magazine, who wrote such a laudatory feature on Edward, back in 1992. 'There is no doubt,' says Jack, 'that the most unpopular haulier, amongst the private, as well as the publicly owned firms, has been Eddie Stobart . . . I'm only telling you what the rest of the haulage industry thinks. They think it, of course, because of the success of the firm and because of the way Edward has aggressively achieved his success.

'I speak to many local haulage firms out in the provinces. They're always telling me how Eddie Stobart has outbid them on jobs. Let's say a firm in Exeter quotes £300 for taking a load from Exeter up to London. That's the best price he thinks he can do it for. He'll then reckon on getting £150 for some sort of load back to Exeter, if he can find it.

'Eddie Stobart comes along and quotes £225 for Exeter to London, thus undercutting the little local firm. But he'll also be able to quote £225 for a return load, from London to Exeter. He knows he can get this somewhere, because he has a national network, with jobs coming in all the time.'

Of course, this is just normal business. The total for the round trip, in this hypothetical case, comes to the same for each haulage firm. Eddie Stobart Ltd doesn't run at a loss, by under-pricing: it just runs on tight margins. Jack agrees, 'Yes, but it upsets the local haulier who loses a London job. He can't do it cheaper, because he hasn't got a national set-up to secure him the return load. I was speaking to a haulier in Yorkshire only yesterday who has thirty lorries. He dreads Eddie Stobart competing with him on jobs; with his thousand lorries and national network of depots, Stobart will always outbid him.

'Local hauliers don't fear the PLC companies, the big boys like Exel with four thousand lorries. PLCs like to do deals with other PLCs – they tend not to compete with the small, local firms. They can't make the small jobs pay: but Eddie can. He's done very well to get some of the big contracts, and compete with the PLCs while still taking on smaller jobs. Eddie has always been willing to be flexible.

'His greatest single achievement, which is how he's been able to compete with the big boys as well as the small ones, is to create a national network, yet control it centrally. The old BRS of forty years ago had a national network, but they were split into regions and failed to get each depot to work together. They had them competing, instead, with their own cost-centres. They didn't help each other: you need central control to make the most of the whole system.

'With central control, you can double-shift your lorries, making sure they are working twenty-four hours a day. Local firms can't do that, nor can regional depots either, if they work separately, as many still do.

'The people who say they resent Eddie for undercutting them and taking their business will, at the same time, admit they admire what he has done. TNT was the haulage firm of the eighties for what they did for the parcel business. Eddie Stobart has been the haulage firm of the nineties. Not just in his commercial success, but in presenting clean vehicles to the public. He did help raise standards all round in the haulage industry.

'He's also a good negotiator, very good at doing deals. He usually manages to get prices well down when he's buying trailers or leasing trucks. He's very acute. The result of being a national name is that customers are pleased and even keen to do business with him. They think it reflects well on them.

'He's also been smart in keeping things simple. If you look at his fleet, you'll find few variations amongst his vehicles. They have a basic wheel-base and a similar h.p., so any truck can pull any trailer. He keeps things regular, disciplined, simple.

'He's always managed to work, so far, on low margins. That's another achievement, although it's a source of complaint from other hauliers. Most important of all, his service is first-class. Personally, I have nothing but admiration for him. I'm just reporting how his smaller rivals feel . . . .'

Jack points out that haulage has always been a tough industry to do well in, or even survive in. 'Josiah Bass was very big in the packhorse business, back in the 1700s, but decided to get out and go into brewing instead, where he did much better. Lord Hanson has always said that everything he knows about business he learned from his early days in road haulage.

'It's always been seen as an unattractive industry. That's one of the reasons why, today, the big PLC companies hardly use the term "road haulage". The buzz word is now "logistics", though hardly anyone outside the industry knows what it means – the PLCs think that "road haulage" has negative connotations. It's good that Eddie Stobart still has "Express Road Haulage" on their trucks. The other private haulage firms are pleased he's done that.'

In Jack's own private life, he's also found a negative image of haulage. Whenever he meets people at parties and tells them he writes about road transport, they tend to change the subject. 'It's a shame, really, that so few are interested. Road haulage is the engine of growth for every economy. And it's a huge employer.

There are 400,000 trucks out there, with about the same number of drivers, plus all the management, back-up staff, ancillary industries. I reckon there must be one million people dependent on road haulage, yet people are hardly aware of the industry.

'They are, of course, aware of Eddie: he's the only one. I've been noticing recently how Eddie Stobart trucks often appear in advertisements, on billboards or TV commercials. If a setting is, say, a motorway, or something to do with travelling, they'll plonk in an Eddie Stobart truck just to establish it. I'm sure Edward is not aware of it, and he's certainly not paying for it. He's got to the stage where he gets product placement for free, which other firms would pay good money for.'

As for the future, Jack is not sure if Edward will succeed in Europe the way he has done in the UK. 'Many have tried and become unstuck. People like Willi Betz and Norbert Dentressangle, each with their 3–4000 lorries, are just so big and powerful. I've met Norbert, and his father. Their own story is much the same as Eddie Stobart's. Norbert's father began with just six lorries.

'Betz and Dentressangle have huge contracts and will make sure their positions are not eroded. Betz uses only Mercedes trucks, so they will not let him lose ground to an outsider. Renault supply Dentressangle and will support them. The British PLCs have tried in Europe, but not done much. It would be marvellous if Eddie cracked Europe. He might do better than the

PLCs, as they tend not to be as efficient as the private firms. But I'm not sure he'll do it . . . .'

But Jack thinks Eddie Stobart might have one small advantage in Europe: the look of the lorries. 'The concept of livery is not known in Europe – Betz's colour is blue and Norbert's is red, but neither does anything elaborate or fancy. Nobody in Europe or the USA has drivers in uniform with collars and ties. So Eddie's trucks might catch on in Europe, as he has done here.'

One of the big boys, the giant PLC companies, is the Transport and Development Group, now known as TDG. Its lorry fleet in the UK is twice as big as Stobart's, with 2000 trucks, while its worldwide staff numbers 7500 and its turnover in 2000 was £424 million. They do a lot of complex work for Sainsburys, Safeway, ICI, Nestlé: some of the big customers Edward has never managed to crack.

Alan Cole was the Chief Executive of TDG from 1990–1999, during which time he kept a close eye on the rise of Eddie Stobart. 'They were a rival, in a sense, but we did the difficult things, like distribute frozen food to two hundred Sainsbury supermarkets from a central site.

'Eddie Stobart's work was a bit simpler, with more full loads from A to B. So, when we heard about their growth, and then the existence of their own fan club, it seemed totally bizarre. It was a mystery to the rest of us how they had done it.

'We knew they had low management costs and

good-quality lorries, which they kept very smart, but we always thought they might get ahead of themselves, having too many leased lorries for not enough business.

'The only explanation we could think of was the financial climate of the times. In the mid and late eighties, it had been pretty easy to get the finance to take on extra vehicles and open new depots. That was how we assumed they were doing it.

'It was true that, in the private sector, things had been fairly unsophisticated for a long time. It was very out-of-date. Old Jimmy would be the traffic manager, scribbling on bits of paper and sticking them on the wall. It didn't take the smartest of brains to run a small-time family haulage firm.

'All the same, we still couldn't understand the attention Eddie Stobart was suddenly receiving. The gossip in the industry was that he worked his drivers very hard and pushed the hours and speeds to the limit. No, I never heard any rumour that he was part of a Mormon plot. The one I heard was that he was being backed by Arabs.

'It was all pure gossip, of course, and, in the end, none of it stuck. We could all see he was running an excellent business. When he received the Haulier of the Year award at the Grosvenor in 1992, we all had to agree he deserved it.'

As for the future, Alan Cole thinks Edward would be daft to try and go public; the haulage industry is not considered financially very attractive at present. 'I think, in the short term, he'll be pushed to keep on growing. The price of diesel keeps increasing and the diesel fuel escalator – in which you do a deal with a customer and agree to share any increases during the term of the contract – doesn't always work. The haulage company seems to end up paying most of it. The second problem is the driver shortage. I can't see that improving in the near future. It's not a glamorous job any more, if it ever was.'

Alan Cole thinks transport hotels or transport caffs are not a bad idea, as it's related to Edward's business. 'He should also think of refuelling depots. The main thing is he should not move very far from lorries. He's built up a good business and must stick to it.'

Professor Martin Christopher is Professor of Logistics at Cranfield University, one of the leading academics in the field. He admits that the word 'logistics' is often misused, to tart up the image of transport. 'Ten years ago, you would get "Joe Bloggs Transport". Then it became "Joe Bloggs Logistics". Now you are getting "Joe Bloggs – Your Partner in the Supply Chain". Meanwhile, it's still the same old Joe Bloggs, driving a truck.

'It's also true that people now go on about "the logistics of a meeting", when all it means is what time they will have coffee. It can be a piece of confusing terminology.

'But what we mean by logistics is planning the whole supply-chain, from beginning to end. The in-flow and the out-flow – not just transporting goods but looking after every stage: supplying management and systems, being able to know why and when demand increases and responding to it. A firm like Exel will do everything in the chain, take it all over, leaving a manufacturer to manufacture.'

Professor Christopher was interested to hear that Eddie Stobart had been doing some of this years ago, when he first moved some of his workers into a Metal Box factory to load his lorries, without ever knowing he had moved out of lorries and into logistics. He doesn't know much about the firm personally, though he admires what Edward has done. 'The big boys are pulling further away from the smaller, private firms all the time. I think he was very clever to spot a niche. He probably now dominates the soft-drinks area. I don't know whether he stumbled into it or worked it out for himself.'

'I sense that people like working for him. He has created a family atmosphere, people feel committed to the brand, the way people feel committed to Branson.

'The industry is particularly tough at present because of the power of the retailers. They are under pressure themselves to save pennies and, in turn, they squeeze their suppliers. Margins are getting smaller all the time.

'The "open-book" system has also made it harder. This is when say a retailer, like Sainsburys, takes on a transport firm on a cost-plus basis. A certain percentage profit is agreed at the beginning, but the transport firm has to open all its books, so everything is known and seen. It means the transport firm hasn't much room to manoeuvre.'

Despite times being so tough, Professor Christopher feels people would still be interested in buying into Eddie Stobart, should Edward ever wish to sell. 'Oh, sure. You might buy him just for his clients, or to get your hands on his fleet, merge them with yours and make cost savings. Or just because you want to take him out of the market. There could be lots of reasons to buy Eddie Stobart.'

As for Edward diversifying into something new, Professor Christopher agrees that this is worth looking into. 'He has built up a very good brand name, so it would be worthwhile exploring, but he should not move out of his core competitiveness – and he shouldn't do it on his own. He needs to find a partner with skill in that area, let them find the properties, let them set them up, but using his name and perhaps a bit of his money.

'Personally, I would have thought a chain of good-quality transport caffs would do better than a chain of transport hotels. From my experience, there are still too many greasy-spoon caffs around.'

One of the leading city analysts in logistics is Clive Anderson of Merrill Lynch. He has been fifteen years in the field, so has observed the rise of Eddie Stobart, but has had no need to do much work on them professionally, as they are a private firm. Fund managers are not much interested, when they can't invest.

'I don't know what Eddie Stobart's thinking has been,' says Clive, 'but he's probably been quite clever in not trying to compete with the big PLCs. If you want to tender for the big contracts, like Marks & Spencer, you have to understand the problems of M&S, analyse their customers, know exactly what they are doing and how. The more complex the supply chain, the more advanced the IT department to do this. Pitching against the big boys can be very expensive. The PLCs have large resources and big financial umbrellas. If you don't win these tenders, it can be very costly.

'My perception is that Eddie Stobart has decided to concentrate on the parts he can supply very efficiently, the basic, simple jobs. In a way, Eddie Stobart is the Prêt à Manger of haulage. Making sandwiches was always seen as a very simple thing to do, but Prêt à Manger set out to make the very best sandwiches. That's what Eddie Stobart has done. He's taken one sector of the market and done it very well.'

As well as hearing the viewpoint of outside analysts, such as Clive, it is interesting to hear what Eddie Stobart's customers have to say about the firm. After all, the firm depends on them, and experience has made them inside experts. They observe and deal with Stobart from day to day, while at the same time knowing all about the rival firms.

One of the firm's top three contracts is with Coca-Cola Schweppes, currently worth £10 million pounds a year. Their connection with Stobart began in 1987. General Manager of bulk distribution for Coca-Cola Enterprises is Mike Griffiths. 'It was around the time of the merger between Coca-Cola and Schweppes. Coke had been using only BRS while Schweppes used a mixture of spot-hire hauliers as well as their own fleet.

'When we all came together, I wanted to reduce the number of hauliers we used, find a simpler system, but we needed hauliers who were flexible. In our business, demand is very seasonal: it's like ice-cream. At certain times of the year, you can sell more than you can possibly produce. Eddie Stobart was already transporting empty cans and plastic items from Metal Box to our bottling plants. It made sense to load them up with our goods on their return journey.'

This version of events differs from the recollections of Edward himself, and others in the firm, who say they were always hounding and pestering companies to give them return loads. But Mike Griffiths is sure it was his idea. 'No, my memory is I suggested it to them. The upshot was we started using them. And we found they were best suited to our requirements because they could cope with having to be flexible. A lot of hauliers tend to be, how shall I put this without criticizing, one-speed hauliers. But Edward himself was smart. With the demise of BRS, he took the opportunity to move into areas where they had been strong.

'Today, they are our biggest haulier, the one we use most. I admire them for the standard of their vehicles and equipment, for their efficiency and attention to detail.

'There was one little thing Edward spotted, which other hauliers had missed or weren't bothered about. On the backs of trailers, you get bars to lock the trailer. When they're closed, the bars obscure the lettering, so you can't read the name of the firm. What Edward did was get them to build the bars into the bodywork so, when closed, you can't see the bars. That was a clever little touch: typical of Edward. Overall, I think what they have achieved in the last ten years has been awesome. Yes, I'd use that word.'

Mike Griffiths is aware that, along with success, Eddie Stobart has had a number of enemies. 'They still have them: it's started again. Not a week goes by without someone in the industry telling me confidentially that Stobart's are going bust. It's all nonsense of course.

'The usual thing people say is that Stobart's got jobs by reducing rates. This possibly happened. But I think a more common reason for jealousy is that Stobart's became fashionable. Directors of firms would tell their managers to give work to Stobart's, because they'd heard about them, were impressed by their reputation.

'I think they were also bad-mouthed because they were a provincial firm. People knew they came from Carlisle. So, when they moved into Kent or Devon, local hauliers would say: "What are these Cumbrians doing down here, we don't want them stealing our local business: they're foreigners." People don't hate

PLC firms in the same way; they don't know where they've come from or who they are.

'There is also a belief in our industry that firms which rise quickly will disappear just as quickly. I can remember firms like John Dee from the north-east, William Nutter from Manchester or Hilton Transport. These firms had phenomenal growth, and some became PLCs. Now they've gone.

'I don't think it will happen with Stobart: they have a very sound business. The cuts Edward has made, reducing overheads, had to be done. But now they've made them. Their warehousing side is very successful and valuable and I'm sure the haulage side will be making good profits again next year.

'I think they can succeed in Europe. Their tremendous attention to detail and absolute integrity will bring them a lot of work. But there's still a lot of scope for them in the UK. I think that's probably where they should concentrate at present.'

THE STOBARTS TODAY

John Stobart, father of Eddie and grandfather of Edward, died in 1997, aged ninety-four. By that time, he had seen all four of his sons create businesses bearing the Stobart name. First son Eddie gave the nation Eddie Stobart Ltd. The other three built up purely local firms, though thriving businesses nonetheless.

John Stobart never moved away from the Hesket Newmarket and Caldbeck area where he first farmed. He spent his last few years at a residential home in Caldbeck, and his funeral was at Caldbeck church, attended by seventy-one members of the Stobart family.

The success of his large family has been remarkable, as is the fact that almost all of them today, two generations later, are still living in the same area. Three of John's four daughters married local farmers and one married a joiner. Country folks, you see, they stick to their roots.

Like Edward and William, the other present-day Stobarts don't care for personal publicity, preferring to go about their businesses quietly and unostentatiously.

Founder of Stobart empire

John Stobart, of Hesket Newmarket, aged 94

● **JOHN STOBART:** Businessman and devout Christian

YEARS of hard work, based upon unswerving Christian principles, enabled John Stobart to lay the secure foundation upon which members of his family were able to build their own thriving businesses.

So, today, we have a national road haulage concern, a flourishing farm feeds manufacturing and retailing business, a busy garage company and a well-known lubricants and fuels enterprise, all proudly bearing the Stobart name.

Without John Stobart, who has died aged 94, none of this would have been possible.

Born into a farming family at Howgill, near Sebergham, he worked there until he moved to nearby Bank Dale Head in 1930, armed with his strong Christian beliefs and very little else. At only 33 acres, his farm was small and he arrived with just £300 to his name.

In his first year he made a profit of just £5, but the important thing was that he kept the business afloat in hard times, when others were going under.

With farming going through a dismal period, he branched out into contract work, which entailed using a horse and cart on Cumberland County Council business and eventually, in 1946, he was able to buy his own tractor, a Ferguson.

This meant he was able to go into threshing and other agricultural contract activities within a 30-mile area around his home, and eventually, in 1960, he moved into farm feeds manufacture.

This company, now owned and run by a later Stobart generation, is thriving and still expanding.

However, despite his toil and hard-won success, Mr Stobart was known for something he considered far more important than business enterprise – his life long commitment to Christianity.

He never worked on the Sabbath and, while others would read books or newspapers, he would read the Bible. He was a Methodist local preacher from the age of 19 until he was into his 80s and he was a founder member of the Gideon Bible Society's work in Cumberland.

He was also a member and trustee of the Scripture Readers' Trust, set up by Wigton philanthropist, George Moore.

One of the high points of the year for Mr Stobart was to join thousands of other Christians from all over the country at the Keswick Convention and he went every year for most of his life.

His first visit was made when he was 12, in a horse-drawn cart to Troutbeck station and then by train. to Keswick, in time for the morning Bible readings.

His last visit was made, only a few years ago, in his wheel chair.

Although a staunch Methodist, Mr Stobart still had an ecumenical turn of mind and great respect for Christians of other denominations. So it was somehow fitting that his funeral service should take place in the Anglican church of St Mungo, at Caldbeck. The building was packed and, among the congregation, were 71 members of Mr Stobart's family.

He leaves his widow, four sons and four married daughters. All live and work locally except for one, who has moved to Sedbergh.

They are proud of what Edward has done, as well as amazed and a bit stunned, but they don't want to appear to be riding on his coat tails in any way. Edward is also rather proud of what the family has done. 'Aye, they've all got good businesses. None of them have gone bust . . . .' Which is an achievement in itself, considering they are mostly in agricultural-related enterprises. Edward today might think haulage is tough, with the fuel prices and driver shortages, but he did well to get out of the agricultural world when he did. The small-holders and hill farmers of the northern fells have had a terrible time these last ten years, often making no profit at all, even before BSE and the foot-and-mouth epidemics came along.

The latter had a serious effect on the cattle-food business of Edward's Uncle Ronnie – Eddie's younger brother. He runs J. Stobart and Son, the firm he began with his father. They are still at Hesket and still own Newlands Hill, where Eddie's business first began. Cattle food and farm feedstuffs are not the best lines to be in when there's an epidemic around but, even so, they managed a turnover of several million in the year 2000. There is a staff of eighteen, including Ronnie's wife, Margaret, and their children: Richard, Peter and Linda, who are all directors.

Uncle Alan, Eddie's half-brother, has his own oil-and-lubricants firm, also based in the Hesket area. Within the family, Uncle Ronnie's cattle-food business is thought to be the most successful – after Eddie Stobart Ltd, of course. John Stobart's fourth son, Jim, had a garage business in Dalston until recently.

Amongst the next generation, the brothers and sister of Edward, Anne, the oldest, still lives near Hesket. She and her husband, Ken, have continued in the area in which father Eddie first began: lime-spreading. They have two tractors and a wagon and employ one man. They'll also shift sand and gravel if required.

Anne and Ken have three daughters: Fiona, 28, is married with three boys; Heidi, 26, is a nurse in Newcastle; Janette, 24, is an office-worker. Anne and Ken are both still committed Christians, and are very active members of Eddie's church.

In 1980, Anne sold out her shares in Eddie Stobart Ltd to Edward, and gave up her directorship. When she was originally given them, aged eighteen, by her father, she never thought of asking for the money. 'There seemed to be no option. I didn't really understand what they meant anyway.'

Anne was always known as the clever one in the family. 'I didn't really want to leave school at fifteen and work at home. But my mother was ill and my father said he needed help. So I never took my "O" levels. But it worked out okay in the end.

'I remember my father, when I'd just started working for him, saying "Some day, we'll have an office in Carlisle and you'll be there." I don't know whether he was just saying this to encourage me to work for him, or if he really was thinking ahead.

'As for my brother Edward, he didn't appear very ambitious when he was young. I never heard him saying "One day I'll have a hundred lorries." It just sort of happened. I think he's more ambitious today than he was as a lad.

'He has done well, but what surprises me is people's amazement. To us, it's all just been gradual. It just sort of seemed to happen, bit by bit. As for the fan club, when I heard about that, my reaction was: why?'

John Stobart, Edward's older brother, was eighteen when he took his inheritance in cash instead of shares in the family firm. 'When my Dad said I could have shares or £1000, I went off to Troutbeck market and bought fifty Swaledales. I paid top price for them – that was between three and eight pounds. I rented some fields from my grandfather and started farming. This was in 1961. I've been doing it ever since.'

Today he farms at Howbeck, just outside Hesket Newmarket, very near the primary school which he and his siblings attended, now a private house. He has three hundred acres, about one-third of which are owned by Edward and William, on which he has 740 ewes and 90 cattle. He farms all on his own, apart from occasional casual labour.

He and his wife, Christine, have three children: David, their eldest, works in Uncle Ronnie's cattle-feed business; Joanne, until recently, worked in the office at Eddie Stobart Ltd in Carlisle; Sarah, aged eight, is still at school.

John spends a lot of his time with the local hunt and has become joint Master of the Cumberland Fox-hounds. This is not the posh, red-coated, southern form of hunting but the on-foot, tramping the fells version. Within the Stobart family, John has always been regarded as the laid-back, easy-going one – not as one of the entrepreneurial Stobarts who like doing deals. 'Oh I'm not that bad,' he says. 'I will bargain when I have to, but I could never have been a businessman like Edward.'

Looking back, John says he never imagined for one moment what might happen to his younger brother. 'Edward was always keen on wagons, mind: tractors and wagons. Very keen on them. But I never thought he'd do all this. But then you don't, do you, when you're young? When you're young, you imagine life always going on the same. I thought my dad would be in charge for ever. So I never thought of Edward or William ever running anything.'

William today is Group Operations Director of Eddie Stobart Ltd, and is joint owner of the firm with forty per cent of the shares. He's still in charge of all the trucks and drivers, as he was when, back in 1986, he gave up driving and moved into the office.

He has enjoyed every moment of the ride so far, though he admits the year 2000 wasn't much fun. 'But you have to accept that, after twenty-nine excellent years on the trot. The main problems are still the same as they always were: utilizing the trucks to the maximum and giving customers the best and cheapest service.'

At the age of forty, William still looks rather young and boyish. It was only in the last ten years that Edward stopped addressing him as 'boy' and started using his real name. He's always known as William in the firm, never as Bill or Will, just as Edward is never Eddie or Ted. It makes them both sound like Victorian patriarchs.

Today, William is quite stocky with floppy, fair hair

which gives him something of a public-schoolboy look, despite his advancing years. He smiles more than Edward, appears more sociable and relaxed, less suspicious about the world.

He got married in 1988 to Helen, a girl from Appleby in Cumbria who was working as a cook, doing school meals. Their family home is still near Appleby. They have two children: April, aged eleven, who is at Austin Friars School in Carlisle, and Edward, aged ten, who is at the village school. 'I called him Edward after my brother and father,' explains William, 'even though Edward is one of the words I still can't say. I just wanted to keep the name in the family.'

Young Edward's passion in life is football. He plays for a local team in Penrith and has attended Bobby Charlton's coaching school. 'I can't see him ever coming into the firm,' says William. 'He's not at all mechanical. He's got no interest in trucks or driving, the way we had at his age.'

William, for the last year or so, has been mainly based at Daventry, now the biggest depot in the Stobart empire. He has a small modern estate house nearby, where he sleeps several nights a week, returning to Appleby at weekends. He misses his family but doesn't mind being on his own: 'I like solitude.'

His stammer is still apparent when he meets people for the first time, but it hardly inhibits him now. And he still uses his own form of phonetic writing, although, with all their computers and computer experts, there's little need for him to ever write down anything these days. The present fashion for text messages on mobile phones has amused him: many of the words are written in the same sort of ungrammatical, bad English shorthand he devised for himself many years ago.

Business-wise, he is confident that the firm will soon leap forward again. 'We are now one of the big boys. Once this blip is over, we will continue to grow and get bigger. I can see us expanding our haulage business in Europe and also the warehouse side in Britain.

'But I think we'll continue to be ninety per cent general haulage, unlike the real big boys, the PLCs. They have huge, exclusive contracts and don't worry about returning with empty loads. We have always worked on payloads: going from A to B with a load for a certain sum, then from B to C with another load, and so on.'

One thing that has changed recently within the company is board meetings. For the firm's first twenty-nine years, they didn't exist. 'We have to have them now: we're in a different era. We can't do everything by our two selves. Edward can't just work any more on his gut reactions.

'What happens now is that we have a board every two weeks, just six of us. We have hired these very good people, put them in charge of vital things, so they have to be consulted and listened to. It means at board meetings, Edward does now get asked questions.

He even gets cross-examined. Aye, he'll just have to get used to it in future.'

William has thought about his own role in the future, but doesn't see it changing much. 'Oh, I'll carry on as before. Follow behind Edward. Then pick up the pieces . . . .'

Eddie and Nora Stobart, Edward and William's parents, live today in Dalston, just outside Carlisle, near the secondary school that Edward and William attended. Their house is a large, luxury bungalow with an extensive and meticulously laid out landscaped garden. They can see Warnell Fell just a few miles away, up the hill that leads to Caldbeck and Hesket Newmarket.

Since Eddie's retirement from full-time business, some years ago, they have spent most of their time working in some way for God. They are active members of the Free Evangelical Church, and most of their time is now spent on the church they helped fund at Low Moor in Wigton. It is a very modern, imposing construction, hard to miss when you come into the town.

Eddie still does a bit of preaching and they regularly entertain visiting preachers in their home. Nora has worked for many years with the Gideons and, until recently, she was President of the Auxiliaries, the women's branch of the Gideon movement.

They are naturally very proud of what Edward has done, how he has put the family name on the national map. Eddie, however, now says that he would never have set up the business in his own name if he had known how big it would become.

Despite Edward's success, his parents are naturally saddened by the failure of his marriage. 'Edward's got everything money can buy,' says Eddie, 'but he lacks what money can't buy. I have a wife I've been happily married to for forty-nine years and thirteen lovely grandchildren.'

'I think it was with trying to achieve too hard all these years,' says Nora. 'That was what ruined his family life. He was hardly there at home. It's very sad.'

'He sat there and told me when his marriage was collapsing,' says Eddie. 'He told us his life was in a mess.' 'But I suppose he's no worse than thousands of people today,' says Nora. 'So many marriages have collapsed.'

'Life is for living,' says Eddie. 'But Edward, even as a very little boy, was always more interested in work than living. He wanted to achieve things, not go out and play or go and enjoy himself. That's just the way he was made. I don't suppose he'll ever change. But you have to admit he has achieved a lot.'

EDWARD TODAY

Edward still lives in Cumbria, when he's not rushing round the country or round Europe. He has a large country house with a long drive and some very modern security gates, about five miles from Carlisle. It was bought originally to be the firm's administrative HQ, but that plan was changed and Edward decided to live there himself, though he does have an office in the house.

Edward's marriage to Sylvia ended in 1996. After that, he was on his own for some time, till he had a relationship with a local woman, Mandy, with whom he has had a daughter, Ellie, born in 2000. He showed me her photograph with pride. They appear happy together, but he says he has no plans at present to get married again.

When he comes home, Edward enjoys taking off his smart suit and sparkling white shirt, putting on an old pair of jeans and T-shirt, and mucking around with his dumper. He has recently created a four-acre lake which involved lots of digging and moving mounds of earth around. He decided to do most of it by himself, as it took his mind off the business and is a good form of relaxation. This, of course, was how his working life all began, aged fourteen, thirty-two years ago, bunking off school to work on the motorway in his dad's JCB.

Apart from the house itself, there aren't many signs of affluence or self-indulgence. Edward does have a Ferrari, but hasn't used it for some time. It was about his only fantasy as a child, wanting to be a racing driver like Stirling Moss. In 1994, Edward made a visit to the Ferrari factory at Modena in Italy to see the cars being made. He liked the look of one model, which of course he then wanted immediately only to find there was a very long waiting list, so he came away very disappointed. Behind his back, William put in an order and, later that year, as a surprise Christmas present from the firm, Edward was presented with the £95,000 Ferrari. He now hardly drives it, preferring instead his BMW. 'The Ferrari's in a garage in Newcastle at the moment. I'm now thinking of selling it.'

But Edward still has his motor-racing painting, the one done by Alan Fearnley, of Damon Hill winning the Grand Prix. He has the originals of the ten Eddie Stobart lorry paintings also done by Fearnley.

As for other luxuries, in 1995 he acquired a £225,000, luxury yacht on Windermere. It was forty-four feet long, with eight berths, and was kept for company hospitality and also to amuse Edward's four adopted children, but it was hardly ever used and was soon sold.

Edward doesn't work quite such long hours as he used to but, nonetheless, he rarely takes a holiday. He isn't keen on going abroad anyway. He has no hobbies, doesn't collect things and has no interest in sport of any form, despite sponsoring Carlisle United FC. He doesn't go to their matches and doesn't watch football on TV, though each Saturday he'll take in the football results, just because he knows many of his colleagues at work are football fans.

He began sponsoring Carlisle United in 1995, which meant that the words 'Eddie Stobart Ltd' appeared on the front of their shirts. It did bring the firm a bit of publicity, when the team twice got to Wembley: firstly, for the final of the Auto Windscreens Shield, and then when they won it in 1997. I was there both times, waving aloft my inflatable sheep. Such excitement, at least in Cumbria, but it did make the football-watching nation aware of CUFC's rather natty deckchair-like strip in the Eddie Stobart colours of red, green and gold.

When Carlisle sank to the bottom of the Third Division in the 1999–2000 season and, oh ignomy, again the following season, most marketing or commercial managers would immediately have decided that sponsoring such a lousy team was a waste of good money, but Eddie Stobart Ltd soldiered on. If the team ever gets relegated from the Football League, that might be another matter.

'We never did it for publicity,' says Edward. 'It's not like, say, Leicester City having Walker's crisps on the front. They are advertising direct to their customers. No one at a football match sees our shirts and thinks hmm, I just feel like some haulage . . . .

'I did it for Carlisle. A city like Carlisle needs a league club. When we were at Greystone Road, I used to watch grandads, dads and sons all walking to the match on a Saturday afternoon. I think football does help to keep families together.

'I didn't go as a boy, partly because I didn't know anyone who did go, but also because I came from a very religious family. Going to a football match was something you didn't do. It was a sort of worldly activity. My dad always told me to keep away from three things: keep away from fast women and slow horses. There was a third, but I've forgotten what it was.'

As for Edward's personal wealth, on paper, in 1999, Edward was worth £100 million, according to the *Sunday Times* annual list of Britain's top one thousand richest people. They made him joint 227, along with such worthies as the Duke of Beaufort and David Bowie. In 2001, they estimated he was only worth a measly fifty million pounds, as things had been tough in haulage. He was therefore dropped to joint 669th in the pecking order, along with the Duke of Buccleuch and Rod Stewart.

The subject makes Edward smile, but he has no interest in it and has no idea how true it is. He has no intention of selling, so there is no need for him to play the game of working out how much his assets might be worth. These days, he doesn't have much money tied up in vehicles, as the tractors are all on their three-year leases, though the trailers are mostly owned. Similarly, only around half of his twenty-eight depots and warehouses are owned, the rest having been sold and leased back.

One way of estimating a company's value is on its annual profit. In 1999, Eddie Stobart Ltd made around £5 million, which, in theory, made it worth £100 million. Then there's the value of the depots, say £20 million, plus assorted properties, the goodwill of the company and what, of course, someone would be willing to pay just to own the firm.

Whatever this sum might come to, Edward could easily have sold up some years ago and never needed to work again. 'I've never even thought about that for one moment,' he says. 'This is still exciting. Retiring to a villa in Spain wouldn't give me a kick at all. I did take a week's holiday in Spain a couple of years ago, but I didn't enjoy it much. A long weekend would suit me better, from say Thursday to Monday. That way I wouldn't get out of touch with what's happening.'

However, what's normally happening at work these days is very often what's happened before, in the past. Problems in haulage tend to repeat themselves, as in most industries. Fuel costs and finding good drivers have been a problem for the last twenty-five years. Edward, nonetheless, doesn't find this repetition boring.

'But I like the problems. There's something wrong with a business if there are no problems. Our business is much bigger today, the figures are bigger, the size of everything is greater, but the problems are not really any bigger. It's now more like steering the *Titanic*, trying to get it round corners and not crash into obstacles. But I don't lie awake at night, restless, any more than I did twenty-eight years ago.'

In the early days, Edward always had targets. When he got to fifty vehicles, he wanted a hundred. When he reached five hundred, his aim was to make it six hundred by the following year. That has slowed down in the last year, once the company got to one thousand lorries and the economics of haulage forced them to do some trimming.

'But I still have targets,' maintains Edward. 'I want to make a bigger profit every year; I got very upset when it went down. I still have lots of challenges. I still have to find a way of paying the drivers more.'

Despite working fewer hours, he doesn't really appear to find distractions. His mind is still constantly thinking about the firm. 'I don't need to wind down because I don't allow myself to wind up. I am more relaxed today. Amn't I, Deborah?' Deborah doesn't reply. Just smiles.

'Deborah, back me up.'

'You still do get very wound up, Edward . . .'

'Well, aye, but not as much as I did. I don't think I do. Anyways.'

Edward sees his four adopted children fairly regularly, as they don't live too far away, and he is providing for their education. However, despite the presence of his girlfriend, Mandy, he does seem to move through life alone, whether at home or work.

'I've always felt lonely: it's nothing new for me. I was lonely at Greystone Road. I had good people I enjoyed working with but, at the end of the day, I was on my own. I only ever saw my dad at weekends. I've always made the decisions on my own. That's how I've wanted to do it.'

There are other company bosses who are on their own at the top, making the big decisions, but they can still have a rich social life. They have partners, friends and colleagues whom they can bounce ideas off, share thoughts, worries and emotions with. Edward was never one of those. At school, he didn't feel connected, either to the system or to his fellow pupils. Even while married, he still often preferred his own company. As his father has observed, that would seem to be in his nature.

Edward himself has no complaints about the temperament he has been handed. But what he suspects people don't properly appreciate are the things that you lose in life by being a lone figure at the top. 'I don't think any financial rewards can ever equal the life you give away, the sacrifices you make on life's journey. I chose to make them; but you have to make these sacrifices, if you want to succeed.

'If I had let the firm stay at ten lorries, there would have been no growth. You can't run a family or give your staff security, not on ten lorries. You either go forward, or stagnate, so I worked all hours in order to go forward. I cancelled dates with ladies to take a lorry out. I didn't see it as a choice – it had to be done. If you want something in this world, it's waiting there for you, but you have to be prepared to make sacrifices.

'People then think, when you become a boss of a big, successful firm, you can then do what you want. But you can't. For weeks now, I have been working on things I don't want to do, meetings I didn't want to attend, decisions I didn't want to make. But you have to. The business needs it done, it's not because I personally enjoy it. Those are all part of the sacrifices I'm talking about, which outsiders don't see.

'People say, "Oh, hasn't he done well," or, "Hasn't he been lucky?" That's most people's first reaction. What they never say is, "I wonder what he's sacrificed?" That should be their first question.

'I'm not saying I haven't liked being alone. I quite enjoy it. I'd rather sit and stare at a wall than have some of the conversations I have to have. When I first got divorced, and was on my own, people did invite me out for Sunday lunch. I used to make excuses because, really, I wanted to be on my own. I preferred it. It was so peaceful, being alone. I can always cope with business problems better than personal problems.

'The important things in life are knowing and believing in God, family and friends and work. That's the correct order: how it should be.

'The problem with those important things is finding the right balance between them. There will always be gaps. Sometimes, the gaps have been wide, as they have been with me. You have to decide your own balance, what's correct for you. With me, yes, looking back, the balance could have been better at times.'

All the same, Edward won't admit to any serious regrets, things he definitely wishes he hadn't done, or that he would do differently if he were to start all over. Not even his lack of formal education. He has never for a moment wished he'd stayed on longer at school and gone to college. William has much the same attitude, but thinks that what he and Edward did, starting their careers at fourteen, would not be possible today. He believes that some sort of qualifications are needed today to get started in any sort of business, or at least the ability to use a computer.

Edward, however, is not convinced by William's argument. 'I think you can still pick up things on the job, or later on, or hire others to do them. So, no, I don't regret what I did. I don't think I missed anything.'

Like his father, Edward now often thinks it might have been better if the firm had never used the name Eddie Stobart. Tens of thousands of fans will be distraught at the very thought. Surely the name, and all it has come to imply, is an integral part of his success?

'I don't know about that. When I moved into Carlisle, I perhaps should have made a clean break from my father and called the firm "Cumbrian Carriers", or "E.S.L." – just something not personal. No, I take that back: it was a silly thing to say. Of course I like the firm's name. I didn't really mean it that way . . . .'

Edward's point, perhaps, is that the firm's name and success has thrust personal publicity upon him, which would not have happened if the name had been more anonymous. As well as giving up using any personalized car numberplates, he has also stopped using his own credit card when getting petrol, just to avoid being recognized. 'There's usually someone in a filling station who says: "Oh, Edward Stobart, you're not him are you?" When I'm abroad, it's not too bad. But in Britain, it was always happening. That's why I now buy petrol with cash.

'On trains, if a stranger starts to talk to me, I'll never say what business I'm in. I know what they'll get round to asking, so I always change the subject. Hotels are not too bad. Receptionists don't really take in a name. But it sometimes happens that people come up to me and say: "Are you who I think you are?" I never know how to answer that. So I usually just smile and try to get away.

'I was in Marks & Spencer a few weeks ago, not far from our Daventry depot, at Leicester Fosse Park. I was staying overnight in a hotel and I went out to buy some socks and underpants. These two women – perfectly nice, middle-aged women – came up to me and said: "We know who you are, you're Mr Stobart, we're in your fan club and we've seen your photograph!"

'There was no way out of that. So I stood and chatted to them for a while, then wished them good spotting and moved away. But, when I was standing looking at the socks, I could see they were still watching me. And they were even telling other people, pointing me out to strangers, nudging them. So I left – I never did buy the socks or underpants.

'When I got divorced, there was a tabloid journalist after me for about a year, convinced there was some other woman, which there wasn't. They were interested just because of my name. Yet I'm a nobody: why should anybody be interested in me?

'I find being recognized anywhere very embarrassing. I'm not a pop star or TV star. If the Eddie Stobart fans enjoy being Eddie Stobart fans, spotting the lorries, then that's fine. I'm pleased they're enjoying themselves. It's just a shame it's my name which has become public property. It makes me feel as if I've lost my freedom.'

So why, one may wonder, has Edward allowed this book to be written? Well, it is primarily to celebrate thirty years of Eddie Stobart Ltd – a factual record of the firm and all the people who have made it into a success. As well as revealing what the firm has achieved since 1970, it will hopefully also make the general public a bit more aware of the haulage industry generally, its history and problems, its contributions to the economy.

Edward perhaps did not expect so many details of his life to emerge, in order to tell the story of the firm. But, whatever he says, it is basically the story of one man. He built it up, created it his own way, in very much his own image. His obsession with targets, always wanting to achieve, get to the next stage, never saying no to any work, is part of both him and of the firm. His passion for clean lorries was always a personal thing, resulting in attractive vehicles and distinctive drivers. This led directly to the fan club, even though such a creation, with him as the figurehead, had never been on his mind.

The firm's story, its rise and rise and the problems encountered along the way, is a story of our times. It takes in modern-day methods of transport, motorways and supermarkets, fuel crises and traffic problems, global companies and PLCs, and the increasing sophistication of distribution and logistics.

Yet, at the same time, Edward Stobart is not of our times. His is a private, family firm in an industry dominated by global corporations. He has become rich and successful in what is essentially a very old-fashioned, traditional business. You expect multi-millionaires in their forties today to have done it through IT or computers, or by city-dealing and takeover bids, not through something as mundane as lorries.

In his business philosophy, such as it is, Edward has never had any time for the received wisdoms of modern management courses, business schools or MBAs. He has done it his way, almost in a vacuum, though often by chance coming to the same conclusions and systems as the great brains in his industry.

His business is unique, however, in the way it is run, with no advertising, no company announcements or mission statements. I'd like to think the firm's story will be studied by business experts – if only as an example of how not to do it, or how to do it in a different way.

Edward cannot be said to be personally charismatic, which is something we are led to believe most great entrepreneurs are. He is not fluent in speech, not easy in public, not a great persuader, not a ranter or raver, displays none of those characteristics we tend to associate with the self-made man or the high-achiever.

As a person, Edward shies away from what we are told most humans want or expect these days: our fifteen minutes of fame. His personality, his values, his way of life, are in contradiction to our media-obsessed, celebrity-fascinated world.

One has to admire the way Edward has succeeded, the way he has done it, for doing it his way. Who knows what the next stage will be, for him and the company. One thing we can be sure of, though, is that he'll keep on trucking.

APPENDICES

A Haulage Glossary
B The Stobarts: a Who's Who
C Eddie Stobart Limited: Chronology
D Lorry Names
E Eddie Stobart Fan Club
F Eddie Stobart Depots
G Top Haulage Firms: 2000

Appendix A

HAULAGE GLOSSARY

- **Lorry, truck, wagon**: any heavy-goods road vehicle bigger than a van. At one time, 'truck' was mainly N. American usage, while 'lorry' was British. 'Wagon' was more ancient, from horse-drawn wagons. But now all three terms are interchangeable and non-specific.

- **Tractor unit**: the front part of a lorry, containing the engine and driver's cab. Often simply called 'the tractor' or 'unit', which can be confusing, e.g. 'I was belting down the M1, just with my tractor unit.'

- **Articulated lorry,** or 'artic': a tractor unit with a semi-trailer hitched on closely behind, so they look like one unit.

  IVECO EuroStar Artic.

- **Semi-trailer**: a trailer that hitches behind the tractor unit. Sometimes just referred to as a 'trailer'.

DAF 95XF Drawbar

- **Drawbar**: a rigid vehicle with a close-coupled trailer.
- **Juggernaut**: unflattering term first used in the seventies to describe these monster lorries. Not, of course, a word used within the haulage industry.
- **Susie couplings**: nothing to do with any Susie, but the air and electrical links between lorry and trailer.
- **Shunt**: short for 'shunter', a vehicle that shunts trailers around inside the depot.
- **Dayman**: a driver who only works days.
- **Nightman,** or **trunkman**: a driver who only works nights, but sleeps at home.
- **Tramper**: a driver who sleeps overnight in his cab.
- **Shed**: term of contempt applied to a driver with a scruffy lorry and/or cab, e.g. 'Your lorry is a complete and utter shed.'
- **LGV licence**: formerly known as HGV, for heavy-goods vehicle. An LGV licence is much the same as the old HGV licence but comes in two forms: an LGV licence, category C, is needed to drive a rigid vehicle over 7.5 tonnes; categories C and E are needed to drive an articulated lorry pulling a trailer.

Appendix B

THE STOBARTS: A WHO'S WHO

John Stobart, farmer and agricultural contractor, born Sebergham, Cumbria, 1903–1997.

Married 1) **Adelaide**, died 1942; two sons: **Eddie** born 1929, **Ronnie** born 1936.

Married 2) **Ruth**; two sons, **Jim** and **Alan**; four daughters, **Mary**, **Ruth**, **Dorothy** and **Isobel**.

Eddie Stobart, son of **John**, born Hesket Newmarket. Began Eddie Stobart Ltd 1970, agricultural contractors.

Married **Nora Boyd** 1951; one daughter, **Anne**, born 1952; three sons, **John**, born 1953, **Edward**, born 1954, **William**, born 1961.

Edward Stobart, son of **Eddie**, born Hesket Newmarket, 1954. Moved Eddie Stobart Ltd into Carlisle, 1976.

Married **Sylvia** 1980, divorced 1996.

Appendix C

EDDIE STOBART LIMITED: CHRONOLOGY

1970 Firm founded as agricultural contractors at Hesket Newmarket, by Eddie Stobart, Senior, specializing in lime-spreading. Turnover £118,000.

1973 Eddie opens farm shop in Wigton. Turnover £279,500.

1976 Eddie's son, Edward, moves into rented premises at Greystone Road, Carlisle, with eight lorries and twelve staff.

    Eddie Stobart Trading Ltd formed to look after the agricultural business. Eddie Stobart Ltd now concentrating on haulage, run by Edward.

1977 Turnover £455,000.

1980 Move to new premises in Kingstown industrial estate, Carlisle, near the M6.

1987 50 vehicles; turnover £4.5 million; 100 staff. Second depot opened at Burnaston, Derby.

1990 130 vehicles; turnover £16.4 million; 500 staff. Collars and ties for drivers introduced.

1992   Awarded Haulier of the Year. Eddie Stobart
        fan club formed.
1993   300 vehicles; turnover £34 million; 1300 staff.
1995   500 vehicles; turnover £52 million; 1600 staff.
1997   Daventry depot (500,000 square feet) opened
        by the Princess Royal.
1998   700 vehicles; turnover £102 million; 2000
        staff.
1999   Three depots opened in Belgium.
2001   1000 vehicles; turnover £150 million; 2200
        staff; 27 depots.

Appendix D

LORRY NAMES

All Eddie Stobart lorries have female names. It all began in the 1970s, when the first one was named Twiggy, soon followed by Tammy, both chosen personally by Edward as he quite fancied them.

Later on, drivers were allowed to choose their own names, such as those of their wives or girlfriends, which often led to complications, when they fell out with or changed their wives or girlfriends.

When the fan club was formed in 1992, members were given the chance to suggest their own choice of names. There is a long waiting list.

Today, you have to join the fan club to get the exclusive and total list of current names, which gets updated all the time. Here is a selection from the 1999 Fleet Manual, just to whet the appetite, in case you feel an urge to become an Eddie Stobart spotter.

VEHICLE MAKE	NAME	VEHICLE MAKE	NAME
VANHOOL COACH	DEBORAH JANE	DAF 95	GRAINNE
SCANIA R144 LHD	HEIDI	DAF 95	CATHERINE
VOLVO FH12 GL	TINA ANN	DAF 95	DOMINIQUE
DAF 95	MAIRHEAD	DAF 95	CHANTELLE
SCANIA R124	ISABELLA	DAF 95	CORRINE
VOLVO FH12 GL	BETHANY MARIE	DAF 95	ANDREA
SCANIA R114	KELLY VANDA	DAF 95	MARY CONSTANCE
VOLVO FH12 GL	PORTIA LOUISE	DAF 95	BILLIE JEAN
VOLVO FH12 GL	NICHOLA EMMA	DAF 95	CHRISSIE JO
ERF EC11	LUCY HANNAH	DAF 95	RUTH ERICA
DAF 85	TAOME	DAF 95	CATHERINE ANNE
SCANIA P114	SUSAN CIBIE	DAF 95	SHARONA
RENAULT MAGNUM	GIGI	VOLVO FH12 GL SE	BONNIE
VOLVO FH12 GL	NICOLA JOANNE	VOLVO FH12 GL SE	TINA
VOLVO FH12 GL	CAITLIN ERIN	VOLVO FH12	BRENDA
SCANIA P94	ERIN	VOLVO FH12	DELIA
DAF 95	SEONAID	VOLVO FH12	HONOR
SCANIA R124 TL	LAURA 'B'	VOLVO FH12	BLOSSOM
SCANIA R124 TL	LEEANN HELEN	VOLVO FH12	LAVENDER
MAN F2000 ROADHAUS	ANN NATASHA	VOLVO FH12	MANUELA
RENAULT MAGNUM	YVONNE CLARE	VOLVO FH12	MURIEL
SCANIA R114	ELAINE SUSAN	VOLVO FH12	CAMILLA
IVECO RIGID	DAISY	VOLVO FH12	CELESTE
IVECO EUROSTAR	ELEANOR JOAN	VOLVO FH12	EILEEN
IVECO EUROSTAR	MANDY ELIZABETH	VOLVO FH12	GENEVIEVE
IVECO EUROTECH	HEATHER ELIZABETH	VOLVO FH12	HENRIETTA
DAF 3600 SPACECAB	CHARLOTTE	VOLVO FH12	JOCELINE
ERF EC11	JOSEPHINE JULIE	VOLVO FH12	MARIANNE
DAF 95 XF	MARION MARIE	VOLVO FH12	MIRANDA
DAF 95 XF	SARAH RACHEL	VOLVO FH12	PRIMROSE
VOLVO FH12 GL	JEAN JEANNIE	VOLVO FH12	SELINA
VOLVO FH12 GL XL	MARCIA ROSE	VOLVO FH12	ANABEL
VOLVO FH12 GL XL	GEORGIA KATE	VOLVO FH12	CECILIA
ERF OLYMPIC	ANN EILEEN	VOLVO FH12	SHELLEY
VOLVO FH16 GL LHD	MARY MAY	VOLVO FH12	VERONICA
SCANIA R124 TL LHD	JOELLA	VOLVO FH12	DANIELLA
SCANIA R124 TL LHD	MOLLY BESS	VOLVO FH12	SUZETTE
SCANIA R124 TL LHD	ELENA PETA	VOLVO FH12	ELEANOR
VOLVO FH12 GL	JULIA BETH	VOLVO FH12	CHERICE
DAF 95	CATRIONA	VOLVO FH12	BRONWEN
DAF 95 XF	DEBORAH HEATHER	VOLVO FH12	MAXINE
DAF 95	ISABEL	SCANIA 8 WHL	BARBARA ANN
DAF 95 DRAWBAR	SARAH ELIZABETH	MERCEDES/ACT	CAROLE ANNE
VOLVO FH12 GL	BONNIE JEAN	MERCEDES/ACT	CLAIRE B
VOLVO FH12	CHRISTINA JEAN	MERCEDES/ACT	EIRA
SCANIA R114 DRAWBAR	JULIE MARGARET	MERCEDES/ACT	JULIE DAWN
DAF 95 XF	SORRETA	MERCEDES/ACT	JULIE RUBY
DAF 95 XF	LUCY MOIRA	MERCEDES/ACT	ALEXANDRA THEA

VEHICLE MAKE	NAME	VEHICLE MAKE	NAME
SCANIA R114	CAVELL SOPHIE	MERCEDES/ACT	DRIS
SCANIA R114	STEPHANIE HOLLY	MERCEDES/ACT	CHRISTINE PAMELA
SCANIA R113	JASMIN ANNE	MERCEDES/ACT	ANDREA
SCANIA R113	GEMMA LOUISE	MERCEDES/ACT	KATE
SCANIA R124	OLGA	MAN F2000	VIOLET
SCANIA R113	AMY LISA	MAN F2000	CHASTINE
SCANIA R113	MHAIRI GARIAN	MAN F2000	KATRINA
SCANIA R124	JULIE MARIE	MAN F2000	ELSIE
SCANIA R124	AMY LOU	MAN F2000	GRETA
FORD TRANSIT	FIFI	MAN F2000	CAROLIND
FORD TRANSIT	DORIS	MAN F2000	ASHI
SCANIA R124	MELISSA NATASHA	MAN F2000	NOVA
SCANIA R114	SUZANNE PATRICIA	MAN F2000	DIAN MARGARET
SCANIA R124	SUSAN ANN	MAN F2000	LAUREN JESSICA
SCANIA R124	MARGOT OLGA	MAN F2000	ANGELA MARY
SCANIA R124	LOUISE	MAN F2000	IRIS MAY
SCANIA R114 TL	SAMANTHA LAUREN	MAN F2000	ANNE MURIEL
SCANIA R114 TL	HEATHER LOUISE	MAN F2000	LYNNE
DAF 95 DRAWBAR	FRANCES LINDA	MAN F2000	JESSIE
RENAULT MAJOR	ANGELIQUE	MAN F2000	NADINA
RENAULT MAJOR	ROSIE	SCANIA T CAB	KERRY JANE
VOLVO FH12 GL	CHELSEA	MAN F2000	SHARLEIGH
SCANIA R143 TL	EMILY KIM	MAN F2000	VIVIENNE
SCANIA R114	VICTORIA AMANDA	MAN F2000	JILLIAN
SCANIA R114	SOPHIE ANNA	DAF 95 XF	GRACE TAOME
SCANIA R114 TL	SALLY AMANDA	MAN F2000	VELVET
RENAULT MAGNUM	LILY	VOLVO FH12	DENISE
VOLVO FH12	MAXINE WHITNEY	VOLVO FH12	NINA CHRISTINE
IVECO EUROTECH	LEANNE LYNDSEY	SCANIA R114	AMY ELIZABETH
SCANIA R113	MARY LUCY	VOLVO FH12	CHARLOTTE REBECCA
SCANIA R113	SHEILA MARY	VOLVO FH12	SHEILA AMY
SCANIA R113	EMMA JANE	VOLVO FH12	KAYLEIGH RHIANON
SCANIA R113	EMILIA VICTORIA	VOLVO FH12	MONICA
SCANIA R113	MARY LOU	VOLVO FH12	JULIE ANNE
SCANIA R113	JANINE EMMA	VOLVO FH12	RITA GRACE
SCANIA R113	AMELIA JANICE	VOLVO FH12	SARAH DENISE
VOLVO FH12 GL	SALLY NICOLE	VOLVO FH12	STACEY JEAN
VOLVO FH12	SHERI LOUISE	VOLVO FH12	EMMA STELLA
VOLVO FH12	LORNA JADE	VOLVO FH12	OLIVIA JOLENE
SCANIA R124	SHEILA BELLE	VOLVO FH12	PRISCILLA
SCANIA R124	GAIL ELIZABETH	VOLVO FH12	MARTINA
SCANIA R113	RACHEL LOUISE	VOLVO FH12	SHIRLEY
SCANIA R113	ANN MARIE	MERCEDES VAN	NICOLE
SCANIA R113	KATHLEEN ANNE	VOLVO FH12	ANDREA MAY
SCANIA R124	PENELOPE ANNE	VOLVO FH12	HEATHER
SCANIA R124	MARGARET	VOLVO FH12	FIONA BELLE
VOLVO FH12 GL	LEONIE	VOLVO FH12	ANNE
VOLVO FH12 GL	ALICE	VOLVO FH12	CHRISTINE JEAN

VEHICLE MAKE	NAME	VEHICLE MAKE	NAME
DAF 85	SASHA	DAF 95	JO BETH
DAF 85	SHAUNIE	VOLVO GLOBE	EMILY ROSE
DAF 85	DAVENA	VOLVO FH12	STEPHANIE RACHAEL
IVECO CARGO	BELLA	IVECO CURSOR	SUSAN MARY
IVECO CARGO	JOSEPHINE	IVECO EUROSTAR	CATHERINE KELLY
IVECO CARGO	DIANE	IVECO EUROSTAR	SHIRLEY LISA
IVECO CARGO	VANESSA	IVECO EUROSTAR	AUDREY MARION
IVECO EURO	SUSAN	MAN F2000	LYN
VOLVO F10 D/B	HELEN ANNE	DAF 85	SUSAN ANNE
DAF 95 D/BAR	CAROL ANNE	SCANIA P113	JULIE ANGELA
DAF 95 D/BAR	KIMBERLEY	SCANIA P113	ALINE MARIE
DAF 95 D/BAR	CARRIE	SCANIA P113	MELVA DENISE
DAF 95 D/BAR	GEANIE	SCANIA P113	JANE LOUISE
DAF 95 D/BAR	DEBBIE	SCANIA P113	LITTLE ROSIE
DAF 95 D/BAR	SINEAD	SCANIA P113	ENID IRENE
DAF 95 D/BAR	CAROLYN	SCANIA P113	JILLY FLEUR
MAN F2000	JOANIE	SCANIA P113	JENNY ELSIE
ERF E14	CHERYL	SCANIA P113	CARA MAY
VOLVO FH12	JANINE	SCANIA P113	ROSITA MARY
VOLVO FH12	DEANNA LEIGH	MERCEDES/1834	VASHTI
VOLVO FH12	PAMELA ELIZABETH	MERCEDES/1834	ANNYA
VOLVO FH12	MARION JOYCE	MERCEDES/1834	CARLA
VOLVO FH12	EVA LAURA	MERCEDES/1834	DAMELZA
VOLVO FH12	STACY LISA	MAN RIGID	HELGA
VOLVO FH12	TONI FRANCES	MERCEDES/1834	GEORGINA
VOLVO FH12	SHARRON JOY	MERCEDES/1834	GHISLAINE
VOLVO FH12	CHARLOTTE LOUISE	MERCEDES/1834	JADENE
VOLVO FH12	JACKIE MARIE	MERCEDES/1834	JANET
VOLVO FH12	BERYL ANNE	MERCEDES/1834	MARIA
VOLVO FH12	GEMMA VICTORIA	MERCEDES/1834	MARSELLA
VOLVO FH12	CHERRY	MERCEDES/1834	MISTY BLUE
VOLVO FH12	CHLOE JAY	DAF 2700	SAHRA LOUISE
VOLVO FH12	LUCY CLAIRE	MERCEDES/1834	RENA
VOLVO FH12	TRACEY SANDRA	MERCEDES/1834	ROWENA
VOLVO FH12	DOREEN LISA	MERCEDES/1834	SADHBH
VOLVO FH12	PAULA JANE	MERCEDES/1834	SANDY
VOLVO FH12	LINDA MARIA	MERCEDES/1834	SEETA
VOLVO FH12	FIONA GAY	MERCEDES/ACTR	MARY ANNE
VOLVO FH12	HEATHER SIMONE	MERCEDES/1834	DIANA
VOLVO FH12	CORRISE ELIZABETH	IVECO D/BAR	CONSTANCE
VOLVO FH12	GEMMA LOUISE	IVECO D/BAR	FRANCESCA
VOLVO FH12	MARILYN KELLY	MERCEDES/1834	SEANNAH
VOLVO FH12	SAMANTHA JADE	MERCEDES/1834	HIRLEY
SCANIA P114	LANA REBECCA	MERCEDES/1834	TRACEY
SCANIA P114	TIERNEY	MERCEDES/1834	MEGAN JADE
SCANIA P114	BARBARA KAY	RENAULT/PRIV	SUSAN SHIRLEY
SCANIA P114	EMILY	RENAULT/PREM	MARLENE
SCANIA P114	ALICIA MARIE	RENAULT/DIST	POPPY

VEHICLE MAKE	NAME	VEHICLE MAKE	NAME
SCANIA P114	HAYLEY	VOLVO FH12	EMMANUELLE
SCANIA P114	PENNY	VOLVO FH12	ANN HAZEL
SCANIA P114	ANDREA MARGARET	VOLVO FH12	TRACY CLAIRE
SCANIA P114	LAUREN	VOLVO FH12	PENELOPE ANN
SCANIA P114	MIIA	VOLVO FH12	RACHEL
SCANIA P114	JESSICA	VOLVO FH12	WANDA
SCANIA P114	PAMMIE	VOLVO FH12	BERYL JOAN
SCANIA P114	SHEENA	SCANIA R124	FLORENCE MARY
SCANIA P114	HELEN	SCANIA R124	ELLIE MAY
SCANIA P114	PAMELA JOYCE	SCANIA R124	LINZI ADELE
SCANIA P93	BARBARA ANN	MAN F2000	DESNA
VOLVO RIGID	ANASTASIA	MERCEDES VAN	NO NAME
VOLVO RIGID	BELINDA	MAN RIGID	ALAINE
VOLVO RIGID	CARMEN	MAN RIGID	MILVIA
VOLVO RIGID	DAPHNE	F/T MINIBUS	LOIS
VOLVO RIGID	DELORES	SCANIA R124	JUDITH
S/ATKINSON	CAROL ELIZABETH	VOLVO FH12	MARILYN
VOLVO FH12 GL SE	CHELSEA	VOLVO FH12	KAYLEIGH
DAF 95 D/BAR	NO NAME	VOLVO FH12	LILLIAN
DAF 95 D/BAR	NO NAME	VOLVO FH12	JANICE
DAF 95 D/BAR	REBECCA	VOLVO FH12	GWENDOLINE
DAF 95 D/BAR	LORNA ANNE	VOLVO FH12	JESSICA ROSE
DAF 95 D/BAR	TAMZIN	VOLVO FH12	ESTHER
DAF 95 D/BAR	HOLLIE LEANNE	VOLVO FH12	JEANETTE
DAF 95 D/BAR	FLORENCE	VOLVO FH12	DOROTHY
DAF 95 D/BAR	TIFFANY	VOLVO FH12	CHRISTINA
DAF 95 D/BAR	TONI	SHUNT	NO NAME
DAF 95 D/BAR	LINSEY MARIE	SHUNT	WENDY
DAF 95 D/BAR	GERALDINE	SHUNT	ROZALA
DAF 95 D/BAR	VIRGINIA	SHUNT	NO NAME
DAF 95 D/BAR	DONNA MARIE	SHUNT	GILLY
DAF 95 D/BAR	ASHLEIGH ANNA	SHUNT	NO NAME
DAF 95 D/BAR	LAUREN ELIZABETH	SHUNT	ANITA
DAF 95 D/BAR	BETHANY ANN	SHUNT	SOPHIE
DAF 95 D/BAR	DAWN LOUISE	SHUNT	ELIZABETH
DAF 95 D/BAR	ELAINE PATRICIA	SHUNT	LESLEY ANN
DAF 95 D/BAR	MARGARET ELEANOR	SHUNT	PETRA ANNE
DAF 95 D/BAR	LAVINIA	SHUNT	CRYSTAL
MERCEDES/1834	DEBORAH	SHUNT	NO NAME
DAF 85	PRICILLA	SHUNT	ELIZABETH
DAF 85	SIAN REBEKA	SHUNT	SARAFION
DAF 85	MELANIE JAYNE	TUG	CATHERINE
DAF 85	KHIANNON MARIE	TUG	GAYNOR DIANE
DAF 85	CENYS ELIZABETH	TUG	CHRISTINE ANNE
DAF 95	BEVERLEY EMMA	FORD ESCORT VAN	JOAN
DAF 95	MAUREEN PAMELA	FORD ESCORT VAN	ADRIENNE
DAF 95	LUCIE MARIE	FORD ESCORT VAN	ELSA
DAF 95	TALITHA	FORD ESCORT VAN	CAROLINE

Appendix E

EDDIE STOBART FAN CLUB

Fan club address: Brunthill Road, Kingstown Industrial Estate, Carlisle, Cumbria, CA3 0EH
Tel: 01228 514 151; fax: 515 158.
E-mail: promotions@eddiestobart.co.uk

Official website, for members as well as anyone else:
www.eddiestobart.co.uk

The fan club began in 1992. It now has 25,000 members. Each month, around 500 new members join. Subscription to become a new member is £10, thereafter £8 per year. Each new member receives a special pack containing: membership card, member's badge, fleet manual, sticker and, at Christmas, an Eddie Stobart calendar.

Members also get a regular magazine, full of news, competitions for children and adults, and a catalogue of Eddie Stobart merchandising, most of it exclusive to members. This includes: toy models of Eddie Stobart trucks, Eddie Stobart clothes, Eddie Stobart tea and Eddie Stobart teddy bears.

The Official Fleet Manual, which all members receive, is the bible for Eddie Stobart spotters and lists all current vehicles, their fleet number, registration number, make, livery and female name – with room to tick where and when you spotted each one. It is regularly updated and is exclusive to members of the fan club.

Fan club members can register a name of their choice with the fan club, but it is not guaranteed that it will ever be used. Unusual christian names, such as Ffion, wife of William Hague, have often got more of a chance. The fleet life of every lorry is three years, so old and common names do come round again. Good luck.

All fan-club members can enjoy a tour of an Eddie Stobart depot, to gaze at the lorries, close up. Guided tours are available at Kingstown and Daventry depots, but members should ring in advance to book a date.

The fan club shop, open to all, is at 27 Castle Street, Carlisle. Tel: 01228 515 166.

Appendix F

EDDIE STOBART DEPOTS

INTERNATIONAL DEPOT OFFICES

BELGIUM
Oeverstraat 9
Lokeren

BELGIUM
Nijverheidsstraat 1
8630 Veurne

BELGIUM
Kapelanielaan 8
B–9140 Temse

NORTHERN REGION

CARLISLE
Brunthill Road,
Kingstown Industrial Estate,
Carlisle,
CA3 0EH

GLASGOW
23 Cook Street, Glasgow,
G5 8JP

GLASGOW
29 Saracen Street, Hamilton
Hill Industrial Estate, Possil
Park, Glasgow, G22 5HT

WORKINGTON
Lillyhall Estate, Branthwaite
Road, Lillyhall, Workington,
CA14 4ED

PENRITH
Haweswater Road, Penrith
Industrial Estate, Penrith,
CA11 9EU

NORTH-EAST REGION

NORMANTON
Don Pedro Avenue,
Normanton Industrial Estate,
Normanton, WF6 1TD

WAKEFIELD
Kenmore Road, Junction 41
Industrial Estate, Wakefield,
WF2 0XE

KNOTTINGLEY
Hazel Road, Knottingley,
WF11 0LG

SHERBURN-IN-ELMET
Warehousing Site
1 Moor Lane Trading Estate,
Sherburn-In-Elmet, North
Yorkshire, LS25 6ES

SHERBURN-IN-ELMET
Transport Site
2 Moor Lane Trading Estate
Sherburn-In-Elmet, North
Yorkshire, LS25 6ES

NORTH-WEST REGION

LEYLAND
Hazelmere Industrial Estate,
Thomlinson Road, Leyland,
PR5 1DY

WARRINGTON
Hawleys Lane, Dallam,
Warrington, Cheshire,
WA2 8JY

WARRINGTON
Kingsland Grange, Unit 12,
Woolston, Warrington,
WA1 4FE

SOUTHERN REGION

DIRFT SOUTH
Railway Approach, Daventry
Int Rail Freight Terminal
South, Northamptonshire,
NN6 7ES

DIRFT WEST
Crick Traffic Office, Watling
Street, Rugby, Warwickshire,
CV23 8YE

DIRFT EAST
Dancs Way, Daventry,
Northamptonshire, NN6 7GX

BURTON ON TRENT
Derby Street, Burton on
Trent, Staffordshire, DE14 7F

STAMFORD
Woolfox Lodge, Stretton,
Oakham, Leicestershire

BIRMINGHAM
Trinity Street, Oldbury,
Birmingham, B69 4LA

SHARPNESS
Sanigar Lane, Sharpness,
Berkeley, Gloucestershire,
GL13 9NF

POOLE
Factory Road, Upton Industrial
Estate, Upton, Poole, BH15 4LJ

READING
Worton Grange, Worton
Grange Industrial Estate,
Reading, Berkshire, RG2 0TG

DARTFORD
Manor Way, Littlebrook
Business Park, Dartford, Kent
DA1 5PT

BRIDGWATER
392 Bristol Road
Bridgwater
Somerset
TA6 4AT

Appendix G

TOP HAULAGE FIRMS: 2000

Each year, two esteemed organs of the haulage industry compile lists analysing the top performing companies. *Distribution Business* profiles the top fifty leading players. *Motor Transport* has a top one hundred.

There are many ways of rating the various firms, depending on profits, turnover, staff, number of depots, number of trucks, number of trailers. In each survey for the year 2000, the UK's biggest company by far was Exel. After merging with the Ocean Group, in February 2000, Exel became the world's second-largest company in 'supply chain management solutions'. That's the technical description for the distribution industry. The merger resulted in Exel having an annual worldwide turnover of £3.5 billion: rather out of Eddie Stobart's league.

In their surveys for the year 2000, Eddie Stobart Ltd came 13th out of 50 in the *Distribution Business* listing and 29th out of 100 in *Motor Transport*'s. In each case, all the companies ahead were PLC companies, or parts of larger groups with many interests, their income coming from many sources.

Eddie Stobart is a private, family firm, wholly owned by Edward and William and not connected with any other company. So, like is not being compared with like. However, the lists are interesting as they show the sort of competition Eddie Stobart Ltd faces, the league it is now in.

In the compilation, below, listing the top twenty UK firms in 2000, Eddie Stobart comes out 10th.

Firms that are not strictly 'lorry' firms, such as DHL and Parcelforce, have been excluded, as they deliver documents and parcels, not heavy goods in heavy lorries. Each is listed according to their UK, not worldwide, turnovers, based on their published figures covering the year 1999. Some will now be out of date, and more mergers might have taken place.

Out of the twenty, only three are independent, private firms: Eddie Stobart (no. 10), Sutton and Sons (no. 18) and Lloyd Fraser (no. 20). All the others are PLCs or parts of groups, many of them global. In a list of independent firms, Eddie Stobart would therefore be Numero Uno.

	Name	U.K. Turnover	Staff	Vehicles
1	Exel	£1 billion	22,000	4,000
2	Wincanton	£660 million	15,000	3,900
3	Christian Salvesen	£660 million	14,000	3,248
4	Securicor	£632 million	1,500	700
5	Tibbet & Britten	£597 million	14,000	2,380
6	Hayes Logistics	£300 million	8,000	1,500
7	TGD	£294 million	6,400	2,000
8	BOC	£254 million	3,800	800
9	P&O Trans Euro	£235 million	2,280	1,288
10	Eddie Stobart	£135 million	2,500	950
11	TNT	£115 million	2,800	2,000
12	Taylor Barnard	£96 million	2,200	750
13	Hoyer	£90 million	1,050	500
14	Ryder	£88 million	1,642	800
15	Gefco UK	£80 million	500	120
16	NFT	£75 million	1,290	320
17	Bibby	£74 million	1,400	400
18	Sutton and Sons	£70 million	550	350
19	Fiege Merlin	£68 million	1,109	500
20	Lloyd Fraser	£68 million	2,600	430

INDEX

355